The Soul of God

A Theological Memoir

Wipf and Stock Publishers
Eugene, Oregon

Wipf and Stock Publishers
199 West 8th Avenue
Eugene, OR 97401

www.wipfandstock.com

The Soul of God
By Ray S. Anderson
Copyright©2004 by Ray S. Anderson
ISBN: 1-59244-778-3

Table of Contents

Preface   7

Part One: The Soul of a Theologian

Introduction   9
1. I Have Decided to Follow Jesus--No Turning Back   11
2. From the Prairie to the Pulpit: Exegeting the Humanity of God   19
3. The Soul of a Preacher: A Kierkegaardian Diary   31

Part Two: The Soul of God

Introduction   57
4. Guide Me, O Thou Great Jehovah   59
5. Thou Didst Leave Thy Throne   67
6. The Love of God   75
7. There's a Wideness in God's Mercy   87
8. Amazing Grace   97
9. When I Survey the Wondrous Cross   107
10. I Serve a Risen Savior   117
11. Spirit of God, Descend Upon my Heart   127
12. Sweet Hour of Prayer   137
13. My Faith Looks up to Thee   147
14. The Church's One Foundation   157
15. Under His Wings   169
16. All the Way My Savior Leads Me   181
17. Abide With Me   191
18. Jesus Lives, and So Shall I   203
References   213
Bibliography   228
Index   234

He broke fresh ground—because, and only because, he had the courage to go ahead without asking whether others were following or even understood. He had no need for the divided responsibility in which others seek to be safe from ridicule, because he had been granted a faith which required no confirmation—a contact with reality, light and intense like the touch of a loved hand; a union in self-surrender without self-destruction, where his heart was lucid and his mind loving.

[Dag Hammarskjold]

Preface

A colleague recently commented that contemporary theology, with all of the debate and discussion over doctrine of God has lost touch with the soul of theology. I agreed, but went on to suggest that what we have lost touch with is the soul of God. We have come to use the word 'soul' as the expression of the vital essence of some thing, movement, or person. It is in this sense that I have chosen for this book the title, The Soul of God, which I write, of course, out of my own soul. The book is not an autobiography, but rather a theological memoir. By writing in this style one runs the risk of self-indulgence if not narcissism. At the same time, it is impossible to write about the soul of God without engaging the soul of the theologian. In his classic book, *Care of the Soul*, Thomas Moore cut right to the core when he said, "The great malady of the twentieth century, implicated in all of our troubles and affecting us individually and socially, is 'loss of soul.' When we neglect the soul, it doesn't just go away; it appears symptomatically in obsessions, addictions, violence, and loss of meaning. Our temptation is to isolate these symptoms or to try to eradicate them one by one; but the root problem is that we have lost our wisdom about the soul, even our interest in it."

After years of preaching and teaching from a seminary context, I have come to feel the same way about a good deal of what passes as academic theology. To the degree that our minds fasten on abstract concepts of God rather than on personal knowledge of God, we not only divest God of soul but produce a theology that is bereft of soul. I fear that a good bit of traditional theology (mine included) becomes stone instead of bread for those who hunger for the Word of God (Matt. 7:9).

The soul of theology is rooted in the soul of the theologian. Karl Barth spoke of the 'wonder' and 'astonishment' which stood at the center of every theological perception. "If such astonishment is lacking," he warned, "the whole enterprise of even the best theologian would canker at the roots." The soul of the theologian is a sixth sense which goes beyond those senses by which we experience ordinary life. This uncommon 'sense of the soul' may begin as a form of spiritual hunger that awakens within us unrest, if not uneasiness. We become seekers, unsatisfied with religious dogma and hungry for a spiritual connection with some ultimate meaning. The sense of the soul is a form of spiritual wisdom to which we must appeal when life renders us otherwise senseless.

What follows in this book is the result of a process by which I discovered my own soul as a minister and theologian over 45 years of theological study and ministry: 3 years of seminary study, 11 years as full time pastor, 2 years of graduate theological study, and 32 years as theological teacher. I have preached virtually every Sunday for 36 years. While I began ministry and teaching in a traditional style, my soul-sense was more maverick. Perhaps my Viking ancestors or immigrant forebears were still alive in my genes. Being a maverick is not something that one claims for oneself but an appellation asserted by others. David Hubbard, former president of Fuller Theological Seminary, once wrote: "No faculty could handle a whole crew of Ray Andersons. But any faculty would be the poorer without at least one." I took that as a compliment *and* a challenge from an elder I admired, helping me to identify my place in the community of a seminary I served for 28 years.

Some of my most creative theology took the form of musings rather than tightly-written and carefully-argued theses that will appear here as I find the style more suited to a 'soul theology.' This book is also a sequel to my earlier book, *The Soul of Ministry* (Westminster John Knox Press, 1997), where I argued that ministry precedes and creates theology. It is only as we reflect on God's ministry as Creator, Reconciler and Redeemer that we gain insight into the soul of theology.

As an elder theologian, I paraphrase the poignant though somewhat self indulgent words of the 'old soldier,' General Douglas McArthur in his farewell speech to Congress: "Old theologians never die, they just find themselves amusing!" I am not ready to give my farewell speech, but offer this theological memoir in the hope that it will encourage others who have some maverick in their genes, and anyone with hunger in their souls.

Part One: The Soul of a Theologian

Introduction

Two influences from Scandinavia were formative of my theological origins and development. From my Norwegian father and his ancestors I gathered a genetic predisposition to the 'maverick syndrome.' My mother was Danish, and the writings of Danish theologian, Søren Kierkegaard, revealed a theology of paradox mediated by self awareness and exploration into God which had existential roots.

Part One of this book traces both of these influences in the formation of my theological profile. The first chapter is in the form of a theological biography leading to my installation as the founding pastor of an Evangelical Free Church near Los Angeles, California. The second is an account of the move away from academic theology into the open field of theological reconstruction, tracing out the contours of divine revelation in the life of Jesus as a living document. The third is a theological diary written during the early years of that ministry, intended originally as private reflection and musings on the human soul in its encounter with God.

These chapters form the context of what was to become a theological hermeneutic by which Scripture and human experience could be read on the same page. While the 'musing's only occasionally found their way into the sermons of those early years, I found their style more theologically relevant than the most strident and self-assured dogmatic utterances. It was, I realized, just this style that Jesus found so effective. Through this process I discovered the soul of a believer, from which developed the soul of a preacher and finally theologian.

The journey through which I discovered my own soul as a theologian continues to this very day as explorations into the soul of God (Part One). In our worship of God we express the theology of the soul inspired by the poet The task of the theologian (Part Two) is to trace the contours of the soul of God inspired by the Spirit. Each is part of the whole.

Chapter One

1
I Have Decided to Follow Jesus--No Turning Back

Life must be understood backwards but lived forwards.
[Søren Kierkegaard]

My Scandinavian ancestors immigrated to the United States in the middle of the 19th century and settled on the untamed and unforgiving soil of the South Dakota prairie. God knows why! Or, according to their view of providence, perhaps even he did not.

As it turned out, their theology was shaped more by Viking courage and curiosity than by a Calvinistic view of divine foreknowledge. They were descended from Norwegian Viking forebears who later were to become Lutherans.

At the top of a Slektstable (Family Tablet) on which my name can be found, I can trace ancestral links to Harold Halfdanson Hårfagre, born sometime in the year 860, 1065 years before I was born. My grandmother Kari Sørensen, broke the century-long demographic links in her family chain to come to the United States in 1866 at the age of 16. Thus the saga of prairie providence began. I have seen the gravesite of my great grandparents in the mountain village of Bø in Norway, behind the 800 year old church in which my grandmother Kari was baptized and confirmed before immigrating to the United States. She was the one from whom my father learned Norwegian as his first language—literally his 'mother tongue.'

As I stood at the gravesite of her parents, I pondered the mystery of this woman, who bore within her soul centuries of life lived within the strict confines of faith and family as she crossed that ocean, never to return. Never again to stand where I was now standing, never again to touch the faces of father and mother, in life or in death. Was her soul secured through that amazing adventure by the tightly-knit bond of relatives and friends she found in the strange new land who spoke the same language and ate the same food? No doubt. But within a single generation she made the transition to a new language, new food, and new gravesites to tend. She found her soul within a new community.

What led the first ones to take the railroad as far west as it would go, walk the next hundred miles or so, drop their burdens and dig the sod for planting seed and building shelter? The landscape to the east of the Mississippi River was more hospitable and offered more creature comforts, but they probably were inspired by exaggerated descriptions of lush, boundaryless prairie grass. Stories of the promised land flourishing with wheat and corn can be powerful agents of divine providence, especially to those reading the reports in the dead of winter in the old country. God's providence may be as much a picture in the soul as a divine plan written in stone. Like the children of Israel, inspired by visions of a land 'flowing with milk and honey' to cross a desert, my forebears may have been moved to cross an ocean in search of a land where the soul could stretch as far as the eye could see.

In retrospect, to my eyes, the prairie was providential. My theological roots, generated in a Viking soul shaped by the gods of the north, would likely have produced a meaner version of divine providence shaped by the narrow fjørds of Norway rather than cultured in the broad fields of the Dakota prairie. The vision of divine providence offered in this new land was generous and gracious, even though unstructured and unknown. Providence, as it turned out, was going to be hard work mixed with a sufficient amount of luck. On occasion, the work and the will did combine to produce what might be termed providential results. This providence became my birthright.

I was a middle child, bracketed by a younger sister and an older brother, who shared my environment but not my maverick tendencies. Was it in my genes? My ancestry included a Norwegian grandmother who left her home and family to emigrate to the United States, never to return. She died the year that I was born, so I have no memory of her face. Could her adventuresome spirit have slipped past the unguarded door of her own destiny to beguile an innocent child, a generation removed? The maverick spirit, like blue eyes, may be a recessive gene reappearing in the most unlikely disguise of a middle child, confined by the bookends of predictability and promise.

Her eldest son, my father, was barely 18 when his father died and he quietly assumed the mantle of family provider. His birthright was the soil, his spirit harnessed to the routine of planting and reaping along with the animals which bent their will to his bidding. His one attempt to jump the traces and launch a career in business quickly failed and he surrendered his vision to a destiny more secure and more sensible.

As a child, I was not told the story of my grandmother. As a child is wont, I assumed that what I *had* been told was all that *was* to be told, that what I saw was all there was to see, and that following the footprints of my father would take me to the other side of the narrow sea that was my soul. Yet the spirit of a child echoes the voices which, though silenced by death, still speak in its genes, in its marrow. Destiny, mediated through necessity, provides the early voices of a calling which will one day tame the restless spirit and satisfy the hunger of the soul.

The Rituals Which Set the Rules

There are rituals, sometimes understood only in retrospect, which mark the turning of a page in the story of one's life. Without a hint of self-consciousness my father, like Jacob of old, passed on my birthright in the only way that he knew. It happened in this way.

Two sandwiches, a piece of cake, and a small thermos of coffee. Twice a day, mid-morning and mid-afternoon. This was my father's sustenance while working in the field. At the age of 6 or 7, it was my happy task to carry this repast to him.

While my father quietly ate his lunch, I would pet the resting horses. On occasion I would slip a stolen sugar cube from my mother's cupboard into the mouth of my favorite, enjoying the slobbering lips against my palm as much as the animal relished the sweet cube--some of my earliest experiences with raw sensuality.

By the time my father had poured his second cup of coffee, I was back at his side, strategically placed for a ritual I had come to expect. Eyeing the piece of cake thoughtfully, he would say, "Well son, I'm not sure I'm up to the cake today, so could you eat it for me while I roll a cigarette?"

While he performed his own ritual of shaking a measured amount of tobacco out of the small cloth sack into the thin paper, licking the edges with his lips and striking a match on the sole of his shoe to light it, I devoured the cake, like the horses had my stolen sugar cubes.

The cigarette seemed to loosen his tongue. When he talked it was usually as much to himself as it was to me. My role was to listen. It was not a conversation. At the same time, it was intensely relational.

He talked about the horses. Each had names so that they could be startled out of their laggard ways when pulling the plow by a shout and a touch of the whip. Horses respond to their names and their master's voice.

"Star is limping a bit. I think we better take a look at his hoof tonight." That was not a chore but a promise. That evening we, he and I, would examine the foot and perform the simple operation of removing a stone.

That 'we' was his language of love. He often used it when speaking of his life and tasks including me as a participant. "We will plant corn in this field next year," he would say, as though I needed to know in order to make my own plans accordingly.

I was not just a boy who carried his lunch, but a partner in the family enterprise. He had no need to talk down to me, indeed he had no language for it. Nor did he attempt to treat me as a man with the pretense of 'man talk.'

What a powerful word, that 'we!' It allows for the difference between you and me and yet equalizes the disparity of age, gender, race and even religion. What I did when I was alone or with other children never seemed of much interest to my father. If entering into the games of children and becoming their cheerleader are the skills and duty of parenting, my father was woefully delinquent. He excelled, however, in the ageless and timeless wisdom of the 'we.'

At the time, I had little awareness of how meaningful this would become for me. My life was narrow and my pursuits were trivial. My peers were competitors as much as they were companions. My siblings were rivals as much as relatives. Yet, his utterance of 'we' was as deep as the bond of father and son and as broad as the common destiny on earth that bound man and boy in the struggle between faith and fate.

Without consciously intending to do so, he drew me out of my own childhood into the 'we' of a common life and destiny without destroying the child in me. Perhaps it was out of this wisdom that he was prompted to do something simple that nevertheless forever transformed my life.

We were sitting on the edge of the furrow, behind the plow, facing the freshly turned soil over which seagulls swooped in search of frantic worms. It was the second-cup-of-coffee time.

"Stick your hand down into the soil, son," he said, looking into my face and talking directly to me. As I did, he said softly, "This soil is part of your life—you take care of it and it will take care of you."

There was, of course, no response expected or given. I lived by the same rules. He never spoke of it again, nor did I ever question him about its meaning. It *may* have been the only gift that he knew how to give. The wisdom of desire being fulfilled in destiny.

There is a saying that is as old as the hills. "You can take the boy out of the farm but you cannot take the farm out of the boy." I took this as a kind of 'manifest destiny' for my life, in a paraphrase: "You can take the boy away from the father but you cannot take the father away from the boy." My connection to the soil--through the 'him of we'-- seemed unbreakable.

Following service in the second world war, my sense of attachment to the soil only seemed to grow stronger. While in college, I earned a degree in Agricultural Science and worked part time in the college's farm operations. During my last year, I sold the new car I had purchased with money saved during my military service, and bought a tractor. Arrangements were made to rent a farm back in the community in which I was raised. I did the fall plowing, went back to college, and moved with my family to the farm

That spring my parents came to visit. I was in the barn, milking the cows. My father sat on a stool watching me for a time. Then he said, "Son, it seems you have found what you want in life."

My answer was brief and sure. "Yes, dad, this is where I belong." Having retired from his own farm several years earlier due to ill health, it was as though he were now the boy sitting beside the man. I think he was silently searching for an answer to this question, "Son, are you the 'we' of me?" Having moved away from the soil that was his life, he was now experiencing the connection through me.

Flushed with the excitement of my own venture into life, I do not think I had the wisdom to sense his searching question and reciprocate his great generosity to me. I did not say, "This fall, *we* will need to remodel this barn to make room for more cows."

That fall, he died quietly of the cancer that ate away at the tissue of his throat and destroyed his voice box so that he could hardly speak. The same cigarettes that lightened his load and loosed his tongue, in the end, silenced him.

The Making of a Minister

For seven years I then pursued my vision and vocation of farming, tracing out my own destiny in the good earth. The legacy of my father's love for the soil became my passion. I added a fascination with the modern technology and the exhilaration of buying and using the latest in farm equipment. I bought and sold, planted and reaped, suffered failures and enjoyed success.

Why was it not enough? Was this not my destiny, to wrestle the soil into submission even while it was wresting control of my heart?

At first it was an unformed urge, not yet an idea. Then gradually, like a seedling emerging from the soil, the urge became a desire that began to take shape. My passion, which had been connected to the soil took on life of its own. I experienced a stirring of my soul when teaching the Bible to a class of young people in the church. I thrived on their questions which pushed me beyond the careful fence of the curriculum into the open range where exploration into the truth of God could be done freely and fearlessly. I became a teacher.

Then the thought came into my mind like a plant fully grown with no need for soil preparation and planting. I looked at the pastor who was preaching a sermon from a prepared manuscript and I said, "I can do that!" In fact, what I really thought was, "I can do better than that." I could be a preacher.

Then I awoke one day and knew that there was something pulling me toward a future that had no antecedent in my past. My destiny was calling me. Like the maverick that I was, once I dared to say, "I can do that," I knew that I was bound to do it. The future remained hidden, but destiny had come into view. It was not so much a calling as a conviction. Believing in Jesus meant following him--with no turning back. But could I do that?

With the revitalizing of personal faith in God that had long lain dormant, I found the words of Jesus Christ to be compelling and unavoidable. In telling the parable of the farmer who kept building bigger barns to store the wealth of his harvests, Jesus said: "But God said to him: 'You fool! This very night your life is being demanded of you. And the things you have prepared, whose will they be?' So it is with those who store up treasures for themselves but are not rich toward God" (Luke 12:20-21).

For more than a year, I struggled with what seemed to be two competing and irresolvable demands upon my life. In general, I had no problem with the idea that one could serve God through farming as well as through any other vocation. But one does not ultimately answer the most fundamental questions about life through theological permission but by existential passion. I knew enough about the Bible to establish theological permission for my calling in life to be a farmer and so fulfill a destiny and live out a gift given to me by my father.

What I didn't find an answer for in the Bible was the lack of inner certainty that this was what would ultimately fulfill my own passion for life. Frankly, I was as much troubled by the eventual outcome of my life as a farmer as I was tormented by the question that God had other plans for me. I could fulfill my passion by working the soil, but the soil could not fulfill my passion for a life lived as fully as I knew possible. I had accepted the destiny defined for me by my father, but I was awakening to a call to leave one land in search of

Chapter One

another, in much the same spirit as my grandmother.

God did not call me away from the farm to some form of Christian ministry. I did not leave the farm and attend seminary, preparing for a vocation of pastor and eventually teacher, because I heard a specific call from God. It is seldom as simple as that.

A new and vital life of faith in God, shared with friends and experienced in a community of love and fellowship, opened a door which could never again be closed. Through this door my passion spilled out like a river overrunning its banks. At the same time, warm breezes blew in and stirred sleeping segments of my soul. I awakened to what I thought was the sound of God talking, as my own father once did, "Tomorrow, we will go to those who are like sheep without a shepherd and bring them to a safe place." It was the 'we of God' that reached out and included me.

And so we left--my family and I--to another state and another life, not daring to look back. We did not fear that one of us would turn into a pillar of salt, we feared that respect for the dead and those still living would weaken the resolve to reach the new frontier.

In making the decision to leave the farm and sever the connection that my life had with the soil, I fully expected to suffer a kind of melancholy. It would be, I thought, a kind of death that would leave part of me unattached. In a sense, I felt that I was leaving my father as well as the soil behind.

It was a pleasant shock to discover, even after only a few months, that my new 'calling' to study for the Christian ministry had left no empty space. Nor did I long for what had been or what might have been. What I had thought would be a sacrifice as the 'cross that I had to bear,' turned out to be a successful career change and a quiet and deeply-rooted transplanting of my life from one soil to another.

What my father had long ago discovered, but left for me to find for myself, was that there was neither mystery nor magic in the soil. The mystery and magic, if we dare to use such words, lie in the connection of the heart to the hand. There is no place or task on earth which can satisfy the restless hand if it is not attached to the heart.

My father had not attached my hand to the soil on that day long ago, rather, he had attached my heart to my hand. My inner self had become bound to my outer life. As a result, whatever task to which I put my hand was done with a sense of finality and completeness that brought joy rather than melancholy and despair. I learned my first theological lesson: transplantation without transformation kills the roots as well as the plant.

How to account for the shift of passion from one objective to another? How to explain the inner certainty with which I changed direction without doubting the correctness of the first and without questioning the rightness of the next?

Did I unknowingly stumble into some kind of 'transforming power' through which I reached for more than the soil could offer? It is surely a paradox. My father taught me that work could be measured by how I planted a straight row of corn. This is the same man who *also* empowered me to reach out for personal goal-fulfillment beyond that last row of corn!

Just as my ancestors had arrived with fervor for the new land, I left the prairie with the passion of a pioneer, my heart bound to my hand. I went in search of the plow of God's providence and a different kind of soil. What I was soon to discover was that the distance from the prairie to the pulpit was more a matter of geometry than geography. As a flatlander I was struck with awe and amazement at entering the three-dimensional universe of academic theology--my new world.

2

From the Prairie to the Pulpit: Exegeting the Humanity of God

The transition from prairie to pulpit required traversing three years in seminary, crossing several borders, stepping over countless thresholds, and leaving behind a regional accent as well as a provincial mindset. The homespun philosophy which passed as conventional wisdom in the coffee shop on the prairie sounded like idle chatter to my colleagues in the rarefied rhetoric of the Pasadena classroom. I then knew what it felt like for Jesus to be identified by origin and accent as a Galilean. At the same time, I quickly discovered an appetite for abstract reflection on theological concepts concealed in a faith based on naiveté as much as knowledge. With scarcely concealed arrogance, like Saul of Tarsus, I imagined to have "advanced beyond them all!" Academic theology became a menu from which I chose my daily sustenance.

I was installed as the first pastor of a newly forming congregation just a week after graduating from seminary. I was prepared theologically, in my mind at least, to stand behind the pulpit and preach my newly acquired knowledge. As it turned out, the mantel of theological knowledge draped over my attempts to impart the truth about God was simply a transparent lack of practical wisdom. This Emperor had no clothes.

While in seminary, I had typed up all of my notes for systematic theology assuming that these would provide a resource for sermons. I found texts of Scripture which lent themselves to my homiletical design and proclaimed with passion the doctrine of God, as I had been taught. Years later, I discovered that Karl Barth had warned against just such an attempt when he wrote, "It is a familiar and perhaps unavoidable beginner's mistake of students and assistants, when preaching, to think they can and should confidently take the content of their preaching from their treasured college notebooks and textbooks of dogmatics." Only a few months went by before one of my congregation ventured a word of affirmation along with a note of complaint. "We know that you really like theology, Pastor. Some of what you have been telling us about God we already knew, and some we did not. But it is all quite *irrelevant* to our daily lives." They were asking for bread and I was serving stones, leaving me undernourished in my own soul as well.

Forcing myself to turn away from the instinct to defend myself, I encouraged the man to explain further what he meant. "It is this doctrine of God stuff!" he blurted out. "You say that we should come to understand that God is omnipotent—that he is all powerful and can do *everything*. What we want to know is can he do *anything* in particular, something that affects our lives for instance." He went on to list all of the attributes of God that I had carefully transferred from my systematic theology notes to my sermons. "If God is omniscient, I can easily assent to the fact that he knows everything. What I want to know is, does he know who I am?"

His question stung me. The truth is, I wondered the same thing myself. I remembered the little book recommended to me by my professor of practical theology titled, *A Little Exercise for Young Theologians*, written by Helmut Thielicke, who was a pastor *before* he was a theologian. Referring to a recent graduate of a theological seminary who became a preacher, Thielicke described initial failure due to the arrogance of a theological novice: "Under a considerable display of the apparatus of exegetical science and surrounded by the air of the initiated, he produces paralyzing and unhappy trivialities, and the inner muscular strength of a lively young Christian is horribly squeezed to death in a formal armor of abstract ideas." It is not that theology itself is the problem, he went on to say, theology is a sacred task but it can become diabolical when it becomes "a coat of mail which crushes us and in which we freeze to death." The Apostle Paul put it plainly: "the letter kills but the Spirit gives life" (2 Cor. 3:6). Thielicke adds, "Whoever ceases to be a man of the spirit automatically furthers a false theology, even if in thought it is pure. . . but in that case death lurks in the kettle."

Years later I discovered the book in which German theologian and pastor Dietrich Bonhoeffer had warned students of the danger of theology as a device to arm the preacher with authority. "The greatest difficulty for the pastor stems from his theology. He knows all there is to be known about sin and forgiveness. . . . The peak of theological craftiness is to conceal necessary and wholesome unrest under such self-justification. . . .The conscience has been put to sleep. Theology becomes a science by which one learns to excuse everything and justify everything. . . . The theologian knows that he cannot be shot out of the saddle by other theologians. Everything his theology admits is justified. This is the curse of theology."

Having tried and failed to preach a 'theology from above,' I set aside the notebooks and textbooks and turned to what Karl Barth had done in his own early pastoral life, taking a 'wholly other' approach. "What we need for preaching, instruction and pastoral care is a 'wholly other' theological foundation." Barth turned back to what he called the 'strange new world of the Bible' and began to read the book of Romans as though he had never read it before. This time, he read it solely for the purpose of letting the Word of God speak to him on its own terms.

While my approach was not as dramatic and eventful as it was for Barth, it turned out to be a new direction, with a trajectory which I am following to this very day. The Apostle Paul set forth for me the essence of a new theological task when he wrote of Jesus, "In him the whole fullness of deity dwells bodily" (Col. 2:9). What if one assumed that all knowledge about God is based on God's revealed self-knowledge? In other words, as Jesus stated, "All things have been handed over to me by Father, and no one knows the Son except the Father, and no one knows the Father except the Son and anyone to whom the Son chooses to reveal him" (Matt. 11:27).

It had never occurred to me or my seminary classmates to question the professor who began a theology course with lectures purporting to define the nature of God. Who told you this? Where did you get this knowledge about God? we might well have asked. We simply assumed that the being of God as defined by philosophy as eternal, immutable, omnipotent, and omniscient was a foundational and axiomatic truth upon which theologians could erect a systematic structure of interlocking truths. Each individual truth was supported by selected proof texts extracted from the narrative of Scripture, much like a forensic scientist does an autopsy on a corpse in search of evidence to support a theory. But how does one autopsy a life? And what if it is the life of the Eternal One who never dies? What was never mentioned were the other texts from the same Scriptures which warn that God is both inconceivable and incomprehensible in his nature.

"Can you find out the deep things of God? Can you find out the limit of the Almighty? It is higher than heaven—what can you do? Deeper than Sheol—what can you know?" (Job 11:7)

"He made darkness his covering around him, his canopy thick clouds dark with water." (Psalm 18:11)

"You hem me in behind and before, and lay your hand upon me. Such knowledge is too wonderful for me; it is so high that I cannot attain it." (Psalm 139:5-6)

"Have you not known? Have you not heard? The Lord is the everlasting God, the Creator of the ends of the earth. He does not faint or grow weary, his understanding is unsearchable." (Isa 40:28)

The Apostle Paul--whose own constructs of God were shattered in his encounter with Jesus on the Damascus road--confessed that true knowledge of God comes only through the self-revelation of God through the Spirit: "What no eye has seen, nor ear heard, nor the heart of man conceived, what God has prepared for those who love him [Isa. 64:4; 65:17] God has revealed to us through the Spirit" (1 Cor. 2:9). In an outburst of praise and worship, the Apostle exclaimed, "O the depth of the riches and wisdom and knowledge of God! How unsearchable are his judgments and how inscrutable his ways!" (Rom. 11:33). The God who is inconceivable from a human standpoint is now revealed to humans through the *mysterion* of Christ, the God revealed in the flesh of Jesus (1 Tim. 3:16).

What if one assumed that the life, death, and resurrection of Jesus is the very self-revelation of God's own being? What if we were willing to have our concepts of God reconceived, as it were, through the conception of God's being in human form? C. S. Lewis, who had his own 'shattering' experience of emerging from unbelief to belief wrote: "Every idea of Him we form, He must in mercy shatter."

It was no longer 'what if,' but 'so then.' Jesus Christ is not only one who points us to God but he is Emmanuel--God with us. *So then* let us assume that the only God that we know is the one who "became flesh and dwelt among us," as John said (John 1:14). I asked myself, "Do I dare set aside my theological books and launch out into an exploration into the soul of God revealed only through Jesus?"

I had made the journey from the prairie to the pulpit--no turning back. Now it was time to take the "longest stride of soul" that a human could ever take, as the English playwright, Christopher Fry expressed it. He put in poetic words the theological quest I was undertaking.

The human heart can go to the lengths of God,
Dark and cold we may be, but this
Is no winter now. The frozen misery
Of centuries breaks, cracks, begins to move;
The thunder is the thunder of the floes,
The thaw, the flood, the upstart Spring.
Thank God our time is now when wrong
Comes up to face us everywhere,
Never to leave us till we take
The longest stride of soul men ever took,

Chapter Two

Affairs are now soulsize.
The enterprise
Is exploration into God.

The abstract concepts of God which stirred my intellectual self now left my soul undernourished and unfulfilled. I did not doubt that they were true, but they no longer satisfied my search for truth. The theological knowledge I had acquired through arduous study did not move those who heard my sermons to know God and his purpose for their lives. I was granted a theological degree that would at once establish and bestow some undisputed credibility on what I would preach and teach to my congregation. But this knowledge was disconnected from those people's daily lives. And that was completely unlike Jesus. The expression of his knowledge of God was permeated by a deep and practical understanding of our fallen human nature, our woundings and needs, our quests and longings.

Jesus is not only one who touches our own human souls with grace and truth, he *is* the very soul of God in human form. Theologians call it *incarnation*, which is the Latin translation of the Greek phrase, "became flesh' (John 1:14). John does not shrink from telling us that the one whom we call Jesus is identical in being with God and, in fact, the very *exegesis* of the Father. When we use the term, we refer to the discipline of expounding and explaining the exact meaning of a text of Scripture. John uses that very Greek word when he says that God's only Son, who is close to the Father's heart, "has made him known [*exegeomai*]" (John 1:17).

Jesus is literally the exegesis of the soul of God. The character of God's being as well as the contours of God's love are disclosed to us through the humanity of Jesus. Here was my subject for a year of sermons, *exegeting the humanity of God*. Little did I realize at that time what later was to become, for me at last, a self-evident truth—the soul of theology is found in the *soul* of God.

I began a series of sermons from the four Gospels tracing out the life of Jesus from conception and birth, through his ministry, to the point of crucifixion and resurrection. I did not conceal my approach nor my intention from the congregation. I announced that we were about to embark on a bold venture seeking to probe the depths of that *mysterion* which is no secret, but rather a 'revealed mystery' accessible through Jesus Christ, in whom the "whole fullness of God dwells bodily" (Col. 2:9).

From the beginning, the series of sermons revealed a common thread. At each point in the life and ministry of Jesus his work following his baptism by the Holy Spirit revealed the innermost being of God, his Father. The apostle John captured this truth in the simple, but elegant words of Jesus to his disciples: "The Father loves the Son and shows him all that he himself is doing. . . I declare what I have seen in the Father's presence. . . .the Father and I are one. . . . the Father is in me and I am in my Father. . . .If you know me, you will know my Father also. . . .Whoever has seen me has seen the Father. . . Believe me that I am in the Father and the Father is in me. . ." (John 5:20; 8:38; 10:30; 10:38; 14:7; 14:9; 14:11).

The soul of God's being is not a concept that stands alone and apart from us, but a divine communion in which we participate through the humanity of Jesus. Through this communion we enter into God's self-knowledge, which is the knowledge that the Son has of the Father and the Father of the Son (Matt. 11:27). Through the Holy Spirit we are brought into that inner communion and thus participate in God's self-revelation through the Son, which is the soul of ministry. It is the ministry of God toward the world that reveals the being of God as the one who loves the world (John 3:16).

For the next eleven years I continued the exploration of the humanity of God as the core of my preaching, teaching and pastoral ministry. In a series of final sermons before leaving for further theological study in Scotland, I prepared a summary of what had become known as an incarnational theology. I chose the prayer of Jesus for his disciples as the outline for the series. In this prayer Jesus made the connection between his being in the world as the revelation of the Father to the world and his being in the Spirit as the reconciliation of the world to the Father. "As you have sent me into the world, so I have sent them into the world" (John 17:18).

The soul of theology is found in the *as*, while the soul of ministry is discovered in the *so*. I seized upon the *as* and the *so* as the hinge on which God's self revelation through Jesus turns toward the world for the sake of its reconciliation to God. Only when we discover the content of the phrase, "As you have sent me into the world," can we give content to the corresponding phrase, "so I have sent them into the world." Several aspects of the humanity of Christ reveal to us what it means to say he was sent into the world to reveal and recover true humanity. Jesus demonstrated authenticity, integrity, love, and maturity. He saw people as individual persons, and yet called them into community.

Each of these dimension of the humanity of Christ can be used to form the contours of the soul of theology. First, the *as Jesus was sent* will be described. Then the *so we are sent* will be articulated, followed by a brief statement as to what our commitment should be in light of both.

AUTHENTICITY

As Jesus was: In the midst of a religious culture that prized appearance and cultivated form, Jesus appeared clothed simply in grace and truth. He refused to recognize as spiritual that which was artificial and affected. He valued the truth of being and doing over the righteousness of words and prayers. Both in the street and in the temple, he uses one language for both the saint and the sinner. He stated divine realities in terms of human experience. His life-style was that of a human person living among humans. Because he *was* the truth, he had no fear of exposure, nothing to defend.

Because he was *human*, he had no fear of humanness, in himself or others. Because he came in love, he had no fear of love--he was open to all who were open to him.

So we should be: A real Christian must also be a genuine human being. Spiritual growth is manifested in those who demonstrate the fruit of the Spirit in relationship with others (Gal. 5:22-23). The Christian is to be related to one's own society in the same way that Christ was related to the world (John 17:18). The test for truth in a Christian is what the world sees of Jesus Christ in us, not what other Christians see of themselves in us.

We are *committed* to live a transparent life, willing to be known for who we really are, not only by who we say we are.

We are committed to live in openness toward others, accepting them as Christ has accepted us, having a spirit of tolerance toward others who do not share our concepts or convictions. Yet we know that openness is not permissiveness, and tolerance is not compromise.

We are committed to the fact that a Christian has anxieties, temptations, moods, doubts, frustrations and problems. This is what it means to be human.

We are committed to have no ulterior motive or religious device in our love for God or our love for our neighbor: that is, we are committed to authenticity.

INTEGRITY

As Jesus was: Jesus' spiritual integrity revitalized the spirits of persons amidst the dead weight of tradition and legalism. Where Jesus was, there was life. The moral integrity of Jesus brought an absolute sense of right to specific human situations. Where Jesus was there was truth. In Jesus there was a personal integrity that spoke with authority against the enslaving influences of religious formalism and demonic delusion. Where Jesus was there was freedom.

So we should be: Jesus Christ is the truth of God. One whose life is centered on Jesus Christ thereby has spiritual integrity (Col. 2:18-19). There is no Christ other than the Christ of Scripture as present to us in the power of the Holy Spirit. The integrity of Christ exists in the integrity of Scripture as the Word of God written (John 5:39). The integrity of Christian fellowship rests in the person of Jesus Christ as the object of personal faith and the ground of mutual commitment. Where Jesus is, there is the church (Matt. 18:20).

We are *committed* to include all in fellowship who seek to know Jesus Christ as Savior and who honor the integrity of Christ between us.

We are committed to keep good faith between one another and so preserve the unity of Christ in fellowship. Within this integrity of fellowship there is room for disagreement but not divisiveness. It is the wisdom of the Spirit and the patience of love to know the difference.

We are committed to allow Jesus Christ perfect liberty in the creating of his church in the world. Our concepts, prejudices, traditions, successes, and failures constitute no obligation upon his will.

We are committed to so live, in word and deed, that our motives are perfectly clear and our methods consistent with the message: that is, to have integrity.

LOVE

As Jesus was: Jesus revealed the heart of God to be most loving toward us. He applied God's Spirit of tolerance to the sharp edge of divine justice. His love held back the law long enough for people to discover *why* they were law breakers, and to receive mercy (John 8:1-11). His liberating love loosed the dehumanizing bonds of a religiously structured society. He taught that the sabbath was made for the restoration and renewal of humans, not humans in bondage to the sabbath.

He brought a new dimension of practicality to the word love. Love from God can be worn on the back, put on the table, and sat down beside you—it is human as well as divine, tangible as well as spiritual. It is Jesus.

So we should be: Love is something you do. The feelings, expressions, and words of love have little substance apart from being transformed into actions (James 2:15). Clothing is love to the naked; food is love to the hungry; empathy is love for the solitary prisoner; and a seat beside you is love for the stranger.

When God loves, it means the same thing as when we love. The difference is that it is *God* loving. Therefore, our love for God is evidenced by our love for one another (1 John 4:8,12). Love is the point of contact in the world for Jesus Christ. The love of the Christian for the non-Christian is the bridge by which persons come to God.

We are *committed* to a fellowship that embodies as much of the Spirit of Christ as the truth of Christ.

We are committed to be tolerant of all that seems contrary to us and intolerant of all that is contrary to Christ, and to be willing to learn the difference! Where the Spirit of the Lord is, there is freedom (2 Cor. 3:17).

We are committed to allowing people in the world to see the interior life of our Christian fellowship, and by knowing us, leading them to know God. Where love is, there is God.

We are committed to making no discrimination in our love between the body and the soul, between the spiritual and the personal, between mine and yours. That is, to have love.

MATURITY

As Jesus was: Jesus Christ fulfills the greatest potential and God's highest purpose for human persons. He liberated the spirit from the law and created children of God out of slaves. He lifted the burden of the law by fulfilling it, not by breaking it, and pointed beyond it to a higher fulfillment. Those who become his slaves find their freedom (John 6:63; 2 Cor. 3:4-6). In his own life, he brought both body and soul into balance.

Because he understood and accepted his own humanity, he never condemned another for being human. He demonstrated that a holy purpose can only be completed when the spirit and the flesh become one. He was in every sense a mature person:
  his feelings ran deep, but they limits,
  his love flowed freely, yet within boundaries,
  he was sensitive to pain, but not easily hurt,
  he had a dream, but consecrated his life in duty.

So should we be: Growth is a greater value than conformity. This means that there must be room to grow for the immature and reasons to grow for the more mature. When standards become barriers to growth they must be moved. Responsibility is a higher motive than guilt. Instead of exploiting guilt to achieve results, we seek to enlarge responsibility to produce growth.

Love is a better fruit than work. Only the capacity to love engages the whole person and fulfills the complete law. In learning how to love the Christian brings every part of life into discipleship (Rom. 13:8-10). Freedom is the highest act of personhood. It is achieved by one who is neither slave to self or to the world. Only one who is free can love. It is complete submission to the Spirit of Christ which produces this freedom (Gal. 5:1,13; 2 Cor. 10:5).

We are *committed* to bring each person to his or her highest level of responsibility. With the assumption of responsibility comes the removing of restraints. Responsibility is itself a law of God working within and through the individual's perception of oneself and God.

We are committed to bring each person to his or her greatest capacity to love. This will mean the exposure of each other to the risks of love and the expectation from each other of the fruit of love (Heb. 10:24).

We are committed to help each person become whole—effectively able to receive and apply God's grace, fully equipped to live a creative and purposeful life, meaningfully involved in the functions of the body of Christ: that is, to have maturity.

THE INDIVIDUAL

As Jesus was: Everyone was a person to Jesus Christ. He ignored the categories established within his own society. For him the despised Samaritan was a woman who could give *him* a drink, the self-righteous Pharisee was a man who wanted to talk, the leper was a person who needed to be touched. While people came to him in droves, each had a name. A congregation was not a mob to send home to eat, but individuals to be fed with bread, broken with his own hands.

In a crowd he was never simply pushed by people, but touched by someone who hurt. Within the clamor of a multitude he heard the cry of a blind man, the sigh of a sinner, the murmur of a skeptic. He let people be who they were and offered to help them become who they could be. He had no uniforms for his disciples and no masks for his friends. He did not ask for conformity but for commitment. His style was love, his pattern devotion.

So we should be: Love is to treat people as persons. People are persons even before they become Christians. Young people are persons even before they become adults. Christians are persons even after they become Christians. Ministry is to relate to each person according to their needs, not to impose our agenda. The church exits for the sake of people, people do not exist to serve the church. Outreach is to love people as persons. Every person in the world has a right to be loved for Jesus' sake.

We are *committed* to help each person find his or her particular gift to the body of Christ (1 Cor. 12:7,11). Until the body permits each individual the full expression of his or her personality, we are less than whole.

We are committed to seek the unity of Spirit without requiring conformity of lifestyle (1 Cor. 12:7,11). We recognize the bonds of love but make no one a slave to a system. The greatest difference between us is far less important than the smallest task shared in Christ.

We are committed to see persons as Christ sees them, not as prospects or problems but as persons who bear a name and a need.

We are committed to know that we do not love humankind until we love one person so that he or she comes to know that God loves him or her: that is, to be committed to the individual.

COMMUNITY

As Jesus was: Jesus called men and women out of estrangement and into a redemptive relationship. He came as a Son and introduced God as Father. Out of this relationship he coined new words to explain human problems and possibilities: prodigal, enemy, reconciliation, friend, brother and sister, flock.

He defined spiritual values in terms of human relationships. God forgives us as we forgive one another; to hate our brother is to hate God; to give of ourselves to another is to love Christ. He gave himself as the new standard of judgment for the community of persons. Those who love Christ become his body, with a common life and one heart.

So we should be: There is no such thing as a solitary Christian. One cannot 'come to Christ' apart from coming into the fellowship of his body—the church. This fellowship (koinonia) is not only spiritual, but personal and social. It may not always be structured as an organization, but it will always be an organism. The highest act of the individual is to surrender his or her right to exclusive self-existence in order to create a community of faith and love.

Because each Christian retains individuality, even in community, the community of Christ is a continuing creation. Community is broken whenever the individual acts exclusively of others or loses individuality in the group. Personal spiritual growth is measured in terms of the individual's contribution to the common good of the entire body. The fruit of the Spirit are relational realities: love, joy, peace, patience, kindness. These are evidenced in our relationship with others.

We are *committed* to give priority to the organism of the church over the organization. Organization is the servant of the organism to carry through the functions that contribute to growth and life: the life of one person is of more value than the entire organization.

We are committed to maintain the integrity and health of the body of Christ through responsible participation and loving discipline. The life and health of the body of Christ is more vital than the demands of one person.

We are committed to set no limits on love that are not intrinsic to the nature of love itself as revealed by Christ.

We are committed to go as far as Christ would go, to share as much as Christ would share, to live in fellowship with those in whom Christ lives: that is, to be committed to community.

We have seen how the soul of theology leads to the soul of ministry. Through this process, my own soul was touched--sometimes tormented--but always restored and renewed. My companion in this journey was the Danish theologian, Søren Kierkegaard whose writings provided mentoring for my own soul. It could not be otherwise. An 'exploration into God' must also be a 'soul-sized' endeavor, as Christopher Fry has reminded us. We must take the journey together

3

The Soul of a Preacher: A Kierkegaardian Diary

> In a world of fugitives
> One who moves in the opposite direction
> Will appear to run away.
> J. G. Hamann

In June of 1959, following graduation from seminary, I was installed as the first pastor of a fledgling congregation. Those dozen families had a vision for the founding of a new church. While meeting in temporary facilities during the process of securing land and constructing our first building, I began the transition from prairie to pulpit, described in the two previous chapters. On the way to discovering the soul of theology, I encountered the soul of God. I neither planned nor desired it; it came about, nevertheless, more through my attempts to survive than to succeed. By the end of the first two years, I resorted to journal-keeping, as a way to keep my breath while caught in the undertow of preaching and pastoral care. Only later did it become a creative dialogue with unseen authors and my own alter ego.

During the final year of seminary I was introduced by Edward John Carnell to the 'burden of Søren Kierkegaard.' Carnell was himself a somewhat tormented soul, who wowed our minds with his brilliance and won our hearts with his suffering. He was later to publish a book under that title, and became my occasional lunch partner during the years prior to his premature death in 1967.

It was my own reading of Kierkegaard during those early years, however, that stirred the existential reflections captured in my journal. What follows are selections taken from that journal written during the years 1962-1970. I offer them as a self-portrait of the soul of a preacher on the way to becoming the soul of a theologian. The content of these 'markings,' suggested by the title of the book by Dag Hammerskold, remains faithful to the original. I have resisted the temptation to rewrite or edit them so as to smooth out the rough spots or to bring greater clarity to what may seem to be obscure utterances. Expressions of the soul can be authentic even though appearing to be enigmatic. I invite the reader to walk with me as though wandering through an orchard, picking and tasting the fruit that falls from the trees without the necessity of grasping at every branch.

The Awakening

It is hard to say what has happened to me in the past few years of my ministry. I know this—the decision to leave the farm and go to seminary was still a part of the same compulsive search for a vocation which would satisfy my insatiable hunger for self-fulfillment. I had no fear that it might fail—nothing has ever failed me. I will not permit it. What cannot be accomplished by skill, I do through passion. The important thing is not the product but the triumph of self-respect and the attainment of a personal goal. This is not to say that there was no spiritual dimension to my decision. There was more of a spiritual motive attributed to it by others than by myself I fear. I was under no illusions—even God's will came within the circumference of my own thought.

I remember the attitude I had the first year in Seminary. The problem was simple. The world needed a Savior and I would go to the world with the solution. It did not occur to me that there was anything more complex than that. I conceived of my ministry as largely repetition. There was only one message and it was only a matter of repeating it with a few variations and with new illustrations. The extent of my ministry was unlimited—not because of the possibilities of relating the truth of Christ to the human situation, but because of the population of the world which would provide me with an inexhaustible audience. I finally had found a vocation sufficient to match my tremendous intensity.

Somewhere in the midst of this grandiose project, there was a change.

It might have started with the books. The stimulating reading that was a part of a theological curriculum awakened a sleeping giant. Philosophy was a field assumed to belong to the repertoire of a pre-theological student. It was a stranger to me—an alien intruder into the world of corn, cows and cockleburs. I read—I probed—I questioned, milking the accumulated wisdom of a dozen others. A few months was all that was needed to give me a working acquaintance with the premises of philosophy, from there I could walk alone. Literature was somehow associated in my mind with the drudgery of a thousand hours spent in hopeless English classes.

With amazement I was introduced to the passion of life through the lives and words of others like myself. And then of course, I was not without friends. They disarmed me with their love and captivated me by their genuineness. Not many, but a few. Enough. It does not take a multitude of friends, only one or two who create the dialectic of self-revelation.

The Great Idea

On every side I see persons who have given their lives to the pursuit of knowledge and have become experts in certain fields. Some simply overwhelm me with their fantastic acquaintance with so many truths. Can one person know everything? Of course not. Then what should one know? How is one to choose out of all the possible knowledge in the world that which is required or permitted?

One person can devote an entire lifetime to the study of New Testament Greek and speak with authority in this field. I could do that. But I could do little else. And having done nothing else, would I have more wisdom or less? Or, I could refuse specialization—become a general practitioner of life, so to speak. Would this be a dilution of potential? Would my spirit be so attenuated that effectiveness would be lost?

One thing I have noticed—every person has his or her own distortion. No matter how erudite and skillful his knowledge, he betrays himself at some point when measured against the horizon of reality. Bonhoeffer, for example, in his letters from prison, reveals a tremendous capacity for objective reevaluation of his own first premises. He is constantly going beyond his own thinking (which by the way, is one of the keys to his growth as far as I am concerned), and yet when it comes to the subject of baptism, he emerges with distinct Lutheran presuppositions.

I think I fear distortion as much as anything. It is far too easy to become so accustomed to moving within the boundaries of one's own presuppositions that reality becomes identified with self-concepts. I am not sure, but somehow I feel that the secret of wisdom (and maturity) lies in knowledge without distortion. This means one must move slowly, and constantly keep everything in relationship to reality.

In his Journals, Søren Kierkegaard wrote, "Some ideas only occur once in a lifetime." The great idea: somehow everything relates to everything. The world has meaning and life is not senseless. This means that suffering as well as joy are part of the fabric. From the perspective of the individual, everything can be integrated into a relevant picture as long as there is a constant check for reality. The presence of distortion is so subtle that I spend as much time tearing down as building. Maybe this is part of my present feeling. I am impatient to build —I fear the edifice that I might build, for it may be a distortion.

So here I stand, surrounded with a thousand ideas, helpless to build anything for fear of unreality—or is this building of a sort?

The Virtue of Uniqueness

The difference between uniqueness and greatness tugs at me. It strikes me that uniqueness is to be preferred to greatness. Kierkegaard was a great man. It is incontrovertible, and will manifest itself in yet greater ways through the next generation. However--and here I must qualify my feeling to guard it from presumption-- I possess something that Kierkegaard did not have: the perspective of my own life. All that Kierkegaard was and said can be known by me and to that, I add my own perspective. I see him in relationship to reality. This was impossible for him. I need not add that it is just as impossible for me to see myself in relationship to reality as it was for him, but then there remains the possibility of uniqueness for others!

I only mean to say this: the uniqueness of individuality is both a tormenting and a tantalizing thought! It is not a novel thought, yet it must be discovered by every person. It cannot be taught—only experienced. Yet it cannot be experienced without a mentor. Kierkegaard taught me to discover the uniqueness of my own self—and I promptly treasured my uniqueness more than his greatness.

He would not mind.

This is why I cannot settle for mere greatness and become a scholar. Professional dexterity in any one of the multitudinous fields of human knowledge is far too limited in scope to satisfy the range of individual uniqueness. Let others forage in the dry dust of a career—I shall encompass their labors within the perspective of my own life and use their knowledge to build my wisdom. Not that I am a parasite. I simply do not recognize the copyright of wisdom. What others have learned can be appropriated by me through the process of distillation and related to the great idea. I shall never know the secrets of the professional person—but neither will I spend a lifetime wandering in the labyrinth of ways that lead to only a form of knowledge. I only need to know the relationship of that labyrinth to a hundred others—and this may turn out to be the more prodigious effort.

Suffering for the Great Idea

"Hope deferred makes the heart sick" (Proverbs 13:12a).

Chapter Three

The heart has little patience with the rules of temporal life. Its sickness is not impatience but hope. That which, in time, is called a virtue (patience) in the eternal becomes suffering. That the two exist simultaneously is no surprise to the heart which fears nothing so much as impatience (sin) and immediacy (despair). Living with a sense of the eternal while limited by the boundaries of the temporal is the special kind of suffering to which Kierkegaard referred. This is a different use of the word suffering, but I am strangely drawn to it.

It cannot be denied that the temporal forges chains which the eternal cannot shake off without betraying its own integrity. The weight of these chains is a burden—their sharp edges are irritating—their limits confining. It is the joy of faith to discern the difference between the anticipated freedom from the chains (temporal hope) and the immediate union of the heart with its fulfillment (eternal hope).

"A desire fulfilled is a tree of life" (Proverbs 13: 12b).

It is the dimension of the eternal that promises fulfillment to the heart—the temporal is only an appropriate expression. The triumph of faith rests in the knowledge that it is not within the power of the temporal to limit the fulfillment of the heart—merely its expression. It is a delusion of the first rank to credit the chains of temporality with the power to increase the fulfillment of the heart. This would make love a contingency of fate and the caprice of geography. Better then, as in the days of Augustine when baptism was deferred until just before death in order to have the greatest value, defer marriage until love has exhausted its possibilities in order to gain an unthreatened value.

The heart has its own wisdom and will not confuse fulfillment with immediacy. The tree of life is not gained by patience (time) but by faith (eternity). It is sickness of the heart to have both the tree of life and frustration of temporal immediacy.

In which case the sickness is its health.

The Wall

"The heart knows its own bitterness, and no stranger shares its joy." Proverbs 14:10

It was a formidable thing
Unassailable by the brazen stranger
    Impenetrable by the closest friend
This great wall around my heart.
It is both ageless and contemporary.
Bright new stones set among mossy antiques.

It has always been--yet in constant construction.
    It is difficult to determine its origin--
       was the first stone mortared with prenatal loneliness?
          Or quickly laid with the first fearful awareness of others
?
To those outside - it is an offense and a threat.
 They plaster its uneven surface with stinging labels
         "independent
             proud
                 cold."
But I am aware—I read their distorted labels and watch them
    with curious detachment.
For the wall is strangely built.
    Opaque to those without—
     but transparently clear in its view from within.
 Strange—the thicker it is built, the clearer it becomes.
There are times when the lucid insight becomes unbearable—
    but the smooth inner walls will hold no covering—
        nor will they be darkened.
   I covet their blindness—yet cherish my vision.
     I am alone—but not idle.
     I am silent—but not empty.
There is much to do. The lamp of awareness is an insatiable torch—
    as quickly as the reality of one moment is grasped, the light
    reveals another to be discovered —
          interpreted—
             savored.
With ubiquitous haste I search the illimitable depths of life, distilling the sweet drops of the eternal from the waste of time.
    It becomes increasingly difficult to converse.
    The painful intimacy of family life has no vocabulary.
The casual talk of friends is a laborious and fatiguing pretense.
    The wall is a friend.
    I lean against it with sadness and am comforted by its strength.
      It has taken everything from me—there is nothing left
        but the individual.
        My loneliness is complete—
           I am a prisoner of my own awareness.
It was an imperceptible thing—
    impossible to see directly—only obliquely visible

There was a presence that was not myself.
But it was impossible! The wall was secure—
   no carelessness had left it in disrepair
nor had unguarded moment opened its strength.
   Yet, it could not be denied
   there was a presence—
   not observed but observing...
   not without the wall—but within!
The view was as clear as for myself—both were viewing
the same world—from the same side of the transparent
   wall!
At first it was unbelievable, then inescapable.
   It was enough to realize that the wall was still there
      yet there was a difference.
There were many things to do—and it was difficult to remember
there was no need of haste.
   I proudly revealed the priceless jewels mined
   from a thousand moments of time—and kept
      for just such an impossible showing.
   Often we simply leaned against the wall with
      wordless oneness
         viewing—
           sharing—
              experiencing.
The wall is transformed—what was once a prison has become a
sanctuary.
   The plant that now grows within this shelter is a fragile
thing.
   So exquisite are its flowers that a brush of
      temporal air would wilt its
      imperishable petals . . .
   The fragrance of its perfume so delicate
      that the dust of words would choke it.
The wall is a friend.

The Existing Self

   Obviously I am not searching for existence—I am writing from within it! If I were not 'in relationship' I could not search for relationship. Which is to say, if I were not a 'self' I could not define self. There was a time when I prized loneness (not loneliness) as the sanctuary of self—I built my wall. I no longer fear the world. I have my insecurities, but they are only because I fear to be understood as much as to be misunderstood. It is much worse to fear being understood, and this was the reason for the wall.

Why should one fear being understood? Is it because understanding is an invasion of the secret heart—a breaking down of the uniqueness that keeps me from being lost in the statistics of humanity?

This cannot be the extent of the fear because uniqueness does not disappear in relationship nor does self-revelation make the sacred common. Somewhere in the primordial self a distortion occurred. The tentative movement of self into relationship experienced pain. Instead of acceptance there was exploitation—the other self found the world a threat as well. Instead of mutuality there was struggle for position. I retreated, wounded, to my own world. The distortion was not my wounds—they could heal; I counted understanding to be a threat--enter distortion!

But herein is the pathos of distortion—the crippled image of self reflects its own ideal (and its own reality!). There is no possibility of healing within the horizons of one's own distortions, because there is no disease. Rather, the distortion becomes its own obsession with intuitive power to guard against the distortion (!) of being a part of another through unhindered self revelation.

Now the wall does not only depend upon its massive stone for strength—it has cleverness as well. And year after year, cleverness is added to fear and the self becomes an expert at defending its secret. When necessary, mutuality can be experienced to gain mutual ends—but there is always withdrawal at the last minute. The self will not be captured by involvement—the pain of being understood is greater than the need for self-revelation.

Have I described the process by which my distortion formed? I hardly know for sure. It seems almost too clear—too obvious. Perhaps this is part of the original distortion (did I not say that cleverness was its strength?). Is it presumption for the self to speak within distortion and to say "now I see clearly for the first time?"

Indeed it is—except for one thing: when the self speaks of itself 'in relationship' it has a test for truth. The reason for this is clear. The distortion of the self was precisely that it defined its reality by virtue of being 'out of relationship.' Hence, to be 'in relationship' is to be free of that particular distortion and for the first time, free to measure reality in terms of self-concept without the bias of distortion.

This much I have learned: a self-concept which cannot be reflected through the perspective of another self (not just any self—but a self 'in relationship') without being altered, cannot be held as *real.*

What I mean to say is that a self-concept is not in harmony with reality unless it is consistent with the reality of self-in-relationship. If the self-in-relationship is loved—it can only maintain a self-concept of 'unloved' by denying the reality of the relationship. But here is where the transformation of unreality into reality is most painful. What happens is that we must become 'different' than we have always been in order to conform to the new reality. This is not easy. We have learned to live with the self-concept 'unloved.' It is a familiar face and we are no longer frightened by its grotesque features. In fact, when alone behind the wall—safe in the sanctuary of loneness—its contours are reassuring, its familiarity our only friend.

I have not discovered the self (Kierkegaard will have to wait for another day!), but I have discovered the presence of distortion and the therapy of 'relationship.' I have been understood and I have survived! It is no longer a malignant fear that has sapped the better part of my life thus far. My movements are halting and uncertain. The new world offers so much to be discovered, consumed, shared, that I hardly know where to begin. The therapy has not been a miraculous cure (though a miracle)—I need to be 'cured' over and over again. But I no longer fear. It is amazing what a difference this makes!

Saturday Night Musings

It is Saturday night, my study is warm and glows with the softness of light and love. It is not hard to let the thoughts move at will through the corridors of previous moments. The building is not aware of the past—nor anticipating the future. These walls do not create a sanctuary—but they are consecrated. Not with a formal prayer but with a feeling heart. Lives have moved into an encounter with God in the presence of this silent building. Perhaps the walls know more of the silent agony—fear —desire—and hope of those hearts than I ever shall. Yet I know that life has been lived here, and where life has been eternity has related itself to time in the pathos of the human situation.

These seats shall be occupied tomorrow again. Who shall come?

What do they seek? What shall I say?

The Word of God, you say. And what is that? Printed characters upon expensive paper? Ancient monograms hallowed in their ambiguity by the reverence of centuries?

Or does God speak again?

Does Jesus move among us with disarming glance and searching heart? Does He care about overdue bills, interminable pressures, painful memories, strained marriages? Yes, of course, but then how does He speak? These words are not precise enough to be discovered in the Scripture.

I am to preach, you say; explain the scripture, say the words that are true to both God and the human situation!

It sounded easy once. A hundred years ago I could have accepted the assignment with confidence, tonight I see the pulpit in its unapproachable fascination. If I could not speak I would not be here. My role is consuming, my mission terrible in its attraction. I cannot resist the reality of that crisis when heaven and earth merge in the 'event' of preaching. Yet, having known its reality—I tremble in its recurring demand. So much that is said comes too easily, trite clichés that spin the truth like a top but never move the heart. Over simplified solutions that are easily remembered but better forgotten. (Kierkegaard taught me that!)

So much is premature. Words must be produced to fill the void of thirty minutes with frightening regularity. There is not enough time to suffer, to flee, to return, to believe, to doubt, to pray, to suffer, to think.

But would I ever be ready? No. And this is the truth that makes an impossible situation possible. The point at which I am ready is the point at which it is too easy—too comfortable—too professional (I cringe and cannot look at the word!).

The possibility of preaching lies in its necessity, not in its duty. The necessity is the insatiable search of my own spirit for that reality of communication between my heart and the heart of the one who hears—and this with God speaking through it all. Not through me, but through it all HE IS THERE. This is what makes the words true, not their pious ring or pompous tone. (I cringe again!)

I have never entered the pulpit but that my heart burned. I have never doubted that some thought were mine through my own struggle for reality. It has not come early, and has not been extensive (often barely enough to justify a paragraph), but it has never been lacking and I have never regretted a message because of this.

This does not make it any easier to face the crises—only more difficult to turn away.

It takes an hour to say this—but I can think it in a moment! Is this strange? Has every thought so much content when disciplined out of the realm of the infinite into finite expression? Then what great potential there is for expression and what reason to labor to bring the spirit to bear upon the orderliness of time.

I am such a child—so impatient to transcend everything with a *great idea! I will learn and will be trained and pruned to produce, I know. Yet I am grateful for that which cannot be learned— the gift of a great idea.*

The Soul of a Poet

Why is it that we linger at the side of the poet? Is it only because of the beauty of his words? No, because our secret suffering reaches out to touch his heart.

I remember reading somewhere that John Milton wrote, "A writer ought himself to be a true poem if he wishes to write well . . . in laudable things." I wish I knew what a poet was. There are so many who pass themselves off as poets who only have some ability to manipulate words and to startle the senses with bold paradoxes.

Of course I do know, Kierkegaard taught me: "A poet is an unhappy being whose heart is torn by secret sufferings, but whose lips are so strangely formed that when the sighs and the cries escape them, they sound like beautiful music..."

So then: if one wishes to write well, in laudable things, he must be before he can say. Strange alchemy—that pain produces harmony.

I fear that far too many traffic in lesser things than suffering. Not because they despise—they simply do not understand.

The Virtue of Truth

Life is not a very noble thing if one measures nobility in terms of moral achievement and righteous virtue. Most of us live by futile necessity nagged by a constant reminder of failure. Even success is a discomfort and prestige a cruel tyranny. If Jesus Christ is presented as possessing every virtue and the paragon of righteous religiousness, then the greater part of the world is too weary and sinful to attempt to emulate him.

I am obsessed with the idea that the truth of Christ lies closer to the lives of ordinary people than to the self-righteous theology of the church. Not that I find reality in negation—the church is the historical line of continuity of the Kingdom of God in the world. Yet, the church has a constant danger—that of becoming irrelevant to life.

Truth is not the fruit of immediacy (contemporary existentialism in literature has lost sight of this). It has its own existence; however, the tragedy of truth is its lack of incarnational witness. Jesus brought truth to humans through the incarnation of love and redemption. He was not accepted by his contemporary religious system, but he did not deny his relationship to it. When forced, he always chose the individual over the system. That the system forced him to this choice reveals the contradiction of the system with truth, not the anarchy of his spirit.

It is not that my spirit is alien to the system—but I cannot conform. This is not an easy course. The price is great, not the least of which is the inner questioning of my own life. I think that I fear distortion as much as I do conformity. The humanist has chosen human reality over against a preposterous divinity. It is not to the credit of organized religion that it forced the choice, nor that it gloats in its self-appointed orthodoxy.

I have learned the simple formulas of orthodoxy: All who do not confess Jesus Christ as Savior are lost—turning to Christ insures eternal salvation and immediate release from fear, frustration, and failure. It can be proclaimed with no discomfort and with a thousand inflections as long as one steps up to the crowd and speaks from a box, retreating into the sanctuary of an ecclesiastical bandbox. But to mingle with the crowd! Rubbing shoulders with the individual—this paralyzes the easy movement of preaching and makes it a laborious and prodigious effort. I am immobilized with the problems of taking the simple formula and relating its meaning to the ambiguity of human individualism with its complex meanings.

I am sorry—I simply fail to be moved with the simple statement that my neighbor is going to hell because he does not share my convictions about the theology of Jesus Christ. It is not that I am sure that he isn't, but that it seems too grotesque for words that I must put him in hell before I can love him in Christ! I do believe in hell, for myself at least. That is, I have no illusions about the reality of personal immortality and the possibility of eternal existence as a self without relationship. Perhaps that is why I cling so desperately to relationship.

But my neighbor! Is it sinful (heretical) to give him the benefit of the doubt while struggling to understand him so that he can understand me? He is not impressed with my theological 'proof' of his prodigality nor does he think bad of me for consigning him to hell, he merely pities me.

*Pity is the iron curtain that keeps the church at a safe distance from the world. It is impenetrable to every assault and secure against every strategy but one. There **is** a way—but it leaves the church exposed and defenseless. It is simply HONESTY. This is hard enough with the world looking on—but virtually impossible in the pious fellowship.*

Perhaps this is a clue to my violent reaction against identity with my own profession. The attendant at the gas station this morning made me cringe with his breezy *"Good morning Reverend, fill 'er up?"* I could hardly eat lunch two hours later ! The last time I had such convulsions was with a group of ministers in a restaurant in Bakersfield when one of them began singing the Doxology in a stentorian bass before we ate breakfast! He was happy in the Lord I guess, but I almost drowned trying to crawl into my coffee cup.

To say that I am concerned over my reactions is an understatement. Why I should be ashamed to be publicly identified as a minister has often perplexed me. Most ministers don't seem concerned, and this by no means indicates that they are professional or pompous. They simply appear to be oblivious to that which makes me cringe. It is my discomfort with titles that creates this sensitivity, of this I am sure. The reactions of the public to the image of ministerial professionalism seems respectful, even if a bit condescending.

Jesus chose the individual. I like to think he would have been uncomfortable wearing the distinctive robes of a rabbi. I felt somewhat better after reading Dietrich Bonhoeffer's confession of his own discomfort with being identified as a religious professional. *"I feel how much my resistance against all that is 'religious' growing. This resistance is becoming almost an instinctive disgust, which is surely not good. I am not of a religious temperament. But on the other hand, I must think unceasingly of God, of Christ. I am also strongly attached to authenticity, life, liberty and mercy. Religious dress is what bothers me most. Do you understand this?"*

But who would understand me if I dared to share these thoughts? But now I have!

The Dialectic of Suffering

"The human spirit will endure sickness . . . " *(Proverbs 18:14)*

The human spirit has a capacity for suffering that is akin to the heart of God. This sickness is not a disease of the spirit but the agony of the heart which can see more than it can reach. It is the nature of the heart that it does not prefer blindness to sight.

My own heart sways like the wild movements of a suspension bridge in a hurricane—it seems that every connection is ripped from its socket and all stability sacrificed to the wind. At one moment life is an orderly process of meaning within the comfortable security of known limits. Then self-confidence trembles with new feelings, new desires, and strange delights. I stagger like a senseless man down a strange street—I reach for the familiar holds and look for well-known signs to prove that right and wrong are not distorted and still everything moves. I slide down inclines that have no direction nor end. I look up and recognize nothing. I listen and hear only the pounding of my own heart; suddenly I discover both depth and height to my life. My wild careening was not in chaos, but in relationship. The fearful movements were within the resiliency of my own spirit as it sought to find meaning in new dimensions. God is greater than my fear, and relationship with Him gives tensile strength to the spirit.

I see life as composed of two spheres rather than one. Viewed from above (or from below) the two appear as one, for the two are superimposed in a vertical plane. The upper sphere is the dimension of the eternal, the lower is the temporal. The self moves with familiarity in the realm of both—there is expressive meaning with appropriate language in either realm. Because of this, the self is one, but not single. With deep perception and honest searching of self-in-relationship, the self becomes intuitively aware of its own nature as a dialectic of possibility within a unity of reality.

The fine distinction between the two spheres is first thought and then felt. Through awareness and experience the spheres move apart without separating (though from above or below they appear to be one). The movement is a dialectic. The temporal dimension of self demands immediate fulfillment and advances in the name of self-expression. The eternal dimension of self preserves an infinite perspective to every movement of the temporal and suspends expression in the name of self-preservation (integrity). The hiatus between the spheres constitutes the suffering of the spirit.. This suffering is not an intruder into the happiness of the self, but is self-imposed to preserve reality and meaning. This does not deprive the self of freedom—with exquisite abandon, the self moves as one when the movements of the temporal are appropriate to the needs of the eternal.

The self does not consider the suspension of action a tedious wait—this suspension is itself a meaningful moment which demands all of the passion and seriousness of the human spirit. Thus I ponder the dialectic of existence in time from an eternal perspective.

We always know more than we can tell. There is a knowledge at the core of the self for which we will never find words. It rises up within us without our bidding and cannot be forgotten or erased by the most strenuous act of the will nor by the most delirious ecstasy of emotion. We cannot resolve life into one sphere alone without diminishing the other. I learned this also from Kierkegaard.

". . . but a broken spirit—who can bear?" (Proverbs 18:14).

This, of course, is simply the self deprived of relationship. What first appeared to me as chaos generated growth when the relationship was preserved. When the suffering of the self in dialectic is unperceived and unidentified, the reaction is one of withdrawal instead of inward suffering. The self retreats to heal itself alone and suffering is changed into despair as the relationship disintegrates.

Suffering can be redemptive and renewing. When the movement is one of inwardness in order to preserve relationship--even if it is done with an agony of honesty--the malady is changed from a physical distress to a spiritual suffering—and hope revives, joy permeates, possibility comes alive! But oh how hard to bring the failure within the relationship so that it might be healed!

But a broken spirit who can bear? There is no redemption without relationship. Can there be a relationship with God without one with other persons? I doubt it. Human relationships are made possible by grace and love. It is not the grace and love that make Divine relationship different—but God. If we deny one relationship—the spirit is broken —grace and love cannot redeem.

Relationship is not only redemptive, it is edifying. Our movements are imperfect and often awkward in trying to fulfill the possibilities of self-in-existence. Apart from relationship, the imperfections become repetitions and the self is frozen in its growth. The love of a relationship that renews possibilities promotes mutual edification (at the human level)—the growth that occurs through suffering makes the relationship stronger and the individuals concerned freer selves. This is a mystery and a problem to the temporal dimension, but a joy to the entire self, which seeks the perfection and freedom of the other in order that the relationship may have infinite possibilities.

Time hung suspended while truth searched slowly for unlit corners. Nothing must be left behind--I have promised myself this requirement. And not even the accusing faces of yet unwritten pages will force me to run ahead of myself.

The Edge of Unbelief

The strength of truth becomes a weakness if it is not hazarded against the untried. There are things to be said that I know now to be true even though others will fear their implications. I cannot walk both the way of professional security and personal honesty. I would be sorry to be misunderstood—but I will not hedge with understanding.

I no longer shrink before the question: "If love is absolute, and neither Divine nor human, why are you the only one who speaks in this language?"

The answer is, there are multitudes crying the same truth. They are simply outside the church. Those whom we have long consigned to the dust of delinquency have outreached us in their need. We would do well to overtake them with the truth that can be found only in the echo of despair.

The Love That God Is will now be written. I care little for its destiny, but only for its birth. It will be responsible for its own survival. There is no doubt of its genuineness—it has already been understood; I should say that understanding has necessitated its utterance. My responsibility is not to create novelty, but to unclothe the true. This has always been the more prodigious feat. Kierkegaard was lonely enough to be honest, and patient enough to learn the vocabulary of pure expression.

Now the days shall be counted and the hours bear their interminable toil—for honesty and patience have a great price. I have experienced relationship and now have a reason to pay the price.

Seeking God

"When you search for me you will find me; if you seek me with all your heart" (Jeremiah 29:13).

It is strange that we are so easily led astray by a promise such as this. The search for God is a universal quest, though few will acknowledge the object of their pursuit, and even fewer claim much success.

The pathos of life is not so much that so few are successful in their seeking of God, but that so many fail at finding "all of our heart." The prodigal son never really did find his father, nor did he need to. In the narrative we are told that "he came to himself" (Luke 15:17). Whatever the implications of this may be, at the least there was the beginning of honest self-awareness leading to a measure of self-responsibility. At this point, his father who had been waiting (love is not sovereign) now was free to restore the son while preserving his dignity as person.

Can God be far from one who has found all of his heart?

I talked this week with a young mother apparently suffering from the tormenting pains of terminal cancer. Her first response was not "I am suffering," but "I am afraid." She has not been told that her condition is fatal (it may not be), but the important thing was that her extremity produced reality—fear is an honest reality, pain is only a circumstance. She spoke of her Catholic background and of answers to prayers through some special saint (St. Anthony,

I believe).

It was a refreshing experience to claim with her the promises of God with no need to disprove her faulty theology or heretical aspersions on the doctrine of grace. I have never cared less than I do now for the formal declarations of theological truth (though I do not hesitate to define the theology of redemptive love). The reality of her heart was a compelling evidence of spiritual assurance.

I only say this to make the issue clear: there is no God for the halfhearted.

The thought just occurred to me —if all were halfhearted would there be a God? Do we have the power to destroy God by disallowing love?

Could it be that in the creation of humans (the incarnation of love), the being of God was hazarded in the precarious existence of love?

Does God watch humanity like we observe a candle burning alone in the dark—and if the flame flickers out, turn away to another experiment? Or is he the flame?

The questions are naive (not blasphemous) for I speak not against God but for my heart. I do not live in fear of belittling God but of failing to measure the heart. I have desires and fears that seem alien to the good, but the conditions for knowing God are not virtue but honesty. These desires are who I am—yet I am more than desire, I am desire before God. Knowing myself, there is then the possibility of choosing the good (he has left me this dignity). Is the good God? No —I choose the good of self-fulfillment, God must choose himself, I cannot be God—that would be inhuman.

I have only begun to find all of my heart,
there is nonetheless
an intimation of God.

Virtue and Modesty

There is a form of virtue that is insufferable—and a semblance of modesty that is inappropriate. Both virtue and modesty are attributes of faith, but neither can be claimed by the self in its own behalf. The clothing of the self may be a virtue if the person is unprotected by love—but what is so offensive as clothing for the sake of virtue in the presence of love?

The one who introduces some quick reminder of a pious truth into a conversation of exploration, not only becomes insufferable when cloaked with virtue, but forces immodesty upon us by stripping the relationship of love. This is betrayal—for we are either forced to clothe ourselves quickly (repeat his pious intonations) or allow our inner self the indignity of exposure to an impersonal truth. It is at this point that truth crucifies love.

There is only one recourse to such a betrayal—to cloth ourselves with darkness. "Let only darkness cover me, and the light about me be nigh." (Psalm 139:11).

There is security in this darkness, but no growth. For the self dares not move into relationship lest our uncovering become another's virtue--betrayal again. The one thing that is feared is light (love), because the self must become unclothed in order to be loved. But darkness cloaks the fear with its comforting presence and repels the light with infallible modesty.

We are safe from betrayal—but never was safety purchased so bitterly—nor modesty in such loneliness. The finality of our isolation is absolute, for love must become darkness to be trusted. "Even the darkness is not dark to thee, the night is bright as the day; for darkness is as light with thee" (Psalm 139:12).

The first moment of our uncovering is a painful thing--betrayal leaves a vivid scar. Yet we cannot withdraw, for darkness is the last refuge. Nor can we deny the presence of another, whose searching glance is as comforting as darkness, whose uncovering as gentle and modest as our own instinct. It is unbelievable! Darkness is as light! The one who moves close to us does not prove knowledge by exposure, nor love by exploitation. Our refuge is in darkness—yet love has become darkness so that both can become light!

Only the betrayed know the exhilaration of trust—the extravagance of abandonment—the luxury of self expression.

*"Forget not that modesty is for a shield against
    the eye of the unclean.
And when the unclean shall be no more,
    What were modesty but a fetter and a fouling
of the mind" (Kahlil Gibran)
Love is modesty—and to be loved, the only virtue.*

The Individual

Life is not kind to the individual—on the contrary, normalcy and conformity are equivalent terms in the vocabulary of the well adjusted.

It is in this sense that I speak of the 'curse of awareness.' Nothing can be experienced without being interpreted. Not only does this pose a threat to the 'group experience' (aren't you feeling well tonight?), but the isolation of misunderstanding only increases the intensity of awareness.

It is not surprising then, when another is able to share this isola-

tion (how can isolation be shared?) that communication assumes a headlong rush of uninhibited expression. The need to communicate does not follow from the unknown experiences shared (as a child telling things that happened in school), but from the agony of awareness that must be healed through the touching of another's knowledge. It is not that another knows us with such complete knowledge, but that he knows himself—this is the knowledge of life shorn of all pretense and unreality. It is this reality that comforts our longing to know someone else, but how can we know one who does not know himself? And if he knows himself, does he not know us too?

This experience is not possible for the 'group experience'—only the things held in common can be discussed, and only so that each is reassured that they are really shared. Opinions are traded like so many recipes, but interpretations of life are left buried in the suppressed awareness of individuality. Only the intimate probing of one who reveals himself threatens this secure adjustment to 'life.' This threat is easily enough handled by simply relegating the individual concerned to the category of 'introvert,' and plying him with solicitous questions (what's the matter with you?).

Did I say that life was not kind to the individual? But his life is, and is there any other? His suffering is sweet and will not be replaced by the euphoria of 'adjustment to life.'

And then there are moments of understanding when expression rushes to spend all that has been discovered in one moment. Who else could afford such extravagance!

A Point of Reference for Reality

Inevitably all reason gives way to unreasonable circumstances. The first principle is doubt. Doubt of self that routs dignity with scorn and achievement with bitterness. There is nothing that can stand before this scathing storm—ridicule leads to grotesque shadows upon the wall, cast by plans that were once carefully set in the soil of new beginnings. Even that soil is suspect, for it was ground from the rock of failure by the sharp edges of regret.

Our voice echoes in the cavernous darkness—a chamber of horrors that turns the words of friends into weird laughter that mocks their well-meaning solicitations. Can they be so naive as to miss the obvious discrepancy?

Ultimately every belief gives way to unbelievable pain. The second principle is realism. Now we recognize the matter for what it is—folly. To have not only believed but to have had faith in the believing! Twice fooled, but now this pain bears us on the crest of truth. Realism churns the sand into foam, our eyes sting even as our heart surrenders all claim to truth and every taste is grit between our teeth.

Finally every hope gives way to hopelessness. The third principle is death. Even our realism was endurable for the hope of some new thing churned up out of the depth. But now that changelessness is infallibly locked into the order of days, there is no longer reason to deny the thought that has often tempted us into oblivion —death. An imperceptible joining of the crowd, lest they be frightened by the sudden deadness and reject our corpse (Even death has to avoid the appearance of change—life).

The logic is unassailable. Doubt brought realism and realism justified death. Not even love can conquer such wisdom, unless love dares to include doubt as the first principle of faith. And then moves through its own logic, but now forced to move doubt into relationship finds that it is more important to doubt the one whom we have loved as the greater doubt. For how shall we be secure in doubt if someone yet accepts our love? We have not doubted until we have doubted the greater as well as the lesser. But love does not fear doubt, for it springs not from reason but from reality. The unreasonable circumstances provide only the first stage of doubt, let doubt go beyond, says love, and doubt love if it dares! But beware, that in daring to doubt there is courage to see the undoubtable. That having scoured absolutely the face of love there is strength to accept the reality of ineffaceable absoluteness. That having granted the realism that doubting gives is now unable to reconcile the reality of life .

Nor can we retreat, chagrined and humbled back into the security of our 'dutiful acceptance.' For the struggle was not for victory or defeat but for truth. And where truth is touched pain is healed into awareness and hurt turned into tenderness. There is no 'lesson' to be learned, no vows to make, no promises to offer, and most important, no past to renounce. That which is past for death, through pain has become part of life for faith. There is no time —no past or future, not even present that shall become past—but only now.

Even so, that which was said at the beginning is said for the first time now:

". . . if they fall, one will lift up the other; but woe to the one who is alone and falls." (Eccl. 4:10)

Only God Can Suffer

"Although he was a Son, he learned obedience through what he suffered." Hebrews 5:8.

Chapter Three

Only God can suffer—and those whom He loves.
And if it should seem inhuman to suffer, we are not being as humans but as animals, who have pain but no affirmation of pain. Love bears pain creatively, thus all suffering is redemptive.
The great peril of life is that we are only the problem and God the solution. Like a typographical error, we cling to the mistake that gave us birth rather than accept the perfection that does not need us! There is an instinctive knowledge of pain, and an unerring distrust of panacea. However glittering the phrases that offer freedom from self, we prefer the reality of conflict to the unreality of assumed piety. Those who in desperation claim 'spiritual' victory over emotional needs may be simply experiencing psychological repression supported by theological concepts. Behold we are sterilized! Spiritually aseptic, capable of neither pain nor desire! If this is faith (and God) then we will oblige. Call us unspiritual if you must, but leave us the dignity of at least being lost!
But how much reality can be born without despair? When does death itself become a frightening comfort, or narcotic a necessary anesthetic? Where is there some action—some task—some tangible deed that will sufficiently claim our passion without betraying our hope?
Behold, there is suffering.
God comes to us in the reality of our frustration and does not force us to deny that which is real to affirm that which is merely true. We know what is true, and need not even a Divine reminder of that. If our needs have become our compulsion, at least He knows and accepts that need (His image in us). Meeting us in our frustration he leads us to suffering rather than solution. If this pain be the altar that demands our life, then he leaves us to choose it rather than fight it. Like his Son, who found the cross unacceptable, though inevitable, so we examine the alternatives and choose the pain.
There is no other course which deals honestly with the facts. Suffering turns our emotions into redemptive grief, our tears into healing waters that cleanse the wound without forgetting the pain. We shall never be the same, the loss will never be repaid, the love never substituted. Nor do we really want that. No substitute is worthy to replace the grief for what has died. But left to make the tragic hour a part of our life, suffering weaves the rent sadly into the fabric of faith. From deep within ourselves comes feeling greater than emotion to direct emotion into redemptive grief; a deeper grief than unrequited love to transform love into wisdom, and wisdom into joy. We may never laugh again without a tear, but we will love again. And not with love that moves with desperate anxiety, with

compulsive need, but love enriched by suffering. Love that leaves the other free to love, knowing that only such love is worthy of the name, only such love a sufficient relationship.

And who taught us such wisdom? Only the One who learned obedience through suffering. And is suffering a sufficient action? It is the only action, all else is an idle gesture in the face of time.

There is this about suffering, this ground need not be fought over again. The moment and the victory is ours; this altar is unalterable.

The Inner Life

"By mere words servants are not disciplined, for though they understand, they will not give heed." (Proverbs 29:19)

We deceive ourselves in our understanding for the moment, the exhilaration of new insight seems actually to have changed our position. Yet, the pattern of our life carries on as though determined by some inward compulsion. The reality is this, we change so imperceptibly, even in the most dramatic crises of understanding, that the ordinary patterns of life do not reveal it.

The agonizing truth compels me to listen, for all the words that I have spoken, for all the understanding that I have patiently brought to birth in those who have listened for several years; for all of those who have understood me in my speaking, I have only this to acknowledge: if any have changed, it is only to change into who I am in the inner self. The peril of understanding mere words is not that it is futile but that in the process of understanding one becomes like another through the imperceptible discipline of relationship. Herein the peril is also the promise; change (growth) is a possibility, but who can bear it?

The only profile of my ministry is the dimension of reality and truth in my own life. What is reality and what is the definition of truth? I could assume the righteousness of Christ as a substitute image for my own inner life, and without fear say that when others become like me they are becoming like Christ. This would be easier, that is, if I could accept the initial unreality of self-crucifixion, but in actuality it is distortion. People do not become like who I say that I am, but who I inevitably and existentially am.

Nonetheless, it must be that Christ is involved if there is reality of change into the good. If, instead of the righteousness of Christ as a mental substitute for my own reality as person, I acknowledge the existence of God in the inner movements of my own awareness, and this I claim with assurance in that Christ did send the Holy

Spirit, his own spirit into my life, so that the estrangement of myself from myself and from God could be bridged. I then acknowledge the presence of God in my movements. Those who become a part of me through that perilous exchange of selves involved with genuine relationship, cannot escape being involved in the reality of God in a redemptive way.

But what are the conditions of this reality? It is too late to speak of perfection and righteousness, these never belonged to me, either by birth or choice. There can only be left honesty, which is a form of integrity equal to righteousness.

Nor can this honesty come disguised as some quick purging confession of sin that gives the sensation of atonement without the reality of transparent genuineness is essential to honesty.

To Will One Thing

I am indebted to Kierkegaard for a definition of integrity. "Purity of heart is to will one thing."

The obvious question has the easiest answer, what is the one thing? Anything! For the oneness is the absoluteness with which it is grasped, not the quality of that chosen. It is the good of course that comes into being when we reach that absoluteness of will that makes us a complete person in the moment of will. This is the discipline, refusing to make a distinction within integrity.

I wrote once of 'the great idea,' perhaps more out of desperation than vision. There had to be a unity within the diversity of truth.

I now see that my first movement was one of choosing reality over truth, and thereby forcing truth to be revealed through the prism of reality.

There was a glimpse today of that 'idea' the slightest opening in the wall through which a fragment of a whole could be seen. Behind the reality of my being, stands the being of God, infinitely extending as a personal being through the center of my own soul. There is the being of God beyond my own, separate, yet extending through love inseparably a part of my reality.

There is the reality of ' another,' a thou to whom my being responds as 'I.' In the recognition of the uniqueness and reality of the other, whom I know as thou, a relationship exists that is love. Not love primarily as affection, gratification, or even expression, but love as knowledge, and the trusting of that knowledge by the abandonment of my being to the reality of thou. In this relationship the entire dimension of God is revealed. Not concealed, nor constrained, but revealed, infinitely revealed so that he is always 'beyond,' that is, standing behind the reality of both I and thou, *and yet lying between the reality of personal beings who directly acknowledge the other .*

I do not love everyone, nor am I loved by everyone. Yet, I do look for the "thou" in others and so strive to 'love my neighbor as myself.'

All reality is a finger pointing to God. Each fragment of humanity, even that portion that can only die is a reality that confirms the 'great idea.' Having once made the commitment to reality as the univocal point in truth, the experiencing of life and the reading of creative expressions of that experience does not disintegrate (fragment) me nor simply tear without mercy, but confirms again the ultimacy of love as the reality of God.

I do not strive for the uniqueness of being God, but I no longer distinguish between His reality and my own.

The Greater Suffering

"May, 1842 . . . And it was the delight of his eyes and his heart's desire. And he stretched forth his hand, and took hold of it, but he could not retain it; it was offered to him, but he could not possess it alas, for it was the delight of his eyes and his heart's desire. And his soul was near to despair; but he chose the greater suffering, of losing it and giving it up, to the lesser, which was to possess it without right; or to speak more truly . . . he chose the lesser suffering of being without it rather than to possess it at the cost of his peace of soul . . . and strange to relate, it came to pass that it was for his good." (Søren Kierkegaard)

If I could have only one truth to guide me through life, it would be the truth of 'the greater suffering!' For all that is good issues from suffering for the right thing. And yet this truth can only be pressed to the heart as paradox. When the paradox is resolved there is no longer any possibility of suffering, for greater suffering is only greater unhappiness. But through paradox, greater suffering is suffering for the greater value and this yields joy for it is the uniting of ourselves with eternity through decision.

Now there are those who do not understand this. And they hold that all such talk of suffering is morbid and depressing. I suppose then that they have what they want. But why then do they not have joy? The truth of the matter is that they do <u>not</u> have what they want, or if they do, they realize that they will not always have it. Thus they are left with suffering whether they like it or not! This suffering cannot be willed with the heart, but must be medicated like a headache. Now I understand why my suffering makes their head throb!

No one will understand or share my joy who has not become part of my suffering. Not as one who observes my struggle to relinquish, but as one who relinquishes in order to choose the greater good. There is no room for sympathy in suffering, only joy.

So let the joy be shared! And if this produces even greater suffering is this not the confirmation that the good has been touched with the heart and continues to intersect our lives with eternal significance?

Lord let my suffering be so perfect that all are drawn to thee through my joy.

Epilogue

Edward John Carnell, first introduced me to the Danish philosopher Søren Kierkegaard 45 years ago. During one lecture he read aloud from the last chapter of a manuscript in which he had written about his fascination with the man. "Now that I had to part company with the Dane, I felt somewhat like a wayfarer who, having come a long distance by himself, is suddenly joined by one going to the same country; only to find that when they unexpectedly confront a fork in the road, . . . they must go their separate ways, for each tenaciously clings to his own convictions. Though keenly regretting the loss of fellowship, each must courageously venture the hope that wisdom is on his side."

In coming to the end of my own 'Kierkegaardian Diary,' written almost 40 years ago, I have somewhat the same feeling. It was not so much a fork in the road that caused me to take the 'road less traveled,' as Robert Frost once put it, but the realization that ultimately the journey is not into the depths of one's own soul but toward the soul of God. Or as Christopher Fry put it, "Affairs are now soulsize/ The enterprise/ Is exploration into God."

What follows in this book is the result of that journey which, as it nears the finish line, is closer to the beginning than it was at first. "The fear of the Lord is the beginning of knowledge" (Prov. 1:7). Let us begin.

Part Two: The Soul of God

Affairs are now soul size.
The enterprise
is exploration into God
Christopher Fry

Introduction

I did not intend to be a scholar. I was faithful to that intention for the most part, except for books written to answer the challenge to every seminary professor, 'publish or parish!' The seven-year hiatus in my formal education prior to my three years of seminary study was followed by eleven years of full-time pastoral ministry. I then enrolled in doctoral studies which eventually led to my present teaching position at a theological seminary. At the outset of my professorial teaching career I was soon to discover that being a teacher was quite different than being a scholar. The discipline of scholarship, which I had already discovered during my Ph D studies, involved research and writing by which one's intellectual mettle was demonstrated in critical and continuous footnotes. In these notes, dialogue with other scholars was sustained as a kind of running commentary beneath or alongside of one's own contribution. When one's own writing and thinking became the subject of critical interaction by other writers, then one was considered to be a scholar. While being a professor of theology was considered to be a significant achievement, Karl Barth has reminded us of Søren Kierkegaard's comment when asked, "What is a professor of theology?" To which he repled, "He is a professor because someone else was crucified." Barth added, "That is indeed what the theologian must now pay for."

The playing field was not level, as I soon discovered. Being the maverick that I was, I was left to run the range by myself, relying upon my instincts and intuition. I wore the uniform, punctuated my writing with copious footnotes, and nourished my maverick tendencies into a creature of my own making.

I came to see that theology must be more than merely making

the Word of God relevant to modern culture. Today's relevance can quickly become tomorrow's irrelevance and what is contemporary in one day is already obsolete for another. Theology must be more than useful, for what is useful to one person may be harmful to another. Theology, rather, is servant to Word of God. The mandate laid upon theology is that it be effective Word of God, as God himself said through the prophet, "so shall my word be that goes out from my mouth; it shall not return to me empty, but it shall accomplish that which I purpose, and succeed in the thing for which I sent it" (Isaiah 55:11). I lean toward the purpose of God expressed through the Word and work of God. "Tell the truth, but tell it slant," wrote Emily Dickinson. The soul of theology is discovered and shaped by the 'slant' which the work of God puts on the Word of God.

The average person will never read the various dogmatic theologies which serve as the formal basis for the faith by which its members live and the songs through which they worship. Most will never read the theological utterances of the great Reformer, Martin Luther. When they sing his majestic hymn, "A Mighty Fortress is our God," however, they touch the soul of his theology, and claim for themselves the justifying grace found in the Word of God alone. Those in the Reformed tradition of John Calvin--who may never read his Institutes of the Christian Religion--sing the soul of his theology in the hymn, "To God be the Glory." Generations of those raised in the tradition of John Wesley remain unexposed to his formal writings while expressing the soul of his theology when they sing, "Blessed Assurance, Jesus is Mine."

There is a sense in which all theology has its basis in doxology, as Methodist theologian Geoffrey Wainwright wrote in his book, *Doxology—A Systematic Theology*. Baptist theologian James McClendon argued that experience of God is the context for systematic theological thinking about God.

In keeping with the approach that I have taken, the name of a hymn serves as the title for each chapter. This is not to suggest that the chapter is an exposition of the hymn, rather, each hymn strikes a 'chord' as it were, which serves as a 'call to worship,' through theological reflection. The chapters which follow express my own soul's conviction through an encounter with the soul of God, through the Word of God, empowered by the Spirit of God as the presence of the living Christ. It is my own soul's experience of--and with-- the Soul of God.

4
Guide Me, O Thou Great Jehovah

"The Lord [*Jahweh*, Jehovah] will guide you continually, and satisfy your needs in parched places." Isaiah 58:11

It was Moses who first heard the name Jahweh, from the lips of God . The voice from the burning bush gave voice to the very soul of God, "I am the Lord [*Jahweh*, or Jehovah]. I appeared to Abraham, Isaac and Jacob as God Almighty, but by my name, 'the Lord' I did not make myself known to them" (Exodus 6:2-3).

Through this name, God revealed the tender heart of a loving parent, fiercely jealous of 'other gods' which might steal the object of his love, stirred to wrath by disobedience, moved by mercy to forgive and heal. Out of the soul of God flows pathos, a depth of feeling *beyond* human comprehension, yet embracing humans with divine compassion. Divine pathos, according to Abraham Heschel, denotes a depth of feeling in God as the source of love and compassion, as well as of anger and wrath toward that which threatens the object of love. As such, pathos is the soul of the divine revelation, and the name of this soul is Jahweh.

Jahweh is the soul of God. Through Jahweh's relation to Israel, the soul of theology emerged as the narrative of God's ministry of liberation from bondage, and the formation of a special people as bearers of the divine promise of blessing to "all the families of the earth" (Genesis 12:1-3). God's redemptive purpose and presence in the world became the normative criterion for theological assertions concerning the being of God. The being of God is revealed in the act of God, as Karl Barth reminded us. God's act reveals God's virtues, and through experiencing God's virtues we are able to speak of God's nature. This is the inner logic which opens us up to the knowledge of God.

Attempts to formulate abstract concepts of God's being and nature apart from what can be known of God through his actions lead us astray and even into error. While the Hebrew name *Elohim* is also used in Scripture (usually translated simply as 'God'), it is only through Jahweh (Lord) that one comes to know Elohim (God). This is often obscured in our English translation. "Know that the Lord [Jahweh] is God [Elohim]. It is he that made us, and we are his; we are his people, and the sheep of his pasture" (Psalm 100:3). The name Jahweh is self-authenticating as the name for God which explains the source of the power in the event (cf. Exodus 3; 6:2-8). Elohim is the generic name for God even as *Theos* is the Greek name for God. It is Jahweh who is Elohim, not the reverse. The actions of Jahweh as the covenant-making and keeping God constitute the critical content for knowing the only and true God. It is as Jahweh that Israel knows her God (Elohim). This is the challenge put by Elijah (whose name means: "my El is Jahweh): "If the Lord [Jahweh] is God [Elohim], follow him; but if Baal, then follow him" (1 Kings 18:21). Only Jahweh has the power to be Israel's Elohim because only he **acts**—the other gods are silent, and it is Jahweh who reveals their eternal silence.

This theological formula becomes part of Israel's worship and a frequent refrain in their hymnbook; "O Lord [Jahweh], God [Elohim] of my salvation..." (Psalm 88:1). "The Lord [Jahweh] is my shepherd..." (Psalm 23:1). "O Lord [Jahweh] my God [Elohim], in you I take refuge..." (Psalm 7:1). When we sing, Guide Me, O Thou Great Jehovah, we are not only seeking wisdom and direction for our daily life, but orienting our theological compass so that our minds may follow our hearts in true knowledge of God.

When we begin with the abstract attributes of God we find it difficult to locate God again within the concrete world of time and space. Kornilis Miskotte puts it this way: "When we start from the infinity of God and attempt to reach his particular reality, we destroy the decisive character of the encounters of God in a concrete sense and end up with the theological ambivalence which is characteristic of the silence of the gods. When we start from the omnipotence of God's being, we are merely stating a theory, and then can find no place for the deeds and days which place him in ontic relation with our history. When we start with the equivalence of the so-called communicable attributes, e.g. righteousness, and mercy, we have lost the content of the saving and sustaining work, that is, we have lost the reality of God in his self-communication."

God's act of self-revelation confronts us first of all, not as a mental construct, but a personal summons into relationship. When Moses first hears the voice from the burning bush he is told to take off his sandals, for he is on holy ground (Exod. 3:5). I often tell my students, do not think of it as though God said, "Moses, I want to warn you, take one more step and you will step on holy ground. You have freedom of will so the decision is yours!" No, there is no neutrality, no point where Moses can stand apart and contemplate or verify the voice as coming from God. If he turns and runs it will kill him. If he removes his sandals and exposes his bare feet directly to the holy ground and the very presence of God, he will discover the soul of God.

So, too ,it is with us. Before we ever hear the voice of God speaking to us in God's Word, we already have 'clothed' ourselves with abstract concepts of who God is. From this perspective, we are not surprised to read the first account of human disobedience depicting Adam and Eve as clothing themselves with fig leaves and hiding from God. When God confronts them, the fig leaves are removed and God "makes garments of skin" to clothe them (Genesis 3:7, 21). Our own soul must be naked of pretense, before we can discover the soul of God. The warning of C. S. Lewis is appropriate here: "Every idea of Him we form, He must in mercy shatter."

Naturally we rebel at this, claiming that it is foolhardy to set aside the criteria by which we verify the truth about God before we can trust the Words which come from God. We want to know the truth about God before we release our hearts in commitment to God. Indeed, one of my former theological professors insisted that faith in God can never be granted until we have verified on the ground of human reason that the Word of God is also the truth of God. The human mind, he argued, must be able to comprehend divine revelation as objective truth before one can yield subjective faith and enter into personal knowledge of God. This kind of thinking leads directly to systematic theology but never to the soul of theology.

The mentor for my own theological doctoral studies, Thomas F. Torrance, held a quite different view. Torrance says that God confronts humans as subjects "by addressing them personally and claiming from them personal responses. Thus although theological statements take their rise from a centre in God and not in ourselves, the very nature of the divine Object makes it impossible for us to abstract them from the personal and community setting in which they take place without damaging their mode of reference and indeed without falsifying them." Thus, he concluded, "Knowledge of God takes place not only within the rational structures, but also within the personal and social structures of human life, where the Spirit is at work as **personalising Spirit.** As the living presence of God who confronts us with His personal Being, addresses us in His Word, opens us out toward Himself, and calls forth from us the response of faith and love, He rehabilitates the **human subject**, sustaining him in his personal relations with God and with his fellow creatures."

I particularly liked the phrase, 'rehabilitates the human subject.' It reminds me of God's command to Moses to 'remove his sandals' because he was already on holy ground. It is not only our hearts that need to be converted in order to conform to the Word of God, it is our minds as well. The most difficult thing for theological students to do, I have discovered, is to experience this 'rehabilitation' process as the only way to approach the task of knowing God and to begin the journey into the soul of theology. It is our *thinking* that must be transformed before we can properly think the things of God.

The fact is, the language of the Old Testament has no word for our term 'thinking': *chasaab* and *machashabah* signify 'purposing to do something.' The 'plans' and 'imaginations' of the heart, says Kornilis Miskotte, are already understood to be the inception and beginning of the act, and thus are discernible in the 'work of the hands.' John Pedersen tells us that for the Israelite the act of *thinking* was not the solving of abstract problems, but rather to 'direct the soul' towards something to be known and understood. Thinking thus was an act of the total self, indeed the soul, in grasping a totality. Instead of the verb 'to think' the Hebrew language used words meaning 'to remember,' or 'to make present,' and thus cause the object to act directly upon the soul. In other words, says Pedersen, "There are words expressing that the soul seeks and investigates; but by that is not meant an investigation which analyses and arranges according to abstract views. To investigate is a practical activity; it consists in directing the soul towards something which it can receive into itself, and by which it can be determined. One investigates wisdom, i.e. makes it one's own."

If the actions of Jahweh reveal to us the very soul of God, then the soul of theology must follow the contours of God's innermost being. These are described through the narrative of God's actions as embedded in the 'days and deeds' of the people of God. Jahweh is the soul of God, and the soul of theology is grace. "Grace is an inner mode of being in God Himself," says Karl Barth. Moses discovered God's grace through his own powerlessness and the power of God as redeemer of a people enslaved for more than 400 years.

At the age of 80, Moses was a fugitive and a failure. Forty years earlier he attempted to free a fellow Hebrew by killing an Egyptian, thereby forfeiting his place as the 'adopted son' of Pharaoh. He ended up a powerless wanderer in the Arabian desert. Through *God's* power he was able to lead the people out of slavery into freedom and the journey to the promised land of Abraham and Sarah. Later, Moses was inspired by the Lord to write an account of their exodus, giving, for the first time, a theological hermeneutic by which God's grace could be found (in a tradition going back to the very beginning of creation). Moses experienced God first as redeemer (Jahweh), subsequently as creator (Elohim). The fact that God was known as Elohim from the beginning is only a chronological priority, not a theological one. The theological priority places Jahweh before Elohim, the covenant before creation and grace before law.

In composing the theological narrative backwards, so to speak, from the Exodus event back toward creation, Moses drew upon resources from the oral tradition. Why choose Abraham, out of the hundreds of tribal leaders known to Moses ,as the theological axis on which the divine covenant promise turned toward humanity both intensively and extensively? Was it only because Abraham was a person of such great faith? Possibly. But the inner logic of grace as already made known to Moses through God's ministry of liberation yields a deeper clue. Where in the narrative is there an antecedent to the work of divine grace such as Moses himself experienced? We remember that it was when Moses was both a fugitive and a failure, without any natural or human power, that he became an agent of God's grace through the Word and work of Jahweh. Where in the narrative of Abraham is there something equivalent to this? It is, of course, in the fact that Sarah was barren! Abraham was a man of faith, to be sure. But he invested that faith in human possibility and through Hagar, attempted to produce the son that God had promised (humanly) and that barren Sarah could not produce. Ishmael was thirteen years old when God approached Abraham again and renewed his promised to produce a son through Sarah. Abraham was confused and confounded! "Here he is," Abraham must have said, "he is thirteen years old, and I have taught him every night by the campfire that he is the child of promise! Oh that Ishmael might live in your sight!" (Genesis 17:18). The answer was No! Ishmael must be set aside in favor of the son to be born from the barren womb, from Sarah. So it came to be that Sarah gave birth to Isaac and God's promise was fulfilled. It would be Isaac, not Ishmael through whom the blessing would come, not only to Ishmael, but to the all the families of the earth.

The inner logic of theology is that the grace of God presupposes barrenness. What is presented either by natural or human means as a basis on which faith rests, must be set aside. It is Sarah, not merely Abraham, who represents the crucial theological element in the narrative. The author of the book of Hebrews comments on this by making a point of Sarah's barrenness, saying that though Abraham was 'as good as dead' (the barren womb!) he believed God and Isaac was born (Hebrews 11:11-12).

As the narrative continues, it is Isaac, not Ishmael, that Abraham is asked to sacrifice on Moriah (Genesis 22). This strange and terrifying event cannot be explained on formal ethical terms, but reflects the inner logic of grace. Even that which comes from grace must live by grace. Isaac, having been raised as though from a dead womb, will now be received back, as it were, from the dead on Moriah. Again, the author of Hebrews captures this logic of grace when it is said that Abraham, when put to the test, offered up Isaac: "He considered the fact that God is able even to raise someone from the dead—and figuratively speaking, he did receive him back" (Hebrews 11:17; 19).

As if to make the same point a third time, when Isaac's wife, Rebekah, inquired of the Lord (Jahweh) as to why she had problems with her pregnancy, she received the answer "you are about to have twins, and the elder shall serve the younger" (Genesis 25). Once more, the inner logic of grace is revealed through the story. The natural right of the first born according to custom and culture is set aside in favor of the one that God chooses to inherit the blessing.

Indeed, one can find this inner logic of grace written into the story of creation itself. In Genesis 2, the creation of the first humans is told, this time, as though the first man is created as a solitary being with no other humans. The divine verdict is that it is "not good for the man to be alone." When animals are created out of the ground and brought to the man so that he can name them, there is apparently some expectation that the missing element in the human creature would be found. In the end, it was not to be. The man was put to sleep and, as the story goes, a rib was taken from his side. What is important from a theological perspective is not the rib nor the surgery, but the awakening moment, "this at last, is bone of my bones, flesh of my flesh; this one shall be called Woman..." (Genesis 2:23). What the English translation of the Hebrew does not reveal, is that the term for 'male' is not used in this story until there is a 'female!' It is not that we have a perfectly complete male who only lacks a female. No, what is lacking is not just a 'helper' but another human who can complete the divine image. The soul of humanity is formed by grace, even as the soul of God is found by grace.

In this chapter I have argued that God's self-revelation begins with God's act through which we can discover the inner nature of God's being. What God *does* reveals who God *is*. I have called this a hermeneutical formula; that is, the method by which we interpret Word of God is derived out of the work of God. The work interprets the Word. This is the inner logic of grace or, as I have said, it is the very soul of theology. The very word 'theology' contains this inner core. The Greek word for God is *theos* while the Greek word for knowledge or reason is *logos*. Theology is thus the *logos of theos*. As human beings, bearing the image and likeness of God, we have a human logos. We are rational beings and we can use our minds to describe, explain, and classify our knowledge. When we apply our logos to the study of the human self (*psyche*) we create the discipline of psychology and produce textbooks which contain the knowledge we gain through self-reflection. When we apply our logos to the study of how humans live as social beings, we create the discipline of sociology. The academic curriculum is comprised of a variety of disciplines of study, each of which represent the result of the human logos applied to the study of something in a way that objectifies it and classifies it.

How then, can we include theology as a discipline of study along with these other academic disciplines? Applying the human logos (reason) so as to objectify divine being and create a discipline of study is not only impossible—no one has ever seen God (John 1:18)—but when attempted leads to the creation of an Ishmael rather than to the birth of a divinely appointed Isaac.

Imagine that there *is* a divine Logos, a Logos that dwells within the very soul of God, would not this become the *logos of theos*? Imagine that this divine *logos* should actually assume humanity and dwell with us, would not this be a supreme act of divine grace? If such a miracle should occur, and that in God of which we humans bear the image, becomes human, could we not, along with this divine/human imagebearer, find in our *imagination* the soul of theology? I imagine so!

5

Thou Didst Leave Thy Throne

> In the beginning was the Word [logos], and the Word was with God, and the Word was God... And the Word became flesh and dwelt among us. (John 1:1; 14)

At the time of Jesus' death, he appeared as any ordinary man, hanging on a cross between two others who were condemned by imperial decree, just as he was. It was exactly as described by the prophet of old: "He was despised and rejected by others; a man of suffering and acquainted with infirmity; and as one from whom others hide their faces he was despised, and we held him of no account" (Isaiah 53:3).

Like other great men before him, death claimed them all. Without his resurrection from that claim of death, Jesus of Nazareth lived and died as any ordinary man, even *with* his extraordinary gifts. Without Easter, there would be no celebration of his birth at Christmas.

It was his resurrection from the dead that confirmed what many had already come to believe, and what then was proven incredibly true. Not only that he was alive, but that during his life, when he spoke of God as his Father, it was with an intimacy of more than one life's acquaintance.

Did Jesus actually have an antecedent existence with some parity in the personal being of God? The Apostle Paul might have been the first to suggest as much. In his letter to the church at Philippi he incorporated what might already have been a 'hymn of praise' chanted in the earliest expressions of worship by the Christian community. It was Christ Jesus, they sang, "who, though he was in the form of God, did not regard equality with God something to be exploited, but emptied himself, taking the form of a slave, being born in human likeness" (Philippians 2:6-7).

This downward movement of humiliation, as seen by Paul, was followed by an upward movement of exaltation in his resurrection and ascension. We remember that Paul had his own encounter with the risen Jesus, not only after his resurrection, but after his ascension to heaven (Acts 9). It was the resurrection that determined for Paul the status of Jesus as not only "descended from David according to the flesh," but "declared to be the Son of God with power according to the Spirit of holiness by resurrection from the dead, Jesus our Lord" (Romans 1:3-4). Long before any of the written Gospel accounts of the birth, life, and death of Jesus appeared, Paul's preaching and writing testified to the divine origin of Jesus.

In the end, after Paul had finished his ministry and died, after Matthew, Mark and Luke had written their accounts of the life of Jesus, the Apostle John wrote of the antecedent existence of Jesus in such simple phrases that, except for their elegance, might have escaped our attention. "In the beginning was the Word, and the Word was with God, and the Word was God. He was in the beginning with God. . . . And the Word became flesh and lived among us" (John 1:1-2; 14). Four words in the original Greek: *ho logos sarx egeneto*. The divine Logos that was with God and which is God, became flesh. In Jerome's Latin translation, the Greek phrase *sarx egeneto* became *incarnatio*, from which we have the English word 'incarnation.'

John was not through, however, he went on to remind us that "No one has ever seen God. It is God the only Son, who is close to the Father's heart, who has made him known" (John 1:18). The older translation of John's words read, "who is in the bosom of the father." This suggests the intimate relation which the divine Logos had within the being of God much like John who spoke of his own intimacy with Jesus at the last Supper as "reclining next to Jesus" (John 13:23). The phrase, 'reclining next to' is translated in the older versions as 'bosom' and is the same Greek word used by John in 1:18 to speak of the relation of the divine Logos within the being of God. John intends for us to understand that Jesus has an antecedent existence to his own human life for which the closest and most intimate human relation is only a metaphor.

This is not all. John says that Jesus, having this existence within the very being of God, has "made him known" (1:18). Here again, a single Greek word lies behind the English translation, 'made him known'—it is the word *exegesis*. Students who study the text of Scripture so as to determine as closely as possible what the words mean do what is called exegesis. Biblical exegesis is a standard part of the curriculum for scholarly study of the text of Scripture.

Quite literally, then, Jesus is the 'exegesis' of God. Not only is Jesus anointed by the Spirit of God, and thus the promised Messiah (Christ), but as the incarnate Son of the Father Jesus is the very presence of God. The 'logos of God' is the same as 'Son of God' for John (1:1,14,18). In becoming the Christ (the Greek term for the Hebrew word *Messiah*—anointed one), Jesus is anointed by the Spirit of God to do the work of God. It is the work of God which testifies to the very being of God, as Jesus himself said. "If I am not doing the works of my Father, then do not believe me. But if I do them, even though you do not believe me, believe the works, so that you may know and understand that the Father is in me and I am in the Father" (John 10:37-38). Jesus did not **become** the Son of God by being anointed with the Spirit of God and by doing the works of God; rather, because Jesus **is** the Son of God, the works which he does testifies to that inner relation.

Some might be tempted to say that the language which speaks of Jesus as the Son of God and as the Anointed One, is primarily descriptive and not ascriptive. That would be to say, Jesus was essentially a human being who, in being anointed by the Spirit of God, functioned in such a way that he described and pointed to God, but that one should not ascribe to the person of Jesus the quality of divine being. In response, one should consider that Jesus not only performed a miracle of healing as a work of God, but insisted that the miracle of healing pointed to his divine authority to forgive sin. When Jesus healed the man who was paralyzed, the announcement of forgiveness preceded the healing (Mark 2:1-12). His critics rightly stated, "Who can forgive sin but God alone?" The point of this story is that Jesus clearly asserted his divine authority in forgiving the man's sins.

At Easter we sing the hymn, Christ the Lord is Risen Today. Then we look back to Christmas and sing, Thou Didst Leave Thy Throne. John the Apostle, like John the Baptist, extended his literary finger as if to say, "Behold the God who has left his throne to live humanly with us, and divinely for us."

In 1970, during my first term at the University of Edinburgh where I was enrolled in doctoral studies, I listened to the lectures of my mentor, Thomas Torrance. Having completed eleven years of pastoral ministry following my seminary work, I expected exposure to academic theology to be something like having the paramedics using a defibrillator to jolt the chest of a patient whose heart had stopped beating. I was prepared for the shock, with the *hope* that I would come alive, perhaps with a new appreciation for life. I might add that I had read two books by professor Torrance prior to leaving for Scotland, and knew that I was heading into pretty deep water. I still have the book where I marked one sentence that took up two-thirds of the page! I felt like Amos who protested, "I am no prophet, nor a prophet's son, but I am a herdsman, and a dresser of sycamore trees" (Amos 7:14). Or, as Dorothy said after her tornado-tossed home set down in Oz, "Toto, I have a feeling we are not in Kansas anymore!" (*The Wizard of Oz*, 1939)

Well, it was quite unlike what I expected. In the classroom, Professor Torrance was as much worshipper as scholar. He brought us into the inner sanctuary of the loving intimacy between Jesus the Son and God the Father. At the very outset, Torrance cited the words of Jesus: "All things have been handed over to me by my Father; and no one knows the Son except the Father; and no one knows the Father except the Son and anyone to whom the Son chooses to reveal him" (Matt. 11:27). Listening to Torrance's lecture was like a guided tour through the expanding spaces, the deepest valleys and highest peaks of the divine heart. Indeed, he took us to the very soul of God, as poured out in human life and love through Jesus. It was no surprise, then, to have each class session concluded with a benediction, something no other teacher has done in my experience.

Some years later, I was reminded of an experience recounted by Karl Barth in his student days at Marburg University in Germany, when he sat under the teaching of W. Herrmann. It was through Herrmann that Barth discovered a way around the formidable wall that historical criticism had erected around Jesus by raising questions about the authenticity of the text. Herrmann, according to Barth, argued that knowledge of God is like a 'secret in the soul,' and that it cannot be objectified and passed on as 'mere information.' The Gospels present both an 'outer life' of Jesus and an 'inner life.' It is this inner life of Jesus in his relation with God that constitutes the truth about God, taught Herrmann. "Herrmann was *the* theological teacher of my student years," says Barth. "I soaked Herrmann in through all my pores." The soul of theology for Karl Barth seems to have begun at that moment: "The decisive thing was the christocentric impulse, and I learnt that from him."

Perhaps the soul of theology began for me during my own days of study, discovering for the first time, after all those years, what the soul of the preacher had longed for. I had preached and taught an incarnational theology, now I was being introduced to a theology of the incarnation. In our worship service we sang *Emmanuel*—God with us—during the Advent season. An incarnational theology that was first song now became substance–the soul of God weeping human tears. My preaching had sought to bring Jesus within the confines of my own humanity, using incarnation as a metaphor; this new knowledge brought my humanity within the communion of God through the humanity of Jesus. "If you know me, you will know my Father also," Jesus said. "From now on you do know him and have seen him" (John 14:7). I soaked it in through my pores!

What the Apostle John described in cosmic terms—a heavenly logos assuming earthly form—the Apostle Paul proclaimed as a sacrament of salvation. "In him all the fullness of God was pleased to dwell, and through him God was pleased to reconcile to himself all things. . . " (Col. 1:19-20). In the person of Jesus Christ, the double movement took place simultaneously, *not* sequentially. At every moment during the life of Jesus, the inner being of God was being revealed through the words and actions of Jesus. This is the movement of revelation through which we come to know the truth of God. At the same time, every word and action of Jesus was a movement from below to above, reconciling humanity to God.

We do not just know about Jesus, but in being brought into relation with Jesus by the Spirit, we are brought into the realm of God's own 'self-knowledge.' Remember the words of Jesus? "No one knows the Father except the Son and no one knows the Son except the Father" (Matt. 11:27). This refers to God's self-knowledge which is a knowledge that resides in the very being of God as mutual love. It is this divine self-love, manifested in the relation of the Son to the Father, that is the basis for God's love for the world (John 17:26).

To know God is to be reconciled to God, and in being reconciled to God we come to know God. We cannot separate revelation from reconciliation so as to make out of divine revelation an objective truth which we have at our disposal. This does not mean that the truth of revelation depends upon our own subjective apprehension of it. Rather, our subjective self is brought within the sheer objectivity of God's self-knowledge. This is why, when Peter confessed that Jesus was really the Messiah who was the son of the living God, Jesus reminded him, "Flesh and blood has not revealed this to you, but my Father in heaven" (Matt. 16:17). Nicodemus received the same instruction from Jesus after professing "We know you are a teacher who has come from God;" Jesus replied, "No one can see the Kingdom of God without being born from above" (John 3:2-3). In his prayer for the disciples, Jesus asked the Father to "sanctify them in the truth." Then, referring to his own relation to the Father he added, "And for their sakes I sanctify myself, so that they may also be sanctified in truth" (John 17:17,19). Sanctification, in this case, involves sharing in the relation that Jesus has as the Son with the Father. Both revelation and reconciliation thus have an objective basis so that our own subjectivity is bound up in the mutual subjectivity of Father and Son.

Jesus is the Word which comes into the world and to human persons. As such, he is the revelation of God through both his divine and human being. His divine being anchors revelation on the divine side, and establishes the content of revelation. His human being establishes the reality of revelation as a true presence and knowledge of God which exists in creaturely and temporal form. True knowledge of God is thus possible for human beings through the humanity of Jesus which serves as the 'sacrament' of revelation.

Jesus is also the response which humans make to the Word of God. Thus, revelation is complete in Christ, both as to its source in God and its response from the human side. His divine being establishes the content of this response, guaranteeing to us that what the Word of God demands has been perfectly fulfilled in the holiness of Christ. His human being establishes the reality of this response as the authentic response of humans bearing in his own humanity the contradiction of sin and the penalty of death. Therefore, in Christ, nothing can destroy or invalidate the Word of God and the faith which it produces.

It would not be wrong to say that Jesus is the true believer, whose own faith in the Father becomes the basis for our faith in such a way that we are freed from the ambivalence and inward uncertainty which always plague our own attempt to believe. It would not be wrong to say that Jesus is also the true disciple, whose own obedience lived out in the face of temptation in such a way that we are freed from our own instability and unreliability of will. I remember the day when Professor Torrance elaborated most eloquently on the way in which the divine Logos assumed a human will in the person of Jesus that was bent away from God and turned back in on itself. Every day of his life, Jesus took that human will and bent it back in perfect obedience to his Father so that in being joined to Christ our will is graciously conformed to his own willingness, which exists to this very day in the humanity of Christ now glorified and existing within the very being of God. This is the basis for our assurance in union with Christ through being made partakers of Christ through the Spirit. There is part of God in us through the indwelling Spirit of Christ. The Christ who in us, says Paul, is our "hope of glory" (Col. 1:27). At the same time, Paul says, our "life is hidden with Christ in God" (Col. 3:3). This means that there is something of us already abiding in the very presence of God through Christ!

In this way both revelation and reconciliation take place through our being in Christ and Christ being in us. In the account of Jesus' life and ministry while he was on earth, the inner life of God has opened up to us a life of selfless love. In reaching out to the 'lost sheep' of the house of Israel, Jesus revealed to us the compassionate heart of divine love. These 'lost sheep' were the excommunicated, the publicans, sinners, the disinherited. They were excluded from the synagogues. Jesus deliberately associated with them, thus enacting the messianic parable of those who will come from the east and from the west and sit down with Abraham, Isaac, and Jacob. Jesus broke down the 'dividing wall' which separates us from God and leads to hostility between one another (Eph. 2:14).

If there are two sides to humanity, I wrote in the doctoral dissertation which issued out of those days, Christ will be found on the wrong side. By this I meant to say that God not only appeared in the world where humanity is broken and burdened with sin and failure, but God assumed that broken humanity through Christ in order to overcome the estrangement humans suffer from God and from each other. This is the divine act of reconciliation which issues from the very core of God's love and is fulfilled through Christ's own love for the Father from the 'far country,' so to speak, as in the parable of the prodigal son where Jesus placed himself in the parable as the lost son (Luke 15).

The late James Torrance put it so eloquently that I cannot help but quote him in full: "Christ does not heal us by standing over against us, diagnosing our sickness, prescribing medicine for us to take, and then going away, to leave us to get better by obeying his instructions—as an ordinary doctor might. No, He becomes the patient! He assumes that very humanity which is in need of redemption, and by being anointed by the Spirit in our humanity, by a life of perfect obedience, by dying and rising again, for us, our humanity is healed *in him*. We are not just healed 'through Christ' because of the work of Christ but 'in and through Christ.'"

The very person of Christ thus continues to be the 'primary sacrament' through which all of humanity is taken up and bound to God. The sacramental life of the church is grounded in the objective sacrament of the real humanity of Christ, so that the water and faith of Baptism, the bread and wine of the Eucharist, are freed from the ambiguity of our own subjective faith. Karl Barth says: "A sacramental continuity stretches backwards into the existence of the people of Israel, whose Messiah he is, and forwards into the existence of the apostolate and the church founded upon the apostolate."

At this point in his lecture, Professor Torrance paused and then went on to say something like this: The humanity of Christ holds us 'at arms length' from God, permitting relation, decision, commitment, worship and fellowship. Yet, within this 'arms length,' God is in touch with us, so that reaching out to Jesus is literally embracing God. God's love has a human face, human arms, and a human heart, filled with divine compassion, inviting all to accept the embrace.

It was time for the benediction. Class was over, but the moment lingered—and does to this very day,

6

The Love of God

> God is love, and those who abide in love abide in God,
> and God abides in them. 1 John 4:16

Edward John Carnell, president and professor of philosophical theology at Fuller Theological Seminary taught us that love is the imperative essence of the being and law of God. In expressing his conviction that love is the true test of orthodox theology, he urged tolerance toward other views, respect for persons with whom we disagree, and grace as the indispensable virtue of truth. For many who were committed to the rational formulas of faith as weapons to be used in defending the truth, this not only appeared to border on heresy but worse, was a betrayal of the consortium of fundamentalists whose legacy still clung to the name of Fuller. This cost him dearly, not only the emotional and mental pain resulting from the rejection which he felt from his colleagues but perhaps in the end, his own life. He announced his resignation as president during his address at my commencement service in 1959. The few years that followed led to his premature death in 1967 at the age of 48. He never received the recognition that he so richly deserved, except among his former students who carried it in their own hearts, my own among them.

In a book published during this time, *The Kingdom of Love and the Pride of Life*, he wrote: "Since one language is spoken in the kingdom of love, there is no confusion of tongues." Ah, but we seem to have lost at birth the language of love and now struggle to find the words that echo in our hearts. I did not know this until I read the poignant words of the novelist, Thomas Wolfe, who lamented: "Which of us has known his brother? Which of us has looked into his father's heart? Which of us had not remained forever prison-pent? Which of us is not forever a stranger and alone? .... Remembering speechlessly we seek the great forgotten language, the lost-lane-end into heaven, a stone, a leaf, an unfound door. Where? When?" We cannot love in word and deed until we learn the language of love. Carnell knew this and, somewhat like his erstwhile traveling companion, Søren Kierkegaard, spoke out of his own suffering soul. He became for some of us, the finger of John the Baptist pointing to the one who came to put the language of love in our hearts and its words upon our lips.

I took Carnell at his word. We must always speak the truth in love, he urged us. Upon graduating from seminary I became the founding pastor of a new church. On the first letterhead I created for the church were the words: *Speaking the Truth in Love* (Eph. 4:15). This was to become the mantra by which we measured our lives and the mandate by which we defined our mission.

The syntax of the language love speaks is pure and potent. "God is love, and those who abide in love abide in God, and God abides in them. . . . No one has ever seen God; if we love one another, God lives in us, and his love is perfected in us. . . Whoever does not love does not know God, for God is love . . . There is no fear in love, but perfect love casts out fear" (1 John, 4:12-18).

The semantics of love (that to which the term itself refers) are clear and unambiguous. "In this is love, not that we loved God but that he loved us. . . ." (1 John 4:10). At the time, I was tempted to say that if God is love, then love is God. But this is only true if we maintain the asymmetrical relation between God's love and human love. We can say that God is love, but the reverse cannot be said: love, by human standards, is not God. The reductionism of divine love to human love leads to a confusion of tongues. When the absolute demand (gift) of love is relativized to our love of the neighbor without God as the middle term, love collapses into mutual self-love. "We love God because he first loved us" (1 John 4:19). At the same time, if we say that we love God but do not love others, our professed love for God is a lie (1 John 4:20).

The Apostle John knew well the story of the birth of Jesus. By the time he wrote his own gospel, Matthew and Luke had written their own versions of the nativity story and we could assume that John had them at hand. It was John, as I wrote earlier, who heard the 'heartbeat of God' as he reclined on the bosom of Jesus (John 13:23). Surely, at the time, he only felt the human side of love from Jesus and thus referred to himself only indirectly as 'the disciple whom Jesus loved.' As the other disciples were no longer living by the time that John wrote his gospel, such pretentious modesty was a privilege against which they could not protest. If one should protest, however, he would simply respond that each could well say the same thing. Jesus' love was available for all to claim if they dared! Love is a costly grace, and to acknowledge that one is the object of God's unconditional love demands that one express love in response, unconditionally.-

It is far easier to say that one believes in God than to say that one is loved by God. In the end, Jesus did not press his disciples to say that they believed in him, but asked simply, "Do you love me?" The fact that this question was first put to Peter is noted by John's own account of the moment, as if to suggest that Peter had to learn what John already had discovered (John 21:15-19).

What John came to see as theological truth is that the love which he experienced in reclining on the bosom of Jesus had its origin in the prenatal life of Jesus as the divine Son reclining in the bosom of the Father (John 1:18). In using the same word (bosom) for the heartbeat of human love and the heartbeat of divine love John grounds the soul of theology in the soul of God. Jesus is not the incarnation of divine reason, but of divine love. John's use of the Greek word *logos* as that aspect of God's being which was 'in the bosom of the Father' and which 'became flesh' places 'reason' within love. Love is not 'irrational' as we tend to think of it, defying all logic. Rather, love is itself the very logic of God. This love is the core of rationality, as the Scottish philosopher, John Macmurray wrote. "The capacity to love objectively is the capacity which makes us persons. . . It is the core of rationality." What is irrational, is to tear reason and logic out of the heart of love and to define the truth of God in impersonal doctrinal formulas which issue from and are under the control of a human logos. As it turned out, those who charged Carnell with introducing subjective truth into the truth of God, were themselves irrational and ultimately, unreasonable.

You will now understand more fully why my own theological pilgrimage began with the newly discovered language of love as the lexicon of truth. It is, after all, truth that brings assurance to the heart that loves. Having experienced the love of God through Jesus, the disciples still wanted to know, "Is it true?" I learned that the response to a sermon which attempted to put in human words the stunning revelation of the divine Word was not, "I enjoyed the sermon, pastor," but, "Is it really true?" That Jesus was actually the very truth of God seemed too good to be true! The love of God for the world (John 3:16) brought sent forth a Son who was a friend of the fallen and the savior of sinners--this should cause us to 'disbelieve for joy!' (Luke 24:41). It's too good to be true—the love that God is.

In those early days I wrote in my journal, "*The Love That God Is* will now be written. I care little for its destiny, but only for its birth. It shall be responsible for its own survival. There is no doubt of its genuineness—it has already been understood; understanding has n*ecessitated* its utterance. My responsibility is not to create novelty, but to unclothe the true."

Even now, I am not sure that it can be written. The hymn-writer who provided the title for this chapter, reminds us that the only adequate way for us to express God's love is to confess our inadequacy.

> Could we with ink the ocean fill,
> And were the skies of parchment made,
> Were ev'ry stalk on earth a quill,
> And ev'ry man a scribe by trade,
> To write the love of God above,
> Would drain the ocean dry,
> Nor could the scroll contain the whole,
> Tho stretched from sky to sky.

I do not want to be like the disciples who blurted out to Jesus, "Now we know that you know all things. . ." (John 16:30), to which Jesus replied, in effect, "Do you really!" One must be careful however. To say too little about the love of God may be worse than attempting to say too much. On the other hand, It may be the case that to take hold of but a portion of divine love is to grasp the whole.

My former mentor, Professor Thomas Torrance liked to say that we can apprehend God even if we do not comprehend him. He then used the illustration of a small child who grasps the finger of an adult fully confident that with that one finger, everything that the adult is beyond the child's comprehension is apprehended in that one finger. Indeed, Jesus himself said that he was, in effect, the 'finger of God' (Luke 11:20). I think I have hold of that finger, and I will not let go, like Jacob of old, who said, "I will not let you go unless you bless me!" (Gen. 32:26). I would rather say, with Paul, "Now I only know in part, then I will know fully, even as I have been fully known" (1 Cor. 13:12).

I will tell you of the part that I know.

The love of God is passionate but not promiscuous. God loves intensely but not indiscriminately. Books have been written and sermons have been preached, I am afraid, insisting that divine love is 'disinterested love,' that is, to use the Greek words, God's love is *agape* not *eros*, and only in a secondary sense, *philia*. Those who like to use these terms to set divine love apart from human love think that they are protecting God from the kind of 'need-love' which seems to drive human love with quiet (and sometimes not so quiet) desperation. *Agape* love, we are told, is love without regard for a response. It is purely gratuitous, freely given out of divine altruism. The fact is, God's first language is not Greek but Hebrew, the *lingua franca* of the chosen people and the mother tongue of Jesus. The Apostle Paul made no effort to examine the shades of difference and meaning between *agape* and *eros* love, for he discovered the essence of love in his own spiritual encounter with Jesus Christ.

In the case of God, love is a verb before it can be a noun. We discover that God is love only because God acts in loving ways. So then, love does not exist apart from the act of loving. At the same time, the New Testament appears to avoid the use of *eros* in favor of *agape* when speaking of God's love. Why this is so, writes Karl Barth, may be found in the Greek translation of the Old Testament where *agape* was chosen to translate the Hebrew word for love, *aheb*, which was frequently used to express the kind of love between husband and wife and in all kinds of familiar and family relationships. In fact, Barth adds, the Greek word *agape* was actually a quite colorless term devoid of passion and feeling. The Hebrew language, however, made no distinction between the love which is theologically significant and that which was later called 'erotic.' What is quite strange, said Barth, is the use of an abstract and empty term such as *agape* to translate the Hebrew word to depict the marriage between Yahweh and Israel and in the Song of Solomon. This love is nothing, if not erotic. In actuality, the use of *agape* to express the love of God is to impoverish the biblical content of the word. In his classic work, *Eros and Agape*, Anders Nygren contrasts *eros* with *agape* attempting to show that *eros* is a lower and less worthy kind of love. To some extent, C. S. Lewis in his equally well-known book, *The Four Loves*, does the same thing. But this is to create a contradiction which does not appear in the biblical narrative.

We should not shrink from expressing God's love in terms that reflect the passion of God by which he enters into the human situation so fully that it requires him to enter the depths of human estrangement.

This is prefigured in Jahweh's relation with Israel as depicted by Hosea, who quotes the words which come out of the very soul of Yahweh; "How can I give you up, Ephraim? How can I hand you over, O Israel? . . . My heart recoils within me; my compassion grows warm and tender" (11:8). The love of God for the people who became unlovely is itself lovely. This passionate pursuit of that which love cannot bear to lose and leave, depicts God as Francis

Thompson's 'Hound of Heaven.'

In his epic poem, Thompson, describes his own the tortuous plunge into prodigality on the streets of London. There he is shown hospitality by women of the street, finding at last in human love the 'lost-lane-end into heaven.' Thompson wrote:

Halts by me that footfall: Is my gloom, after all,
Shade of His hand, outstretched caressingly?
"Ah, fondest, blindest, weakest, I am He Whom thou seekest!
Thou dravest love from thee, Who dravest Me."

When the poet and the prophet speak of this passionate love that God is, how dare our theologians turn back from the promised land of love to the barren desert to stare at the bush which never burns. Knowing the passion of love in our own hearts, even when it leads us astray, we ought to know better than to worship a God who has never felt the hurt of lost love nor the joy of embracing a found child. In knowing the love of God we experience love which is passionate but not promiscuous. Divine love does not go out searching for just anyone to love, it reaches out to touch everyone with love. If divine love is troubled, it is not by anxiety or unrest within love itself. What arouses passion in the love of God is not an unfulfilled need, but a longing to embrace the divine image in another. This longing is the fulfillment of love which may yet suffer the contingencies of time and chance in this temporal life. There is a serenity to love which shines through the darkest clouds.

A decade or so ago, many years after I was the student of Professor Thomas Torrance, he and I were asked to deliver papers at a conference with Chinese Confucianist scholars in Hong Kong. The two of us shared a flat where we spent some time each day discussing our own theological views. One of those discussions turned to the question of divine impassibility—the theory that God does not experience emotion and feelings such as humans do. This view of God's being held that for God to experience emotion would introduce change in God's being, which would conflict with another theory that God was unchangeable and immutable. Professor Torrance was somewhat resistant to my suggesting that God surely must experience emotion and have deep passion as Jesus did. He argued in response that the ancient theologians thought of God's being as ultimately serene, and that the serenity of God precluded the experience of emotions which would disturb that serenity. In response I urged him to consider a mother who sees her small child playing in the street where an automobile suddenly comes careening out of control, about to hit the child. The mother is aroused by feelings of concern and even fear for the life of her child, When she runs into the street she finds that someone has pulled the child to safety and she takes the child in her arms and her heart is at peace. "That is serenity," I suggested to my mentor.

Professor Torrance thought for a long while and then replied, "It is always a joy to be taught by one of your own students!" This tells a great deal about Torrance himself. He is a person for whom wisdom and grace are virtues so obvious as to be ordinary, when in fact they are uncommon and extraordinary. The passion of Christ, Torrance was later to write, "is the very passion of God himself incarnate in him. . . . Jesus is God's very own Son, his only begotten Son—one who came to us out of the Father's Life who belonged to his very Heart and innermost Self. And when the Father did not spare his own Son but freely delivered him up for us all in atoning sacrifice, the Cross became a window into the innermost heart of God and the nature of his love. It tells us that God loves us more than he loves himself."

God's love is grounded in God's freedom to create life and give it freedom to love and be loved. The Incarnation of Jesus Christ into the world does not imply an insufficiency in God's love, as though he needed something or someone other than himself to exist in order to love well. It is not a question of self-sufficiency or of self-need at all. Rather, the concept of a divine self-sufficiency is a 'philosophical myth,' according to theologian Catherine LaCugna. When personhood, as with God, is an ultimate basis for love, then "Eros can be thought of as arising out of plenitude not need, because it is out of fullness not emptiness that the lover wishes to give himself or herself to another."

That can only be true in Jesus Christ himself. "What has come into being in him was life," wrote John, "and the life was the light of all people" (1:4). The life of God does not belong to God alone." One might add to what LaCugna has said stating it this way: "The life of the Father does not belong to the Father alone, but also to the Son, and those who become partakers of that life." The divine love of which Hosea wrote came to fulfillment when God himself embraced humanity in the person of Jesus who, in solidarity with humanity under sentence of death, restored humanity through resurrection. As a result, it is this 'love of God' which is poured into our hearts by the Holy Spirit, writes Paul (Rom. 5:5).

This is what I know in part. Love creates possibilities beyond what can be realized and desires which can never be fulfilled on the stage of life. The curtain always falls on this stage, at the end, where the dreams we dream and the longings we feel are left hanging in the empty space long after the applause.

Forty years ago I preached a sermon with the title: "The Silent Tears of Unborn Sin." I wish that I could remember what I said in the sermon as well as I remember the title! I am sure that it was heard as an esoteric and eccentric peregrination over the landscape of my own soul, which at the time, as you already have discovered, was deeply drenched with Kierkegaard and walking on the edge with Ecclesiastes! Nonetheless, there was in the title, at least, something of the soul of a theologian.

What struck me at the time, and still plucks at my heart strings, was the thought aroused by John's statement concerning Jesus in Revelation 13:8. While there are several variations in the translation of this text, the older version (provided as an alternative reading in the NRSV) said that Jesus was "the lamb that was slain from the foundation of the world" (KJV). How far back into the soul of God, I wondered, could we trace the love which led Jesus to the cross to die the death resulting from the sin of Adam and Eve? If, as John had written in his gospel, the life which became the light of the world in Jesus came out of the very heart of the Father, then the death that ensued came out of the same heart and the same love. The tears shed by Jesus at the tomb of Lazarus and over the city of Jerusalem were the tears of God as surely as Jesus is God. God anticipated the risk of creating life with the possibility of death. He might well weep over sins not yet committed. The incarnational love of God presupposes a tragic dimension when the infinite is exposed to suffering the impossibilities of the finite. If that is not what I said in the sermon, it is what I *ought* to have said.

We are each Willy Loman in Arthur Miller's play, *The Death of a Salesman*. Loman is a salesman whose self image is unrealistically pinned to his dreams of success while denying the reality of his failures. Willy Loman is a fictional character, yet his pathetic attempts to rescue his self-identity from the abyss of failure touches a chord in all of us. There is no self so secure but that a bit of him doesn't rise up like a ghost to haunt our dreams with the specter of failure and futility.

Theologian Wendy Farley writes that creation is brought forth by God out of a divine eros. "Created perfection is fragile, tragically structured. The tragic structure of finitude and the human capacity for deception and cruelty together account for the possibility and actuality of suffering and evil... The power to create must therefore include the power to redeem. The fragility of creation requires the continual presence of divine power to resist the evils resident in history." The presence of the tragic is not entirely due to sin but rather to the 'structure of finitude' itself. But the world that God created is the world that God *loves*. Love does not exist independently of the created order. God breathed into humans something of his own image and likeness. From the beginning, before sin entered into this finite structure, the first humans experienced 'love within limits,' as my former colleague Lewis Smedes wrote. "Love is an uncommon power to cope with common suffering, . . . To qualify as sufferers, we must want to be rid of something with such passion that it hurts." To his definition I would add, "To suffer is to hope for something with such passion that we are bound to be disappointed." It was Kierkegaard who taught me that to grasp the eternal in a moment of the temporal is to suffer. For the eternal can only be mediated into the temporal through suffering. That is, to desire what the eternal makes possible but which the temporal forecloses as impossible.

Adam and Eve were immediately thrust by love into an impossible situation. The first moment of mutual awareness was one of ecstasy and fulfillment: "This at last is bone of my bones and flesh of my flesh. . . " (Gen 2:23). Karl Barth once suggested that the woman who speaks in the Song of Solomon might be giving voice to Eve when she says, "Set me as a seal upon your heart, as a seal upon your arm; for love is as strong as death, passion fierce as the grave. . . If one offered for love all the wealth of one's house, it would be utterly scorned" (8:6,7). The thought of death was not insinuated into their minds by the Fall, but by God himself in warning them that death would be the result of eating the forbidden fruit. They were, after all, divinely created beings wrapped in the flesh of mortality.

They could not hold hands forever. In order to survive, even in the Garden of Eden there is work to be done, separations to endure, anxiety to quell. In watching the other walk over the hill the thought occurs, "will he/she return?" The Garden was good, said the Lord God, but it was also very dangerous. When separated, love turns into longing and waiting, hoping and dreaming. Even in the Garden, before sin entered through their disobedience, there might well have been momentary irritations at some personal discomfort, one being preoccupied with a task, the other lost in thought about a personal matter—why does my stomach hurt?

In my imagination I view their 'perfect' relationship as having these normal episodes. One asks, "What were you thinking about?" The other responds, "Nothing!" That is not a good answer, even in a perfect world! The spirit of another person, as the Apostle Paul reminds us, is inaccessible to us (1 Cor. 2). That is the mystery of personal being and the motivation for searching for clues as to what lies behind words and gestures.

My point is this, each have their own bodies and their own space, though they also share the same space. What is a personal and private moment may appear to be a mask of indifference to the other. We should understand that existence in a world of time and space involves risk, negotiation of private and personal feelings and desires, and a sense of limitation. The space between them as the space between them and the world is infinite though fixed by finite boundaries. This is the space that love creates and seeks to preserve without the power to compel the other or coerce the cosmos to yield its own power to the desires of love. Here too there are desires that remain unfulfilled and needs that remain unmet. Can we acknowledge that this is the drama of human existence as originally created by God? On this stage, the curtain will always fall before the play is over.

My students do not like me to talk in this fashion! For some strange reason they feel more comfortable with the idea that all human 'dis-ease' comes from sin. They see no virtue or good in the tragic. They want divine love, at least, to be a deep flowing stream with no rocks or rapids. They do not like the word 'tragic.' They want to erase it from the vocabulary of love as though denying its existence as part of the good world, they can eliminate its possibility from the real world. They finally can accept the tragic as due to sin, but not as a reality of love. Thus, the love of God is preserved (in their minds) as an ideal form of love, and their sense of God's presence and favor as fragile as their faith.

In Christopher Fry's play, *The Boy with a Cart*, Cuthman is sent by his father to watch the sheep. He invents a ritual whereby God guards his sheep by drawing a circle around them with his staff, allowing him to run and play and daydream the hours away. Mildred and Bess, two neighbors come out to inform him that his father has died. He refuses to believe it. They insist that it is true. He continues to deny.

"We were speaking the truth," they tell him.

"You came to make me sorry," he responds, "but you're breaking the sun over your knees to say my father's dead. My father is strong and well."

They persist, "come down with us and see him."

He rejects, "Let me alone. No; if I come you'll take me to a place where truth will laugh and scatter like a magpie. Up here, my father waits for me at home and God sits with the sheep."

Off stage the chorus chants: "How is your faith now, Cuthman?

Is God still in the air now that the sun is down? They are afraid in the city, sleepless in the town. Cold on the roads, desperate by the river. Can faith for long elude prevailing fever?"

The passion of love with its capacity to embrace the tragic is the enduring power of faith. I suffer for those who dare not love for fear of having to let go, in time at least, of that which is loved. Embracing the tragic element imbedded in the act of love at the beginning is not to be afflicted with sadness but to have faith in love. I suffer for those whose faith is fragile because its love is too bright and beautiful to survive the dying of the light. The loss of faith is due more to the failure of love to sustain an ideal than for faith to be grounded in folly. I suffer with those who dare to believe that God is love and who hold that love to its promise, disbelieving the finality of every loss and the futility of every dream. Love is as strong as death; its passion fiercer than the grave.

This is the part that I know. Every act of human love creates not only what must be loved but also what must in the end be lost. Except! Except for the love of God which wept for this loss and sent his only Son so that divine tears might moisten human eyes and run down human cheeks. Jesus wept.

This too I know, and this is the part that is the whole. Divine love not only reaches down into hell, it ascends not just to heaven, but to the Father's outstretched arms. "Father, I desire that these also, whom you have given me, may be with me where I am, to see my glory, which you have given me because you loved me before the foundation of the world" (John 17:24). In the end, John said the whole of love. In his final vision he wrote, "See the home of God is with mortals. He will dwell with them; they will be his peoples, and God himself will wipe every tear from their eyes" (Revelation 21: 3,4).

This is the love that God is.

7

There's a Wideness in God's Mercy

> For the love of God is broader,
> than the measure of man's mind;
> And the heart of the Eternal,
> Is most wonderfully kind.

My professor of pastoral theology at seminary was Dr. Clarence Roddy, a former Baptist minister who brought years of pastoral experience to the classroom and a wealth of anecdotal wisdom for those of us preparing to be pastors, from which I learned more than from his professorial lectures. When he began a lecture with the magic words, "I was a young man, pastor of my first church," we put down our pens and opened our hearts. "A young woman in the congregation became pregnant before she was married. The head elder of the church demanded that she appear before the entire congregation on a Sunday morning to confess her sin. I stood helplessly by, watching the shame flood her face and knew that we had lost a soul. She disappeared from our midst and we never saw her again."

Roddy was a deeply emotional man. Tears glistened in his eyes as he peered back through the decades in search of a different, kinder ending. But there was none. There never is. Each of us has a historian self that diligently records the facts, and though we revisit the scene a thousand times, we find the record chiseled in stone. So he continued, "I knew in that moment that something was wrong with what we had done. Our crime against her was greater than her sin against God. With God there is mercy, with a scolding and scathing spirit of judgment there is none. But I was young and unsure of myself. I was afraid of the elder. The power with which he acted as her judge could, in my mind, as quickly be turned against me."

He paused again, while fire in his eyes burned the tears away, "Within a year that same elder left his wife and ran off with another woman." He challenged us to learn from--and thereby redeem--his regretful mistake. "Don't ever fear to show mercy to those who need it most, and don't ever think that mercy is a minor virtue in favor of God's justice. I know better now."

I heard little of the rest of the lecture. I pondered what he said and made a vow to begin my ministry where he ended--with the wisdom to show mercy. Rather than leave behind a trail of casualties caused by being too quick to punish and too slow to show mercy, I would practice mercy in the lives of those who were abusing themselves with guilt and self-punishment, while I learned the wisdom of a pastoral heart.

It was not easy. I became the pastor of a newly formed congregation where situations arose which seemed to call for moral judgment, if not also discipline. I searched the gospel accounts of Jesus' ministry in vain for instances where his first response was one of moral judgment rather than mercy. There were numerous occasions where he encountered persons who had no moral standing due to their own sin, and not once did he scold or act in a judgmental way toward those who were 'real sinners!' When he did pronounce righteous judgment, sometimes with scathing words, it was always directed toward the self-righteous and those who claimed moral superiority by virtue of their own religious practices. "Mercy tempers justice," wrote Shakespeare. "It is enthroned in the hearts of kings, It is an attribute to God himself; And earthly power doth then show likest God's, When mercy seasons justice."

I began to rethink the relation of mercy to God's moral law. Jesus practiced the moral freedom of God in standing with persons condemned by God's moral law. The woman caught in adultery for instance, was thrown at the feet of Jesus with self-righteous moral judgment by her accusers. They even had Scripture prescribing death as punishment for such behavior. Instead of invoking the moral law of God, Jesus extended the moral freedom of God by making an intervention between her and the law which condemned her. In this way the effect of the law was deflected by his words, I do not condemn you, "go your way, and from now on do not sin again" (John 8:11). God can act quite arbitrarily with regard to extending mercy because he acts out of freedom rather than having to satisfy some abstract moral law. "I will be gracious to whom I will be gracious, and I will show mercy on whom I will show mercy" (Exod 33:19). This verse is cited by Paul in his argument on behalf of God's freedom to set aside natural law in favor of divine election (Romans 9:15). As we will see, the moral freedom of God does not lead to moral confusion and the result of mercy is not moral ambivalence but the creation of a new moral structure of love and community.

It was Jesus himself, 'close to the Father's heart,' who dared to extend mercy to one who had no moral standing before the law. In doing so, he invested his own moral authority in her rather than in the law. Mercy is moral empowerment, while punishment, even justice, tends to dis-empower those who have already lost their moral right to righteousness. God's moral freedom reaches deeper into the divine heart than God's moral law. It is not justice but mercy that drives the moral law of God and so establishes God's moral nature. There is a time and place for justice, but not at the expense of mercy. Often justice can *only* be realized through mercy. Those who are victims of injustice look for mercy on the part of those who have the power to restore justice.

Those who feel compelled to hand out severe moral judgment may actually be moral cowards. They lack the moral courage to extend mercy, fearing that in being merciful they will themselves be guilty of failing to uphold God's moral law. We might ask, what right does Jesus have to forgive those who have committed real moral transgressions? Does he not, in extending forgiveness while requiring neither penance nor punishment, become a lawbreaker? Those who protested against the showing of mercy through forgiveness thought so. But in refusing to acknowledge his divine freedom to exercise mercy they not only felt morally justified in rejecting him but in putting him to death as a result of their moral outrage. I think that we may have as much to fear from those who act out of moral outrage than from those caught in the web of outright immorality. The elder of Roddy's church got his pound of flesh,' but not without drawing innocent blood as well--that of his young pastor. At least that seems to have been the case with Jesus who ended up the 'victim of those who claimed the higher moral ground.

However, my students now argue, did not Jesus tell the woman to 'go and do not sin again?' Did he not impose on her a life of moral behavior as a condition by which her forgiveness would really count with God? The basis of their questions, I discover, is their discomfort with the idea that the grace of divine forgiveness and the mercy which flows from this grace leads to a weakening of God's moral law. There lurks in the heart of most of us a distrust of divine mercy when extended to those who are really guilty of moral faults! Perhaps it is because we have been led to believe that divine justice is poised alongside of divine mercy in God's being, as two quite different aspects which refuse to be reconciled. This view sets up a bipolar tension resulting in moral ambivalence about an extension of mercy without the terms of justice being met. This lies behind what I call lack of moral courage in showing mercy.

What we fail to understand is that justice is -a legal act while mercy is a relational one. When justice takes a legal approach to moral fault it abstracts out of the relational context and seeks to satisfy moral demands by pronouncements of either guilt or innocence. If one is judged guilty, as was the woman brought to Jesus, mercy can only be granted after acknowledgment of guilt and repentance, which was the logic behind the woman being brought before the congregation in Roddy's church. Moral justice ignores restoration of relationship in favor of moral verdict. The fact that the consequence is shame and rejection by the community is of little consequence to the moral law. Those who brought the woman to Jesus as well as the man who brought the young woman before the congregation have already divested themselves of responsibility to preserve the guilty person within community, on the grounds of their own sense of moral justice.

Not so with Jesus. In response to my student's insistence that Jesus imposed an even higher moral demand upon the woman by saying, "go your way and do not sin again," I reply, "No, he did not bind her to a higher moral law of perfection nor did he free her from the moral law altogether." I then ask, "Suppose that someone discovers that she has returned to her old ways and is committing the same sin, what would Jesus say when told about this?" They had not thought about this, obviously, for they had no immediate answer. What Jesus might actually say is, "Bring her to me; I am the one person she will have no fear of facing for I was on her side rather than on the side of her accusers. She needs to understand that I did not merely free her from the law, but I bound her to me." Jesus sought to empower the woman with moral worth so that she could live a renewed life within the moral structure of community. She was to 'go her way' in a 'different way' of life. It was as though Jesus said to her, "You don't have to live like that anymore. You do not need to be driven by your needs or compulsions. I have liberated you from shame and guilt in order that you might live in the moral freedom that I have given you."

Listen. We must understand this! The soul of God is intrinsically a relational soul. The soul of a moral theology must possess the moral instincts of love rather than the insensible letter of the law. "The letter kills but the Spirit gives life" (2 Cor. 3:6). As suggested earlier, the intention of mercy is the creation of a new moral being. Mercy is not an abstract virtue, but a means for maintaining a relationship damaged by moral failure. Mercy is what keeps sin from being fatal.

The 'wideness' of God's mercy is a river of divine love which, at times, overflows its banks, but never becomes a destructive flood.

Chapter Seven

The loving intentions of a Father's heart extended even to the far country in order to embrace a prodigal son. "But while he was still far off, the father saw him and was filled with compassion; he ran and put his arms around him and kissed him " (Luke 15:20). In the parable, the 'far country' is the other side of the world from God, the broken edge that separates all of humanity from the loving Father. In sending his only Son into this world, Jesus found himself in 'human form,' in order to make a path back from the far country to the Father's house, where "God highly exalted him" (Philippians 2:7, 9).

Mercy is the motive behind God's love for the world. This mercy is extended toward 'all the families of the earth' through the seed of Abraham, which extends through the generations to Jesus, according to Paul (Gen. 12; Gal 3:16). Divine mercy guarantees forgiveness and makes reconciliation possible. Forgiveness is offered to all through Christ, and reconciliation is the intended goal. God does not want any to perish, "but all to come to repentance" (2 Peter 3:9). Mercy must be received in order for forgiveness to be realized as a gift of grace. The goal of mercy is not merely the granting of amnesty, which often leaves the one who is estranged free of guilt, but a mercifully restoration with life in community. "Once you were not a people, but now you are God's people; once you had not received mercy, but now you have received mercy" (1 Peter 2:9-10). Receiving mercy, experiencing forgiveness, and being reconciled to God within the people of God is to know the salvation of God.

In 1993, Amy Biehl, a 26 year old Fulbright Scholar, was murdered by 4 blacks in South Africa while registering voters for the nation's first free election. Her murderers were apprehended and imprisoned. Her parents, Peter and Linda Biehl, went to Cape Town to establish a foundation with the goal of violence prevention. This foundation, named for Amy, continues to maintain a presence for peace. Under the government's newly formed Truth and Reconciliation Commission, established to grant amnesty for political crimes to those persons who confess and give the whole truth about their actions, the four men who murdered Amy were given full a pardon and released from prison on July 29,1998.

Commenting on this action which they supported, Amy's parents said, "It is this vision of forgiveness and reconciliation that we have honored." They believed that this is what their daughter would have wanted. Peter Biehl then added, "We're not dispensing forgiveness. We're not God. But we support the decision." Releasing the men from further punishment in no way mitigated their crime, to which they confessed. Forgiveness in this case, however, was an act of mercy which the Biehls saw as an important step in the journey toward peace and reconciliation.

Forgiveness is not always a possibility, but mercy is. There are people who may be beyond forgiveness on human terms, but as persons who have done evil, even they are not to be excluded from mercy. For the dispensation of mercy is in the hands of the judge, not the criminal, and relies on the strength of his or her moral character. Those who fail to act with mercy fail to be authentically human.

"Do you think Judas will be in heaven?"

The man who asked me that question was manacled to a table in Los Angeles County Jail, sentenced to life without parole for the brutal killing of his mother and father. He carried in his hands an underlined copy of a book I had written about Judas which had been given him by one of the volunteer chaplains.

"Can Judas really be forgiven for what he did? I did something worse than Judas, but somehow I believe that if there is hope for him there may be hope for me."

We talked for an hour. He wondered how Jesus could ever forgive Judas and feared that what he had done might finally be unforgivable, even by God. I said, "Let me ask you a question. Suppose that when you die God confronts you with your parents whom you murdered and tells them that they now have the power to make a determination as to your eternal destiny. These are the parents whom you murdered. What will they say?"

He paused for a long while and finally said slowly, "My mother will forgive me, for she loved me, I am sure of that." To which I replied, "Then you know that God can forgive you, for he has taken upon himself your guilt through the death and resurrection of Christ." Difficult as it was for him to internalize the reality of God's forgiveness, the case of Judas became a door through which he could walk.

I presented this encounter as a case for discussion with my seminary students. There was general agreement that if the prisoner had confessed the sin of murder and trusted Christ for forgiveness he could be assured of eternal life with God in heaven. While some questioned the authenticity of such a conversion under these circumstances, it was agreed that only God knows the heart and that there is always some degree of ambiguity in the human profession of faith, especially when it has not yet been tested as to its endurance and growth. We were reminded of the conversion of Carla Faye Tucker, the woman in Texas who had participated in a terrible murder. In prison, under sentence of death she accepted Christ as savior and professed a transformation of life. In her case, several years passed before she was executed. During that time she taught Bible classes in prison and demonstrated a consistent testimony to a new life in Christ. Even the brother of one of the victims affirmed the genuineness of her conversion and, himself being a Christian, expressed confidence that she was forgiven by God and is now in heaven after her execution.

Setting aside the ambiguity regarding the prisoner with whom I had my conversation, the theological issue which troubled some of my students was the thought that God's forgiveness--granted merely upon a person's confession of sin--violated God's justice. Once again, the concept of justice and mercy as a polarity within the being of God was raised. Some responded by saying that God's justice was satisfied with the death of Jesus on the cross so that God could show mercy to the man who confessed to killing his parents. That is the traditional response. It was what I was taught in seminary.

I had anticipated this question in suggesting to the man that God might well hand over to the parents that he had murdered the decision as to his final destiny. For them to show mercy would not be a violation of justice, for they were the victims. For them to offer mercy and forgiveness would not be a contradiction of divine justice for, in my scenario, God had transferred his own absolute power of justice to the parents. I wanted the man to consider mercy as a possibility, not in contradiction to justice, but as a creative act of justice based on love. The fact that he was able to think of his mother only as granting him forgiveness showed that he was holding on to the fact that she could love him despite what he had done to her. "Did his mother have the moral right to forgive her son," I asked my students. They all agreed. A mother's love transcended the legal issue of justice.

I was not through, however. I pressed the matter further. "If we now assume that the man who murdered his own parents can be forgiven out of the moral freedom of God, despite the horrendous act which he committed, what about his parents themselves? This man had the opportunity to repent, confess and ask Jesus for forgiveness while he was still alive. Assuming that his parents had given no evidence or indication of their faith in Christ prior to their death, is it possible that their son, the murderer, would go to heaven based on his conversion to Christ while his parents would end up in hell?"

Some students agreed, though reluctantly, that this indeed would be the case assuming that they had no opportunity to repent and receive Christ as savior before their murder. Their response was determined by the conviction that only those who personally accept

Christ in this life can be saved. One's eternal destiny is determined by one's relationship to Christ and this must take place before death. Otherwise, they said, what motive would there be for taking the gospel of Christ to the unsaved?

Other students were offended by this, saying that it would be outrageous for God to save the murderer while sending the victims to hell. When pressed, they had no basis for their feelings other than it "just didn't seem right!" This, of course, leaves us with the tormenting question with which we began this inquiry—is it possible that the murderer will be in heaven while his victims go to hell because they did not have the same opportunity that he had to receive and believe the gospel? Could not God find in the death of Jesus Christ and his resurrection a basis for mercy on the part of the victims as well?

Such speculation, of course, may already have exceeded the bounds of legitimate theological inquiry (if not also common sense). As Professor Torrance once said in class after making a bold statement about the unlimited power of divine grace, we should 'clap our hands' over our mouths in making such statements, as though to exclaim, "Did I really say that? May God have mercy!" God's mercy runs wide and deep, beyond our own human imagination. Yes I really said that!

In the end, one must resist making a moral law or even a spiritual virtue out of forgiveness as though there are no consequences to wrong actions. We should always remember that even where there is forgiveness, there may well be consequences for one's actions which must be deal with. Some have forgiven those who have murdered a child or other family member, but that person still remains in prison. Extending forgiveness to one who has hurt us means that *we* surrender the right to exact punishment, even though punishment may still be exacted as a legal requirement of the law.

Compassion as an expression of mercy is quite different from forgiveness, and is expected even where forgiveness is not possible. Compassion is grounded in the feeling another's pain, and is the impulse toward mercy. In showing mercy, one seeks to alleviate pain, temper justice, and restore relationships. While mercy is prompted by compassion, it has its source in the moral virtue of promoting the value of a human life when it least deserves it. We applaud acts of mercy because we recognize the moral goodness of such actions which go beyond the legal demands of the law.

While some people show no mercy because they have no compassion, others who have deep feelings of compassion are reluctant to extend mercy in fear of undermining justice. For some, punishment for violation of either a natural, civil, or divine law constitutes the moral content of the law itself. To release one from the consequences of breaking the law is considered by some to be a violation of the moral law.

The moral value of mercy, on the other hand, is grounded in the moral being of God and of humans created in the divine image. Mercy is shown to those who have no power or right to establish their own righteousness and human well-being. Mercy is a moral demand while forgiveness is not. We cannot hold persons accountable to forgive when they have been sinned against, but we can expect them to show mercy where it is appropriate. Where forgiveness is offered, mercy has preceded it and constitutes the moral basis for forgiving.

Some might argue that in extending mercy one has already made a commitment to forgive. Not necessarily. Forgiveness has to do with releasing one from one's own need to punish allowing justice to be done by those authorized by a civil society. To forgive and also allow punishment is not a contradiction in terms. Mercy begins with compassion and a recognition that even an offender is a human person. Mercy can also go beyond simple compassion, by treating humanly one banished to prison, for example.

Forgiveness, as an extension of mercy, is the first step toward reconciliation. Reconciliation is an ultimate goal. Obstacles to reconciliation might be the lack of repentance on the part of the offender, damage done to a relationship which is irreparable, or the death of an offender. For a woman who was sexually abused by a parent as a child, reconciliation might be a possibility as long as the parent is alive. With the death of the parent where no repentance or acknowledgment of wrong occurred, reconciliation on earth is impossible. At this point, forgiveness is no longer directed toward the goal of reconciliation but toward personal healing. In the end, reconciliation as well as forgiveness is a divine gift of grace which one usually receives bit by bit and grows into. At other times, forgiveness comes when one least expects it, like a bolt of lightning out of the blue.

Mercy is a costly grace, as Dietrich Bonhoeffer reminded us. It demands more than pity, it demands compassion directed toward those who suffer at the gates, if not in the very midst of a community of mutual self interest. In Jesus' parable it was the Samaritan who responded to the victim by the side of the road, spending his own money, promising to pay more, who was said to be the 'good neighbor' because he "showed him mercy" (Luke 10:29-37). I have always been amazed by the account of Jesus' casting out the demons from the demoniac who was naked, dragging chains, and wandering amongst the tombs. What amazes me is not that Jesus exorcized the demons, but that the man was found clothed and in his right mind, sitting at the feet of Jesus (Mark 5:11). The mercy was not in the exorcism alone, but in his rehabilitation into the community. Jesus can cast out the demons. But the same community that had driven out the man as a terror restores him to their midst—Mercy! *That* is the miracle that amazes me!

My friend and former student, Matt (a member of the pastoral team of a large church in Texas), began an alternative ministry to young people who felt estranged from the traditional church. It was called Mercy Street, with meetings held on Saturday night. At first the group was comprised of primarily younger people. The format consisted of contemporary worship, a preaching ministry based on the grace of Jesus Christ, and a commitment to mutual support and encouragement. Over a three year period Mercy Street has become a growing, vital community of Christ of more than 300 participating, many of whom are adults seeking to be 'clothed with mercy'--literally as well as figuratively. Each Saturday, vans go out to bring in persons from homeless shelters, domestic violence shelters--women and children--swelling the congregation to double is size.

While there are many stories which come out of Mercy Street, the story of my friend Betsy is a microcosm of this ministry. A single parent whose adult son found support in his recovery from drug abuse at Mercy Street brought her into the fellowship, where she found healing and hope for her own wounds as well as support for financial needs. Now she participates in the ministry of mercy, going to prison to visit one of the members who relapsed, providing encouragement and counsel for those who are discouraged and weary in spirit.

I do not know how Matt came up with the name Mercy Street. But it appeals to me. It also strikes me that it should be the main street of the church, not a side street! Where Jesus is present there is abundant mercy and amazing grace. I want to live on this street!

8

Amazing Grace

> We are born broken. We live by mending.
> The grace of God is the glue.
> Eugene O'Neill

"Grace must first kill before it can make alive." I was sitting on the very front row in the seminary room in New College, Edinburgh, when Thomas Torrance uttered this incredible statement during a lecture on the grace of our Lord Jesus Christ. It was so stunning that I forgot to take notes for a few minutes. That is why I will never forget it. The statement could not be filed away for later reference, it demanded immediate attention, as though someone had rushed into the room yelling "Fire!" And fire it was, burned into my conscious mind before it could be buried in my unconscious self.

Torrance credited his former mentor, Karl Barth, for this insight. It was Barth, Torrance told us, who reformulated Calvin's doctrine of grace as the truth of God revealed to us through incarnation. God himself is given to us through the person of Jesus Christ, not just information about God. "It is this truth which kills and makes alive," wrote Barth. What the truth of God kills, Barth insisted, is an attempt to build a scaffolding out of human reason, religion, or moral principle as a means of ascertaining and verifying knowledge of God. For Torrance, it is God's grace that sets aside as unusable our attempts to complete God's promises in order to create life out of death, as it were.

This indeed is amazing grace, though perhaps even more than John Newton intended when he wrote the text for the well-known hymn.

"'Twas grace that taught my heart to fear, And grace my fears relieved; How precious did that grace appear, The hour I first believed."

It was Jesus, full of grace and truth, who has his origin in the 'bosom' of the Father, who brought grace to us. Therefore, the grace that we experience is not only a remedy for our guilt and fear but a piece of the Father's own heart. Grace is not God's antidote for sin, but it is an original creative impulse within God himself. "Grace is an inner mode of being in God Himself," says Barth. God's grace is a movement of his own heart toward us, expressed first through creation by which Adam and Eve came into existence, and then to save them from bondage to fear and guilt.

Let me tell you how I imagine grace to have been first experienced by Adam and Eve. They are walking along, hand in hand, reveling in the freedom of the garden where God caused them to emerge out of nonbeing into being. "Look," says Eve. "See where you and I were walking along the stream that flows though the garden last evening, there are three sets of footprints in the damp earth. But there are three sets of prints." Adam pauses and says, "Have you forgotten? Our God comes down and walks with us in the garden at the time of the evening breeze. He was with us again last evening" (Genesis 3:8).

In my mind, these are the footprints of grace. In their innocence, the first humans lived 'by grace and faith' in the simple joy of their own love and their God who sustained them daily. This is the grace of God. God's freedom to move out of his own inner being and create human partners with whom to share his life and love. Grace was there in the garden, where there was neither fear nor guilt. When grace is conceived as only a remedy for sin and a response to human disobedience, it makes grace a secondary movement within the being of God. And, in a strange twist, it makes human sin the occasion by which grace comes. This is not how it is! Grace is there from the beginning, as Barth has said, the divine motive for creation as well as the divine means of redemption.

When the first humans sin, they do so in opposition to divine grace. When this sin becomes rooted in human attempts for self-preservation and self--aggrandizement it must be 'killed,' by grace itself, in order for grace to create in humans a true self which leads to self-fulfillment. In the creation story, the 'footprints of divine grace' appear again so that Adam and Eve, from behind the curtain of fear that they have constructed, "hear the sound of the Lord God walking."

"Where are you?" God calls out, and the man responds, "I heard the sound of you in the garden, and I was afraid, because I was naked; and I hid myself" (Genesis 3:8-10). To cover their nakedness, as though self-conscious in each other's presence, they sewed fig leaves together in an attempt to cover the consequences of their sin. They took refuge in the garden in an attempt to hide from the presence of God. Again, this is symbolic of a desire to make the best of a bad situation. They had survival skills and, who knows, with the rudimentary elements of the divine image with which they were originally endowed, could well have used their religious instincts to fashion rituals and idols through which to mediate their sense of shame and guilt. Sin can find its deepest hiding place in human religion and cultural cleansing rituals.

These are things which grace must kill in order to bring new life out of the rituals of death. The fig leaves are the first to go. In their place, God fashions skins of animals and clothes them with grace (Genesis 3:11). This time, grace must first remove what has been used to conceal shame and let go of that which had brought some religious comfort of their own making. The garment that God provides is a garment of grace because it gives assurance of forgiveness and confidence to enter into full fellowship with God and each other.

This is what Paul meant by saying that we must 'put to death' that which drove us away from God and against one another with hostility and malice. We cannot, of our own selves, 'put to death' these instincts which have become natural to us. We need the supernatural power of divine grace to cancel out that which is destructive in order to be 'clothed' with grace and truth (Col. 3:5-17).

The inner logic of grace goes beyond human logic. That is why it is incomprehensible. We should not attempt to fit grace into our own scheme of how things should be, says Torrance; "Grace that is comprehensible is not grace, for it is the grace of God that can be known only as God Himself is known, out of God and not out of ourselves. That is what justification by grace means."

What I have touched upon in Chapter Four, I now want to expand more fully. Grace presupposes barrenness. This is the running thread through the Old Testament story of redemption. Let us revisit the story of Abraham and Sarah and trace out a theology of divine grace.

Abraham was told that he will have so many descendants that they can scarcely be counted, indicating that God's promise will extend infinitely, as many as the stars in the heavens (Gen. 15:5). Not only that, through this promised seed, "all the families of the earth shall be blessed" (Gen. 12:3). This is God's promise that Abraham believes and it is reckoned unto him as righteousness (Gen. 15:6). Sarah is to bear their son who will become the heir through which the covenant promise is to be fulfilled. Unfortunately, Abraham is bereft of an heir due to Sarah's old age and her barrenness.

What occurs is a further development of the inner logic of grace.

Sarah concludes that she is the obstacle, and says to Abraham, "You see that the Lord has prevented me from bearing children; go in to my slave-girl; it may be that I shall obtain children by her" (Gen. 16:2). According to custom, this is both morally and legally permissible. The paternity of the child is the key to the inheritance of the blessing. This was also true in the case of a polygamous marriage at that time. Remember the fig leaves? In the face of what appears to be a human impossibility, human ingenuity finds a solution. Together, they conspire to bring about the promise of God compromising with the end to justify the means. To Hagar, the slave-girl, a son was born, who was named Ishmael (Gen. 16:15). It is worth noting that Moses identifies her as an Egyptian slave-girl (16:3), a thinly veiled reference to the fact that the child represents the slave status of the Hebrew people when they were in Egypt, a condition from which the Lord graciously redeemed them.

Abraham is eighty-six years old (16:16) and, at the time of their clever plan, is apparently satisfied that they have successfully appropriated the promise of God by circumventing Sarah's barrenness. Several years go by and, when Abraham is ninety-nine years old, the Lord appears again to reiterate the covenant promise. He announces the astounding news that Sarah, who is eighty-nine years old, will conceive a child in her barren womb and God's promise will be fulfilled (Gen. 17). No wonder Abraham fell on his face and laughed (17:17)! The birth of a son through Sarah was not only impossible but, in his mind, it was *unnecessary.*

I picture Abraham protesting strongly and pointing to his son Ishmael. "I already have a son, he is already thirteen years old. He is almost as tall as I am. I have taught him every night by the campfire that he is the very embodiment of the promise of God. He is the one who will be chosen to carry on the promised blessing."

"Then unteach him," the Lord might then reply. "O that Ishmael might live in your sight," insists Abraham (17:18)!

"No," replied the Lord, but your wife Sarah shall bear you a son, and you shall name him Isaac" (i.e. 'he laughs' 17:19).

While provision for Ishmael will also be made, he is not the one chosen to bear the promise to others, even for himself! As much as Abraham has invested in Ishmael, he must forsake him and trust God to enable barren Sarah to conceive. "O that Ishmael might live in your sight!" Ishmael represented thirteen years of Abraham's life of faith. Ishmael was an act of faith and obedience on Abraham's part, interpreted by his own context and culture. Ishmael was not produced out of unbelief and disobedience, as far as Abraham was concerned. And yet, Ishmael, along with thirteen years of his own life must be canceled out.

This teaches us that the issue is not so much obedience as contrasted with disobedience, but true obedience as compared with false obedience. It is not so much an issue of unbelief as it is of right belief contrasted with wrong belief. True obedience and right belief are based on apprehending God's purpose and conforming to it. False obedience and wrong belief result from a human way of thinking. This is why faith and obedience must be empowered by grace as a gift of God.

Jesus rebuked Peter for his wrong belief when Peter attempted to persuade Jesus not to go to Jerusalem. "You are a stumbling block to me;" Jesus said to Peter, "for you are setting your mind not on divine things but on human things" (Matt. 16:23). Peter believed that he was acting in accordance with what seemed right, but he was wrong!

When we take up the Word of God on our own lips and proclaim the mystery of God's grace and love, we are not preaching and witnessing in many cases to those who have no belief and to those who are disobedient, in their own eyes. When we preach the Word of God, we are speaking to those who believe in something dear to them, and to those who rely on their own way of obedience. This belief must be stripped away as was Abraham's belief in Ishmael. No wonder Paul exclaimed, "Who is sufficient for these things" (2 Cor. 2:16)?

What is difficult, as we hear it in the plaintive cry of Abraham, is the death of our own Ishmaels. The grace of God must first kill before it can make alive. The grace of God requires barrenness, not our own belief as a precondition. True faith and true obedience come as a gift of God's grace, and the inner logic of that gift requires that where we have inserted a human possibility the grace of God must remove it. This was true for Moses, as he experienced his own failure and futility, only to witness God's power and grace through that weakness.

But what about Sarah?

It is, after all, Sarah who must consent and cooperate with divine grace in order that her barrenness be overcome and she conceive. How does Abraham convince Sarah that they must now turn toward each other and embrace that barrenness with hope and faith? I could well imagine Sarah's reaction. It is not hard to write the script for this conversation which is not recorded in Scripture.

"You have no right to ask that of me. Thank God for the day that I passed the age of bearing children. Yes, I had finally to surrender the hope and dream of producing a child, but that hope is itself a curse.

Each month when I awakened to the realization that I had failed again to conceive, I felt the sharp edge of the Lord's disapproval and the openly expressed scorn of my friends. And, yes, Abraham, you too were disappointed in me. I felt it."

"I have long since given up hope," Sarah continues, "but I at least have accepted my fate and find it comforting and secure. In asking me to hope again you are asking me to risk despair and disappointment again." There is a burden to hope that tears away at the spirit when failure occurs. "Hope deferred makes the heart sick," the proverb reminds us (Proverbs 13:12). Self-blame is only one part of hope deferred. The failure of God to respond as we pray and petition strikes at the core of our faith and trust.

There is a kind of peace that comes when one settles for the inevitable. Surely Moses felt it and used it to smooth over old wounds, to try to forget failed dreams. But the grace of God will not permit that. As Moses was summoned out of his anonymity and silence to speak the Word of God to Pharaoh, so Sarah is summoned out of quiet resignation to her fate to conceive what had never been possible for her, and to hope for that which had always eluded her.

We must understand that the grace of God presupposes barrenness, not fertility; that impossibility from the human side is the condition which demonstrates most clearly the inner logic of grace. We must also learn that humans have a share in the grace of God; that human obedience and faith are not set aside by grace, but are drawn into the grace of God as an indispensable aspect of God's ministry. After all, Isaac did not drop down from heaven on a supernatural parachute! Rather, his birth resulted from a human act as much as did the birth of Ishmael. Grace is not a supernatural addition to a natural life, but the empowering of natural life to realize and produce a divine potential. The miracle of God's grace is not that Abraham could disseminate his seed, but that a barren woman could conceive from it! This is the inner logic of grace and barrenness.

Grace is something like love. Love is not something that one 'gets' by having a prescription filled. I cannot prescribe love, though as a pastoral counselor I have tried! Grace, as with love, is first experienced as a benefit to oneself which leads one back to the source. When we experience grace it is when love shines upon us, drawing us out of dark cold shadows into the warmth of the sun. The sun must first 'kill the shadow,' in order for the light to shine on us. The child who experiences the warmth of the sun on a cold day instinctively moves into the space where the sun shines, only later to understand that it is the sun which provides this 'grace.' Theologian Hans Urs von Balthasar, writing on a theology of childhood, said that love is awakened in the soul when the love of another shines on it. "God, who inclined toward his newborn creature with infinite personal love, in order to inspire him with it and to awaken the response to it in him, does in the divine supernatural order something similar to a mother. Out of the strength of her own heart she awakens love in her child in true creative activity. . . . No man reaches the core and ground of his own being, becoming free to himself and to all beings, unless love shines on him."

When the grace of love shines on us, we experience the benefits of grace and are then empowered to move toward the source of grace--God. The grace of Christ in our lives is first experienced as good. If it is grace it is experienced as good. For that which is experienced as good in our lives to be the grace of God it must lead us directly back to the source so that the content of grace is not merely its effect (the benefit), but that which issues from the heart of God.

The warm sun on a dark cold day is experienced as grace—it feels good—but the feeling lacks the content of divine grace. The grace of God is not a stimulant; if it were, it could be reproduced by ingesting a substance. The grace of God is not an anesthetic; if it were, it could be acquired from the pharmacy with a prescription. The grace of God is not a comfort zone: if it were it could be achieved with a thermostat. Entering the house with frost on one's eyebrows and standing by a warm fire in the middle of a South Dakota winter is a grace that I have experienced more times than I can count. Jumping into a car with leather seats when the air temperature is over a hundred degrees in Arizona, and then having the air conditioning come on full blast, is grace. Out of your own experience you can think of a dozen more examples. The word 'grace,' to paraphrase philosopher Anthony Flew, has died the death of a thousand qualifications. But then things are merely the feelings of grace--not the substance of it, not its source.

We only know the grace of God when we experience the presence and power of God as a supernatural source of what we experience in our natural lives. When I feel guilt and shame due to personal failure or outright sin, I can resort to a stimulant, seek some anesthetic, or find a therapist to regulate my inner life and so move me out of pain into a comfort zone. This is a an attractive temptation to the 'point and click' mentality of our modern culture. As any therapist will say, the greatest difficulty in helping people overcome deep seated emotional pain is the desire to get out of pain as quickly as possible and feel better. As a matter of fact, without stating it in so many words, a competent mental health professional knows that effective therapy must first 'kill before it can bring healing.' The source of the pain must be sought, which may bring more pain than one expected.

"Who told you that you were naked?" demanded God of Adam and Eve. "Have you eaten of the tree from which I commanded you not to eat?" (Genesis 3:11). Though they had, indeed, denial had already become their own 'comfort zone.' Projection of blame was their coping device: "it was the woman you gave me," said the man; "the serpent tricked me," said the woman (3:12, 13). The fig leaves and the thick foliage of the garden were perceived as graces in that they served to conceal them from the penetrating gaze of God. What they feared as divine presence without mercy, however, became merciful grace: "The Lord God made garments of skins for the man and for his wife, and clothed them (3:21).

Now tell me of grace! Paul says that we who once were estranged from God but are baptized into Christ by the Spirit are 'clothed with Christ' (Gal. 3:27). This, of course is a spiritual garment and not a literal one. But grace is a spiritual reality for which we must use metaphors and analogies. The grace of forgiveness and healing from shame and guilt is itself an effect produced in us by Jesus Christ. It is Christ in you, says Paul, which is the hope of glory (Col 1:27). It is Christ himself, Paul adds, who dwells within us, not just *through grace*, but *as grace* ! Christ is the content of grace. Being in Christ, Paul assures us, is being in a state of grace so that our life is 'hidden with Christ in God" (Col. 3: 3). "When Christ who is your life is revealed, then you also will be revealed with him in glory" (3:4).

It is advent season as I write. Luke's account of the Angel's announcement to Mary carries the words of grace, "The Lord is with you . . . you have found favor with God" (Luke 1:28, 30). It was to be a costly grace—"and a sword will pierce your own soul too" (2:35). The conception was supernatural, the birth natural. And the word became flesh and lived among us, "full of grace and truth" (John 1:14). Christ was first known by his benefits. The man blind from birth, received his sight at the words of Jesus. "Who was the one who healed you," the religious leaders wanted to know. Under constant provocation and questioning, he could only say, "One thing I do know, that though I was blind, now I see. . . . If this man were not from God, he could do nothing" (John 9:25, 33). When he then encountered Jesus the second time, he recognized him as the Lord and worshipped him (9:38). He let grace lead him to know Jesus as the source of his healing and salvation.

It is the grace of God that leads us to God, if we are willing to be led. Amazing grace! "Thru many dangers, toils and snares, I have already come; 'Tis grace hath brought me safe thus far, And grace will lead me home."

"I go to prepare a place for you," said Jesus, "that where I am you may be also" (John 14:3). You know the way to the place. But Thomas cried out, "We don't know the way to the place. . . How can we know the way?" (14:5). "I am the way," replied Jesus. Just let grace lead you and you will be with me on the way.

9

When I Survey the Wondrous Cross

> And being found in human form, he humbled himself
> and became obedient to the point of death—even
> death on a cross. Phil. 2:8

"When Jesus returns to earth," my friend asked, "Do you think that the first thing he wants to see is the cross that we use as a symbol of our faith? I would think that it would be the last thing he would ever want to see again!" I was a bit flummoxed at the question. Sensing my discomfort, he pinned me down a bit harder by asking, "What do you think his favorite hymn might be, When I Survey the Wondrous Cross?" If you knew my friend you would know that lurking behind what might appear to be frivolous questions, was an invitation to a serious theological discussion.

While the New Testament has abundant references to the cross and, in particular, the death of Jesus on the cross for our sins, it may not have been the first symbol used to identify one as belonging to Christ. The first century Christians who suffered persecution in Rome hid in the catacombs, we are told, where they inscribed a drawing of the fish on the walls as a secret sign of communication with others. Two curved lines were drawn, converging to form the shape of a fish. In the Greek word for fish—ICTHUS—the early Christians understood the letters to form a simple theological formula: Jesus Christ, Son of God, Savior. In recent years the 'fish symbol' has become a popular form of expressing one's Christian faith, unfortunately, primarily as a bumper sticker!

The cross appeared a couple of centuries later as a common symbol of Christian faith, instigated by the fourth century Roman Emperor, Constantine. He took up the task of making Christianity an official religion after claiming to have seen a vision (or a dream) of the cross in the heavens with the inscription, HOC VINCES—'In This Sign Conquer!' By his edict and influence the cross, for the first time, became an emblem used throughout the empire in both ecclesiastical and secular architecture. Today the cross can be found everywhere, marking the site of roadside deaths, lifted high on cathedral spires as well as gracing the most rustic chapel. Making the 'sign of the cross' has incurred special powers over the centuries in the minds of some, granting permission to enter sacred space without transgressing. It also serves as the preferred defense of choice when confronting the supernatural power of demons. Baseball players 'cross themselves' when facing a power pitcher so as to gain an edge or, as the case may be, to put down their own demons of doubt and anxiety.

I had a student in my class some years ago, who carried a large wooden cross wherever he went on campus. He could be found standing by it in the grassy mall at noon while shouting out his angry invectives and hurtling divine judgments against the school for its spiritual nominalism, religious formalism, and secular materialism. Leaning the cross against the wall when entering the classroom, he joined his classmates in the pursuit of the very academic degree which he had so vigorously derided an hour earlier. At least he had the opportunity which so many of us found elusive, to go out of the classroom and literally 'take up his cross' and follow Jesus. For all of the embarrassment which his outrageous posturing caused his fellow students (which he seemed to relish), his stark and unrelieved passion combined with the pure simplicity of his attachment to the cross, offered a sharp and somewhat compelling contrast to the sophisticated nuances of the theological spin we were putting on the gospel. On one occasion, when my former mentor, the distinguished Professor Thomas Torrance was giving a chapel talk, he burst into the auditorium shouting out words of divine judgment in somewhat the same spirit as the prophet Amos of old. Afterward, I apologized to the good professor for this unseemly incident, but he was not at all offended. In fact, he replied, "What the man said made a lot of sense!" One final footnote to this story. After receiving his degree (thankfully without carrying the cross across the platform!), he left town. No one really knew where he had gone, except for the clipping from a news paper in Grand Rapids, Michigan with a picture of him carrying his cross with the notice that he had been arrested for disturbing the peace. The Dutch Reformed folk in Grand Rapids wanted their religion presented with more culture with the cross on their churches, not on the streets. We were smugly amused, but secretly thankful that no mention was made of Fuller Seminary as his alma mater!

The theological discussion with my friend took a different turn.

It was not merely the cross as a symbol that aroused our interest, but the way in which death on a cross could become paradoxically an entrance into life. Why is it that so many of our songs and hymns focus on the cross and seldom on resurrection, and then only at Easter? Why is there a preoccupation with the 'power of the blood' to wash away sin? Are we really saved by the blood of Jesus? A man in my church once confronted me with the complaint, "Why is there so much talk about blood when we talk about how Jesus saves us? When we sing the hymn, There is Power in the Blood, I don't know what that means!" At the time, while I agreed with his sentiments, I could think of no clear alternative. The blood on the cross evokes powerful emotions, but I am not sure that there is saving power in blood itself.

Certainly the significance of blood is clearly portrayed in the Old Testament. The blood of animals was required for forgiveness of sins and without the shedding of blood there is no forgiveness of sins (Hebrews 9:22). A clue as to the significance of blood is found in Leviticus 17:11, "For the life of the flesh is in the blood; and I have given it to you for making atonement for your lives on the altar; for, as life, it is the blood that makes atonement." Blood is understood to be 'life blood,' so that when an animal 'bleeds to death,' the blood becomes a token of the life of the animal given as a sacrifice. Because it is "impossible for the blood of bulls and goats to take away sins" (Hebrews 10:4), Christ gave his own life (blood) in taking upon himself the consequence of human sin. Thus the blood of Christ became a synonym for his life, given over to death on the cross. Even in the Old Testament rituals of atonement, if one drained a portion of blood from a lamb and left the animal alive, that blood would have no atoning significance when put on the altar. The same with the blood of Jesus. A portion of the blood of Jesus drawn while he was still alive would be meaningless, indeed, a grotesque ritual if splashed on a wooden cross. We know better than that!! It is the death of Jesus that is represented by the 'shedding of his blood,' not the blood itself. Yet, the shedding of blood is a powerful theme running through the whole of Scripture and it can hardly be ignored.

But is this the soul of theology? Does the cross somehow lead us into the depths of divine love? Is the death of Jesus and the shedding of his blood on the cross intended to stir us to devotion—if God loves us enough to die for us, we ought to love God in return? Or, does the entire life of Christ collapse into his death as the only significant work which he accomplished for our salvation?

In a theological examination for a prospective faculty member, one of my theology colleagues posed this question to the candidate: "What work did Jesus accomplish on the cross for our salvation?" I wanted to interrupt and say, "Nothing! A dead man cannot do any work!" But I held my tongue, and the candidate plunged ahead, giving a traditional, and apparently, acceptable answer.

The traditional doctrine of the atonement is almost exclusively focused upon the death of Jesus on the cross as offering complete satisfaction for the dishonor done to God through human sin. The 'work' of Christ, therefore, in this view is taken to be the offering up of his life as a sacrifice to fulfill divine justice and permit God to pardon freely all who accept the death of Jesus as a substitute for their own death. The forgiveness of sin is offered by God based on the satisfaction achieved by the death of Christ. It was Anselm of Canterbury (1033-1109), who introduced the concept that the death of Christ on the cross brought satisfaction to God for the dishonor which sin had done to him. The sinner is held fast by a duty to bring satisfaction of a penal nature. God, as the feudal overlord, demands satisfaction. Only the perfect humanity of Christ (who has no debt of his own) can satisfy God's moral justice through his vicarious death, and freeing God to forgive and pardon sinners. Anselm's vicarious satisfaction concept gradually prevailed, being taken over by the Reformed orthodoxy of the 17th century with some modifications. The strong juridical aspect of the vicarious satisfaction view of the atonement stressed the penal character of Christ's death. The penalty rightly belonging to the sinner is charged to the account of Christ (imputed), and thus not imputed to the sinner; while on the other hand, the righteousness of Christ is positively imputed to the sinner. There is within our theological tradition, a long history which stresses the 'work' of Christ in dying on the cross as the basis for our salvation.

The candidate, I should add, provided exactly this kind of response and passed with flying colors, having guessed correctly what the question was meant to elicit. Wisely keeping silent during the investigation of the candidate's theology, I carried over my concern into my lecture to a group of pastors in our Doctor of Ministry program which followed the next day. It is usually safer to explore innovative theology with students than with faculty colleagues! Even though, sooner or later, the 'cat is out of the bag,' so to speak, and one must be prepared to give account of one's own theological convictions.

"If Jesus had died of a heart attack in the Garden of Gethsemane," I asked my students, "and the disciples carried him out and placed him in a tomb. Would there have been a resurrection?" Only a few hands went up. The rest were stunned by the thought and not prepared to respond.

Some who raised their hands argued that he would have been raised from the dead because he was the Son of God, irrespective of how he died. I then played my trump card. "Assuming that he would have been raised from the dead, would there have been an atonement? Could we still say that he died for our sins?" Now I saw a flurry of hands, and the consensus was that, no, there could not have been an atonement because he did not die on the cross as one rejected by God. They too had learned the 'correct answer.'

Some refused to entertain the hypothesis, feeling that the question was itself irrelevant, if not blasphemous. "Jesus died on the cross in fulfillment of Scripture and as God had determined," one protested. "It couldn't have happened any other way." At the same time, I could tell that there was growing discomfort with this conclusion. Other students were now beginning to do some theological reflection, and one responded, "It was the resurrection that counted anyway. Without a resurrection there would be no atonement, even if he died on the cross."

Amazing! Here was a student coming up with a theological insight I had never heard mentioned in the theological exam of the faculty candidate. I read from Paul's letter to the Corinthians, "If Christ has not been raised, your faith is futile and you are still in your sins. Then those also who have died in Christ have perished" (1 Cor. 15:17-18).

It is the resurrection of Jesus, not just his death on the cross that completed the atonement. The use of the cross as a means of putting Jesus to death was, in some ways, more of an accident of history than a theological necessity. Death by stoning was the method used by the Jews, while the Romans used crucifixion. The fact that Jesus was executed under Roman law rather than Jewish law, led to the use of the cross to carry out the death sentence. The theological meaning of Jesus' death is not determined by *how* he died, but *that* he died. It is not only that sins need to be forgiven, but death as a consequence of sin needs to be overcome.

The consequence of sin is death (Genesis 2:17; Romans 6:23). The great dilemma facing all of humanity is death, not merely sin. Furthermore, if Jesus assumed a human nature subject to death in his conception and birth, then death was inevitable for him, regardless of the means. Yes, there was in retrospect, after the crucifixion of Jesus, ample evidence in Scripture that even the means of death has been foreseen by God. But death on a cross was not necessary, only that the death assumed by Jesus be completed and that he be raised from the dead in order that the atonement could be completed and humanity restored to fellowship with God.

The vision of the cross as atonement for sin is always seen from the perspective of the forgiven person who has experienced transformation from death to life. The cross by itself condemns, it does not convert.

"Wait just a minute!" cried a pastor who was sitting in the seminar. "We have a cross on the wall of our sanctuary behind the altar as a symbol of Christ dying for our sin. We have at least a dozen hymns in our hymnal which speak of the cross and the shed blood of Christ as the atonement for our sins. What about this chorus which we love to sing?"

> At the cross, at the cross where I first saw the light,
> And the burden of my heart rolled away,
> It was there by faith, I received my sight,
> And now I am happy all the day.

"Let me ask you a question," I replied. "If Jesus had remained in the tomb and not been raised from the dead, would we still be able to sing that hymn?"

"Of course not," he shot back, "but the Bible clearly says that Christ died for our sins on the cross, and I happen to have my Bible open to 1 Peter 2:24 which reads: 'He himself bore our sins in his body on the cross, so that, free from sins, we might live for righteousness; by his wounds you have been healed.' What do you say to that?"

Let's go over it again. The atonement began at Bethlehem, in a sense, where Jesus from birth has been under the curse of the law (Gal. 3), bearing the same nature as those who are under the sentence of death (Heb. 2:14). The dilemma of all humans since the fall of Adam is death, the consequence of sin. Sin caused death, and so death must be overcome in order that this fate which came upon all be removed. We can say that in becoming human, the divine Logos assumed a death nature in the form of Jesus of Nazareth, but not a sin nature. In other words, becoming human, God became liable to death through the person of Jesus of Nazareth. The fact that Jesus was without sin does not alter the fact that he will inevitably die, in one form or another, having assumed humanity under sentence of death. This is the basis for the solidarity between Jesus and all humanity and the reason why he could still be subject to death even though without sin. "Therefore, just as sin came into the world through one man, and death came through sin, and so death spread to all because all have sinned. . . " (Ro. 5:12). The death of Christ on the cross could have no meaning except that following his resurrection it be seen as the overcoming of death as the condemnation due to sin. "If Christ has not been raised," argued Paul, "you are still in your sins" (1 Cor. 15:17).

In being raised from the dead, Jesus has removed the offense to humanity which is death. At the same time, sin is also removed along with the guilt which sin causes. The Father does not have to kill the Son to effect atonement, the Son has already assumed death in assuming humanity, and thus the atonement is rooted in God's relation to the Son and of the gracious union with Christ assured through the resurrection and the giving of the Spirit. The forensic nature of Anselm's theory fails to touch the heart of the true vicarious nature of reconciliation as grounded in the entire life, death and resurrection of Jesus as the incarnation of God. When the atonement is treated separately from the incarnation, the work of Christ on the cross is made into a legal act, with God pronouncing a forensic judgment apart from the life of Jesus, and from outside of history. The substitution is not a legal stipulation, but the substitution of Christ's life and death for ours. It is a substitution which does not displace us but which replaces us within God's covenant love and grace.

I remember listening to Professor Torrance in Edinburgh giving the assignment for a final paper to his undergraduate students. "I want you to write an essay on the relation of the incarnation to the atonement. I do not want an essay on the incarnation, and I do not want an essay on the atonement. I want you to write a paper showing the intrinsic relation between the two." I had never heard of this before and, while glad at the time that I did not have to fulfill the assignment (mine would come later as a doctoral dissertation!), I came to appreciate the theological necessity for viewing the atonement as grounded in the very person of Christ, not merely his death on the cross. It was not the death of God's Son that brought satisfaction to the heart of the divine Father, but greeting him alive after coming out of the tomb! This is why Jesus told Mary, who would like to have held him within arm's reach, "Do not hold on to me, because I have not yet ascended to my Father" (John 20:17). Why should we remain at the cross when the empty tomb beckons us to enter into that joyous reunion by seeking the things which are above, "where Christ is, seated at the right hand of God. . . . your life is hidden with Christ in God" (Col. 3:1-3).

The good news of the gospel is not only that death as the human dilemma caused by sin has been overcome through the death of God's Son, but that the human person, Jesus of Nazareth has been raised from the dead and affirmed to be the Son of God in power (Acts 2:22-24; Rom. 1:3-5). It is not only through his death, but through his resurrection and life that Jesus continues to be the advocate for humanity before the Father. This is why the gospel of forgiveness begins with Pentecost as the praxis of the Spirit of the resurrected Christ. The vision of forgiveness and freedom which belongs to the forgiven person is not from the perspective of the cross but from the experience of the resurrection.

The question which plagues most of us who are in ministry is why, despite our preaching on the theme of God's forgiveness through the death of Christ and the atonement for sins completed on the cross, there is still such power of sin, guilt and shame on those who believe that truth. Why are so many Christians turning to psychotherapists to find relief for their emotional problems? Why are the marriages and family relationships of church members so often dysfunctional and abusive? Why, if we confess our sins each Sunday and receive the good news of our forgiveness, is there so little reconciliation, so little justice, and so little peace in our world, not to mention in our lives?

I remembered the story of a woman who in her early years was a Roman Catholic, but who in later days had left the church and had come upon bad times. No longer related to the church, she happened upon a Christian bookstore and went in to browse. The salesperson came over and said, "May I help you?" And the woman said, "Yes, I'm looking for a cross, but do you have one with the little man on it?" I can appreciate what she was looking for, even though she was searching out of the remnants of her tradition rather than out of theological conviction.

I even found such a cross to be helpful in my own pastoral ministry. Asked to visit a young woman dying of cancer who was herself a Roman Catholic by tradition, I found her not only full of anxiety and fear, but angry with God. "Why would God allow me to die, when I have three small children to care for? You would think that a powerful God who can do anything would intervene to help me." It was probably not an uncommon reaction, though it was the first time that I had encountered it in such a dramatic and desperate situation. "I think that the power of God is not of that kind," I responded. "God's power is based on love, like that of a parent for a child. And even parents find it impossible to do everything that is needed for the children that they love."

"Don't we have to believe that God's power is unlimited and that he can do anything?" Finding it impossible to defend God's power in light of her tragic situation, I replied, "No, I don't think that such a concept of God's power is one that we can accept and still hold on to his presence with us."

"Then where is God," she asked? Looking over at the wall in her bedroom I saw a cross, with figure of Jesus on it. "There God is," I said. "He is present with you in the only way that he can be, sharing in your suffering as his own." She thought a long time, and then said, "I never realized what that cross meant before. If Jesus is here with me then I can face whatever I have to face."

In this case, 'the little man on the cross' did have theological significance, and I was quietly grateful that it was not the bare cross which we had on the wall of our church!

The protestant cross is empty, of course, and as such is a rather puzzling point of contemplation. I remember the hundreds of communion services I attended over the years where the focus of the hymns and the homily was always the cross. While I was reluctant to admit it, and even pushed the idea out of my own mind when it sprang up, the focus on the cross was really a rather empty and even morbid exercise in personal piety. The sermons urging me to 'come to the foot of the cross' as a point of spiritual renewal had little effect.

It was only years later that I read an essay by the theologian, Wolfhart Pannenberg, in which he lamented the fact that so much of Protestant theology tended toward what he called, 'penitential piety,' where individuals were urged to identify themselves as sinners for whom Jesus died on the cross. "Guilt consciousness," says Pannenberg, "is not, as such, a type of Christian piety." An unfortunate consequence of the early Protestant emphasis on acknowledgment of sin as a precondition to grace, brought the cross to the forefront as both a theological and experiential basis for one's life of faith. The effect, argued Pannenberg, was to ground personal piety in personal consciousness of being 'nothing but a sinner' saved by grace. The cross thus became both the beginning and end point of one's spiritual self-identity—a zero-point, as Pannenberg called it. Pannenberg went on to say: "But if consciousness of guilt is equivalent to non-identity, this type of piety traps the individual into alienation. There is no escape from such alienation because there is combined with it a fantastic conception of self-identity in the name of salvation. Such a self-conception is doomed to remain fantastic because the permanent self-consciousness of personal sinfulness does not allow the individual to establish a new identity."

The cross is the end of our life as mere sinner, not the beginning. The cross put an end to the law which condemns, says Paul. The cross is not a place to revisit time and time again in morbid fascination with the things that weigh us down and destroy our worth as God's children. "I died to the law so that I might live to God," wrote Paul, "I have been crucified with Christ" (Galatians 2:19). What Paul says of himself is true of every human being. In the cross all of humanity died when Christ died. That is, through Christ God brought the consequence of sin upon himself, so that death no longer has the power to determine human destiny. "It is no longer I who live," added Paul, "but it is Christ who lives in me. And the life that I live in the flesh I live by faith in the Son of God who loved me and gave himself for me" (Galatians 2:20). Not every person can say that, but only those in whom the spirit of the resurrected Christ dwells (Romans 8:9).

"The world behind me, the cross before me," we assert when singing the familiar song, I Have Decided to Follow Jesus. That is so wrong!! I would rewrite it to say, "The cross behind me the world before me!" No one should think that following Jesus leads back to the cross. That is finished! Once and for all. "The Way of the Cross Leads Home," is the title of another song in my hymnal. Another misconception! I don't want to go there and I doubt that Jesus does either! The Lost Lane-end Into Heaven," as the novelist, Thomas Wolfe, wrote, is not found at the foot of the cross but in the pathway marked by the light shining out of the empty tomb. There is indeed a cross in my past, but not in my future. I want to walk in the light and be singing of a Risen Savior when Jesus walks in the door!

10

I Serve a Risen Savior

We know that Christ, being raised from the dead, will never die again; death no longer has dominion over him. The death he died, he died to sin, once for all: but the life he lives, he lives to God. So you also, must consider yourselves dead to sin and alive to God in Christ Jesus. (Romans 6:9-11)

It was in Hong Kong, October, 1986, that Professor Thomas Torrance and I each presented papers as part of a week-long dialogue with two Chinese Confucian scholars, each through simultaneous translation. The theme of the conference was on the nature of humanity from both a Western Christian view and from an Eastern Confucian view. What became apparent during our discussion, in which several participated representing both viewpoints, was that the Confucian view of humanity was grounded in a social network of family and was quite similar to the Hebrew view as presented in the Christian Scriptures. The teachings of Confucius were compared with the teachings of Jesus with many similarities noted. At the end of the conference, one of the Confucian scholars asked a pointed question: "What then is the difference between Confucius and Jesus, why should one be preferred to the other?"

My response was to say, in a gracious spirit, I hope, "Confucius, for all his valuable teaching, died and remains dead to this day. Jesus died, and was raised from the dead so that death no longer has power over humans. Without the resurrection of Jesus from the dead, we would not be here and would have nothing to say. The difference is that we believe that Jesus Christ lives and through his life believe in our own resurrection."

The man stood to his feet and looking directly at me said, "That is a good answer! I myself do no believe this, but it is a good answer."

I sometimes wonder if, in all of our divisions and differences as Christians over doctrinal disputes, ecclesiastical polity, and creedal nuances of the faith, we have lost sight of the 'good answer?' Even with respect to how we understand and articulate our own personal faith I fear that we may too often be attempting to answer the wrong questions. Do we really have a good answer to the question, Why are you a Christian? The question is not, What do you believe as a Christian? If we understand it in that way, we become mired down in apologetics—arguing for what we believe—or taking up the role of public defender for a belief system that is so impoverished by its own lack of credibility that it needs our assistance in presenting its case.

"Do I believe the Bible to be the very Word of God?" I have had that question put to me from both sides. Those who believe that it is need my affirmation to make their own more secure. They have no tolerance for ambiguity in their own lives and no respect for a carefully nuanced yes. I have never managed to give quite the right answer! Those who do not believe the Bible to be the Word of God can make me dance on a hot stove while standing coolly to the side, turning up the heat to keep me preoccupied with keeping all of my evidences from becoming merely assumptions. There is no good answer to that question—believe me!!

When the ten disciples confronted Thomas after the resurrection of Jesus, they simply said, "We have seen the Lord" (John 20:25). This was the good answer to an implied question, "Why are you so joyful?" Sometimes we hear the answer before we have thought to ask the question. Thomas did not raise any questions, he did not demand that they convince him by their own faith. Rather, he was only saying that he wanted to touch with his hands what they had already touched. I think that he was simply saying, "I want the answer for myself." I do not take this as the kind of doubt that demands evidence, but the kind of faith that seeks an answer.

Under extreme duress and distress, Job cried out, "If mortals die, will they live again?" (Job 14:14). That is the right question which calls for the good answer. I do not know that Confucius ever asked that question, if he did my Confucian scholar friend could not ask it in all seriousness for himself. He heard the good answer, but he was not asking the right question.

I have had people question whether or not Jesus was really the divine Son of God. They do not find the Bible gives them sufficient evidence of that. My response is to ask, "Do you believe that Jesus of Nazareth was raised from the dead?" Their response is usually, how can I believe that if I cannot believe that he was the Son of God? You are asking the wrong question, I tell them. If you are unable to get a good answer to the question, Was Jesus raised from the dead?, no other question is worth asking, and no other answer is worth getting. If you dare to ask that question, you must want to hear the answer.

It really does come down to that. When Saul of Tarsus encountered Jesus on the road to Damascus he asked the right question, "Who are you, Lord?" (Acts 9:5). The answer was simple and decisive, "I am Jesus." Blinded by the power of the luminous presence of Jesus (remember, grace must first kill before making alive!), Saul received first the Holy Spirit, when Ananias prayed for him, and then his sight. From that moment, Saul, who later took the Latin form of his name, Paul, not only set aside the misconceptions that drove his fanatical fury against Jesus, a form of blindness that also needed to be healed by grace, but provided the first theological account of Jesus' life and death on the cross. It was the resurrected Jesus, that became the good answer for Paul. The fact of the resurrection led Paul to the conclusion that Jesus was truly the Son of God and the content of his gospel "concerning his Son, who was descended from David according to the flesh was declared to be the Son of God with power according to the spirit of holiness by resurrection from the dead" (Romans 1:3-4). Paul lived and died before any of the gospel accounts of the resurrection of Jesus were written. Surely he had heard first-hand the anecdotal accounts from many of his followers (1 Cor. 15). But he was the first to understand and teach that Jesus Christ is a contemporary reality as well as a historical figure. It was not resurrection itself that Paul came to believe in through the witness of others, it was the living Christ whom Paul experienced as a spiritual reality that enabled him to understand the theological significance of the death of Christ.

The whole of Christian theology as well as the foundation of Christian faith rests upon the fact that Jesus of Nazareth, who was crucified, dead and buried, was raised from the dead and continues to live and reign with God in heaven and through his Spirit in our lives here on earth. I Serve a Risen Savior, is the song that I like to sing when asked, Why are you a Christian? I still think that it is a good answer.

It is tempting to focus on the *concept* of resurrection rather than the One who was resurrected. Even as it later became a temptation to speculate on the miracle of a virgin birth rather than on the One who was conceived in the womb of the virgin. The gospel accounts include the story of the empty tomb where Jesus was buried, but there is no account of a conversion from unbelief to belief at the empty tomb. Having encountered the risen Christ, they could then accept the fact of the empty tomb and the fact that a resurrection had occurred. We do not simply move from 'fact to faith,' as some would argue. Historical 'facts' hide behind the elusive past that can never be brought forth into the present. The 'orthodox' theologians of the seventeenth century built up their dogmatic system upon philosophical proofs for the existence of God and historical accounts of the life of Jesus. Rational argument for the veracity of divine truth was assumed to lead to personal faith. Gotthold Lessing (1729-1789) demolished the underpinnings of rational orthodoxy when he wrote that "The reports of miracles are not miracles." Miracles that one sees with one's own eyes, Lessing said, is one thing. Miracles reported by others is quite another. His most famous critique of attempts to ground faith in historical evidences is summed up in his conclusion: "Accidental truths of history can never become the proof of necessary truths of reason." In other words, if no historical truth can be demonstrated in the present, then nothing can be demonstrated by means of historical truths. Between us and the events of the first century in which we read reports of Jesus' resurrection, Lessing said, there is an 'ugly ditch' "which I cannot get across."

Orthodox theology never really recovered from this liberal attack based on critical historical thinking. The resurrection of Christ as an historical fact succumbed to the same fate as all of the other miracle stories in the Bible. In the early twentieth century Rudolph Bultmann attempted to recover the resurrection story in the gospel accounts as an 'existential reality' enclosed in a myth. From a modern perspective, Bultmann argued, we can say that all of the miracle stories in the Bible reflect a world-view that lacks the historical and empirical credibility which we now hold to be necessary for something to be true. Therefore, Bultmann, said, we must 'demythologize' mythical stories to get at the 'inner core' of the truth which leads to existential content rather than historical fact. In preaching the resurrection accounts in the gospel, Bultmann held that the existential reality of the Christ Spirit can arise in the hearts of the hearers who do not take the stories as literally true but as having the power to create faith. Some have said that, for Bultmann, the resurrection which did not occur literally in the first century occurs every Sunday when the gospel is preached and people come to faith in Christ! This, of course, solves Lessing's problem of the 'ugly ditch' which separates us from the first century, but at the expense of any continuity between the 'Christ of faith' and the 'historical Jesus.'

Karl Barth, a contemporary of Bultmann argued that the resurrection of Christ did occur in the realm of history, but not in such a way that the risen Christ was accessible in the same way that other historical events were available for objective examination. Relying on the German language to make such a distinction, Barth said that the resurrection appearances of Christ were not on the level of *historie* (the bare facts), but as *Heilsgeschichte* (Saving History; that is, as personal accounts of facts). Barth did not intend that the resurrection of Christ was 'unhistorical' but that as an event which occurred within the plane of history, it simply could not be demonstrated on historical grounds. One might suggest that the story of the conception of Jesus in the womb of Mary was a historical reality for Mary, but that she would find it impossible to prove or demonstrate as a supernatural event. She could 'tell the story' as she obviously did, but only those who came to understand that Jesus was himself the very incarnation of God could 'believe' her story. In somewhat the same way, the first hand accounts of the resurrection of Jesus by those who encountered him could not be proven or demonstrated apart from an encounter with the risen Christ. This was the problem confronting the ten disciples when they reported their own encounter with the risen Christ to Thomas. They were helpless to make Christ appear on their own terms. It was only a week later, when they were meeting and Thomas was with them, that Jesus appeared (John 20).

Thomas Torrance, in his account of a meeting with Barth only a few weeks before his death, says that he mentioned to Barth that some of his students had interpreted his view of the resurrection of Jesus as not literal, lacking ontological reality. At that point, Torrance reports, "Barth leaned over to me and said with considerable force, which I shall never forget, '*Wohlverstanden, leibliche Auferstehung*' – 'Mark well, bodily resurrection.'"

When Barth asserted the ontological reality of the resurrection of Christ he meant that the very person who lived as Jesus of Nazareth, the incarnate Son of God, rose from the dead. This was said to counter Bultmann's concept of an 'existential' rather than ontological resurrection. But Barth's concern was also to preserve the continuity of the Christ who rose with the Christ who lived and died as Emmanuel—God with us. Torrance makes clear the importance of this when he says that the relation of resurrection to the person of Christ, "discloses to us that it is *the whole Jesus Christ who is the content of the resurrection*, for all of his life from birth to resurrection forms an indissoluble unity" (italics in the original).

I like that! I don't like to think that when Jesus died, that was the end of the person who invited all to come unto him, "you that are weary and are carrying heavy burdens, and I will give you rest" (Matt. 11:28). I would be quite at a loss if the person who said, "I am the resurrection and the life. Those who believe in me, even though they die, will live" no longer exists, but fell back into the dust as do all mortals (John 11:25). I think I know why Mary Magdalene was one of the first to go to the tomb and thus the first to meet the risen Christ (John 20). This is the Mary who suffered a tormenting mental and emotional disorder from which Jesus delivered her in casting out her demons (Luke 8:2). If the one who had the power to cast out her demons no longer lives, will the demons return? Her reason for being at the tomb is to attempt, even in ministering to his dead body, to cling to the gift by staying near the giver. Her incredible joy at discovering him to be alive that led her to 'take hold of him' is quite understandable (John 20:17). Don't bother asking her whether she believes in a resurrection, she has already given her answer in grasping with her hands what her heart can scarcely believe.

I wonder about the paralyzed man to whom Jesus said, "your sins are forgiven," and as a sign of his authority to forgive, healed his body (Mark 2). Does this man have any interest in what Barth calls the 'ontological reality' of the risen Christ—you bet he does! And so do I! I stake everything on the fact that the one who was raised from the dead is the one who said, "I go to prepare a place for you" and "If I go and prepare a place for you, I will come again and will take you to myself, so that where I am, there you may be also" (John 14:2-3). I am not interested in any other person who might claim to be raised from the dead. It would indeed be something of a curiosity, I suppose, like the not infrequent claims of a sighting of the Virgin Mary in some obscure village that results in a flood of tourists and religious seekers. I would not cross town to be part of a mob gathered to view the miracle of someone raised from the dead. Miracle stories simply do not generate my interest. I have a deeper desire that arises in my soul, that the same person who stood on earth and said, "If you have seen me you have seen the Father" (John 14:9) be in heaven to welcome me to a place prepared for me! This man came from the very soul of God (John 1:18). This is the person who said, "I am the bread come down from heaven" (John 6:41). The Christ who rose from the grave is the one who said, "I am the living bread that came down from heaven. Whoever eats of this bread will live forever" (John 6:51). The one who received and gives the Spirit of God 'without measure' and who embraced that Spirit in his own human life is the same one who breathed the Spirit upon his disciples after the resurrection and said, "Receive the Holy Spirit" (John 3:34; 20:22).

I no longer spend time reading the speculations and theories that continue to cast doubt upon the resurrection stories in the Bible as though to sift the wheat from the chaff. The bread that comes from the oven of those who bake what they cannot break apart by their own skeptical reason offer us loaves that never rise!

When Dietrich Bonhoeffer was in prison, his young fiancé, Maria (only 18 years old!) wrote to him of her growing distaste for sophisticated theological speculations. She told of attending a Bible conference for three days listening to lectures on the resurrection "followed by lively debates during which every conceivable view and opinion was shared. Having endured those days with polite sighs", she wrote, "I came to the following conclusions: Either you believe in the Resurrection or you don't. But if two people can wrangle over minutiae for so long without reaching agreement, there's no better proof that neither of them believes in it!" Good answer Maria!

What has been implicit during this discussion must now be made explicit. Saul of Tarsus is closer to us than to the original witnesses to Jesus' crucifixion and resurrection. That is, Jesus was raised from the dead and ascended to heaven prior to Saul's coming to faith that Jesus was indeed the Christ, the Messiah. The encounter with Christ on the Damascus road took place within the parenthesis that separates us from the original resurrection day. While the followers of Jesus did experience him in his resurrection appearances during the 40 days prior to his ascension, this period belongs to the same historical period as their time spent with him prior to his crucifixion. This was, in a sense, 'altered time' due to the overlap between the 'their time' and the 'time' in which Jesus lived after resurrection but prior to ascension. However, they had direct access to the risen Christ which no one has had since he rose to be with the Father. They touched him, ate with him, and had to 'make room' for him when he stood in their midst (John 20).

What Lessing failed to grasp was that his so-called 'ugly ditch' which separates the present from a historical past was as true for Saul of Tarsus as it is for us. Saul's encounter with Jesus was not based on historical accounts which had to be true in order for him to believe. Rather, his encounter with Christ as a spiritual reality, though experienced within his own historical existence, enabled him to assert the truth of the historical accounts. That which provides the continuity between the present reality of Christ and the historical event of Christ's life, death and resurrection, is not a rational truth but a spiritual reality—that is, the Holy Spirit as the Spirit of Christ.

This is what has been implicit in our discussion. The Holy Spirit is the Spirit of the resurrected and coming Christ. As Paul later understood and taught, Christ was raised by the "Spirit of holiness" and declared to be the Son of God by the same Spirit (Romans 1:3). Because the Spirit of God dwells in us, Paul says, we have the Spirit of Christ (Romans 8:9). Thus, Christ is literally in us, claims Paul, by virtue of the Spirit that dwells in us. "If the Spirit him who raised Jesus from the dead dwells in you, he who raised Christ from the dead will give life to your mortal bodies also through his [i.e. Christ's] Spirit that dwells in you" (Romans 8:11). Paul had no difficulty in affirming that the Christ who was raised from the dead now lives at the right hand of the Father and intercedes for us (Romans 8:34). Indeed, says Paul, "When we cry, 'Abba! Father!' it is that very Spirit bearing witness with our spirit that we are children of God" (Romans 8:15).

In the same way that the continuity between the risen Christ and the historical Christ is established as an ontological reality—the same person who died is now alive—the continuity between our present life and the life to come through the resurrection is ontological—we will be the same person in the resurrection that we are now. In what may have been words spoken at the first funeral service Paul conducted, this assurance is given in his first letter. When Jesus comes again, he wrote, "God will bring with him those who have died,... Then we who are alive, who are left, will be caught up in the clouds together with them to meet the Lord in the air" (1 Thess. 4:14; 17).

I have knelt at the gravesite of my great grandparents behind an old church in Norway, and have stood in reflection at the grave where their daughter, my grandmother and grandfather are buried on the prairie of South Dakota.

These people died before I was born. I have their pictures and can trace their names on the tablet of my ancestors. But I will not need their picture to recognize them when we meet in heaven, nor will they have to inquire as to who this person is that bears some resemblance—as Paul says, then we will know even as we have been known (1 Cor 13).

There really is no good answer to the question, How will this work? Paul virtually called it a foolish question, but then went on to suggest, metaphorically, that we really ought to be able to figure it out! "What you sow does not come to life unless it dies" [so it is that grace must kill before making alive!] (1 Cor. 15:36). Each person has and will have their own body, though the one is a physical body and the other a spiritual body. The continuity is not in the DNA but in Christ. If we are bound to Christ in our physical bodies so we will be bound to Christ in our spiritual bodies, argued Paul (15:44-49).

Chapter Ten

This is what I affirm when I sing, "Spirit of God, Descend Upon My Heart." It is a prayer that has already been answered before it becomes my request.

11

Spirit of God, Descend Upon My Heart

You will receive power when the Holy Spirit has come upon you.... All of them were filled with the Holy Spirit and began to speak in other languages, as the Spirit gave them ability. (Acts 1:8; 2:2-4)

There is no recorded ministry of Jesus prior to his baptism by John in the river Jordan. After being baptized, as he was coming out of the water, "the heavens were opened to him and he saw the Spirit of God descending like a dove and alighting on him. And a voice from heaven said, 'This is my Son, the Beloved, with whom I am well pleased'" (Matt. 3:16-17). From this point on, Jesus himself recognized that in being anointed by the Spirit he was set apart to fulfill the role of the promised Messiah. "Filled with the power of the Spirit," Jesus returned to his hometown in Nazareth and went to the synagogue where he was given the scroll of Isaiah from which to read. When he unrolled the scroll he found the place where it was written, "The Spirit of the Lord is upon me because he has anointed me to bring good news to the poor. He has sent me to proclaim release to the captives and recovery of sight to the blind, to let the oppressed go free, to proclaim the year of the Lord's favor." After taking his seat he said to them, "Today this scripture has been fulfilled in your hearing" (Luke 4:16-21; Isaiah 61:1-2).

Luke says that the baptism of Jesus occurred when he was around 30 years of age (3:23). From his birth to his baptism, no recorded actions of Jesus are found in the gospel accounts except for the brief incident when he was twelve years old. Jesus had gone with his parents to Jerusalem for the festival of the Passover but remained behind when they left. When his parents discovered that he was missing they returned and three days later found him in the temple engaged in theological discussions with the religious leaders. When his mother admonished him for causing them such great anxiety he replied: "Did you not know that I must be in my Father's house?" (Luke 2:41-51) Apparently his parents were not impressed, though his mother 'treasured all these things in her heart.' Luke simply says that he went home with them and was obedient to them. We are left to ponder what the eighteen years that followed might have been like for Jesus as well as his parents. What does seem significant is that there is no mention of any form of ministry or activity of Jesus during those years. Nor is there any mention of the Spirit of God directing and empowering him, not even when he was demonstrating his precocious wisdom in the temple!

I believe that this is significant. It is only when Jesus is filled with the Spirit at his baptism that his life and ministry become evident as a manifestation of the work of God. Jesus himself was very clear about this. "I can do nothing on my own," Jesus said. "The works that the Father has given me to complete, the very works that I am doing, testify on my behalf that the Father has sent me" (John 5:30; 36). "If it is by the Spirit of God that I cast out demons, then the Kingdom of God has come to you" (Matt. 12:28). The ministry of Jesus as Messiah took place under the power and direction of the Spirit of God. The importance of this for our understanding of the role of the Spirit in our lives can hardly be overestimated, as we shall see.

The distinction between the Spirit of God and the Spirit of Christ and Holy Spirit is not always clear in the New Testament. However, it needs to be said that the source of the Spirit is God the Father, that the Holy Spirit is "Spirit of God" (Rom. 8:9); the "Spirit of him that raised Jesus from the dead" (Rom. 8:11), the "Spirit of the living God" (2 Cor. 3:4), and the "Spirit which is of God" (1 Cor. 2:12). Again it is God who has given us his Holy Spirit (1 Thess. 4:8). In the baptism of Jesus, the Spirit descending upon Jesus is the "Spirit of God" (Matt. 3:16), and the passage from which Peter quotes on the day of Pentecost (Joel) says: "God will pour out his Spirit. . . . " (Acts 2:17). While Jesus was conceived by the Spirit of God and the Spirit of God certainly was present in his life prior to his baptism, his anointing by the Spirit at his Baptism marked the beginning of a new relationship between Jesus as Son of God and the Spirit of God.

Jesus had divine authority, even to forgive sins, because he was the Son of God (Mark 2:10). From his very conception, as the very essence of his being, Jesus was "in the form of God" (Phil. 2:6). Jesus did not become the Son of God at his Baptism. The incarnation of God does not result from a 'Spirit-filled' human who somehow morphed into a divine being. We should not confuse his messianic anointing for the ministry of God with his conception by the Spirit as the Word become flesh (John 1:14). At the same time, we must not lose sight of the fact that in the very person of Jesus, the Spirit of God and the Son of God were bound together in such a way that there can now be no Son without the Spirit, and no Spirit without the Son.

I shall never forget the day that I sat in the Library at New College, Edinburgh where I was working my doctoral dissertation and read this statement from the third-century theologian, Irenaeus: "For God promised, that in the last times He would pour Him [the Spirit] upon His servants and handmaids, that they might prophesy; wherefore He did also descend upon the Son of God, made the Son of man, becoming accustomed in fellowship with Him to dwell in the human race, to rest with human beings, and to dwell in the workmanship of God, working the will of the Father in them, and renewing them from their old habits into the newness of Christ."

What an amazing thing to say—that the Spirit of God became 'accustomed' to dwell with humanity through the intimate daily life of Jesus of Nazareth! When I read this quotation to my students I suggested that the wild and untamed Spirit of God, which we so often read about in the Old Testament, was 'domesticated' by dwelling fully in the humanity of Jesus! I even went so far as to say on one occasion, that the Spirit of God was 'housebroken' in living with Jesus! Some students were a bit outraged by that, so I never said that again—until now!

We do not receive the Spirit of God in the same way as Jesus. The Spirit which we receive is the Spirit which dwelt with and in Jesus, already 'accustomed' to dwell with humans. Thomas Torrance reminds us that the Spirit does not come to us as 'naked Spirit,' but clothed with the character and personality of Christ. Karl Barth says that the Holy Spirit is the Spirit of Jesus Christ—The Holy One. The Spirit is Holy (*hagion*) because he is Lord (*kyrion*). "The Spirit is Holy in the New Testament because He is the Spirit of Jesus Christ. He shows Himself to be the Spirit of Christ by the fact that He is given to men by Him, i. e., by the Crucified and Risen, as the power of His death revealed in His resurrection . . . If they have the Spirit, they have the Spirit from Him, otherwise than from it, there is no Holy Spirit, no empowered witnesses, no apostles, no Christians, no community."

Throughout the centuries the relation of the Holy Spirit to Jesus Christ has been the subject of much debate. The Eastern Church (Greek and Russian Orthodox) maintain to this day that the Western Church (Catholic and Protestant) erred in revising the Fourth-Century Nicene Creed (A. D. 325). The Creed as originally formulated confessed belief in the Holy Spirit "Who proceeds from the Father."

The Western Church, under the influence of the church at Rome, altered the Creed to read, "Who proceeds from the Father and the Son." The Eastern church theologians argued that this relegated the Holy Spirit to a subordinate position with the effect that the Holy Spirit can only be allowed to work where directed by the Son. When the Western church defined the authority of the papal office as that of Jesus Christ (the Pope being the Vicar of Christ), the freedom of the Spirit became constrained by the legal stipulations of canon law, according to the Eastern Church. The fact that this constituted one of the major reasons for the division between the Western and Eastern Church in the eleventh-century which continues to the present day, demonstrates how serious this matter is for the theologians of the church.

While admitting that the insertion of the phrase 'and the son' (*filioque*) into the Nicene Creed was as a matter of process, illegitimate, Karl Barth argued that the intention lying behind this change was theologically correct and practically significant. For us to understand the Holy Spirit as having no relation to Jesus Christ, says Barth, undercuts our own relation to God as constituted by the real humanity of Christ. Our own humanity cannot serve as the bearer of the Spirit without confusing the Holy Spirit with our own human spirit. From a theological perspective, Barth reminds us that we are baptized into union with Christ by the Spirit, rather than being 'baptized into the Spirit.' It is Christ who is our mediator and intercessor with the Father. Thus, from a practical standpoint as well, the Holy Spirit unites our own humanity with Christ so that we do not fall back on our own human weakness in prayer and worship but rather, empowered by the Spirit of Christ from within, our own spirit is permitted to be fully human without confusion and distortion. As an attempt to mediate this dispute, theologians on both sides of the debate are moving toward the expression the Spirit proceeds from the Father 'through the Son.' The Father is the source of the Spirit, while the Son mediates the Spirit to humans through his own inner life with the Father.

Why should we be concerned? Are these theological distinctions with no real difference?

In 1959 when I completed my seminary training and became the pastor of a newly forming congregation, controversy and confusion regarding the so-called 'Charismatic Movement' spread like wildfire throughout many Protestant (and some Roman Catholic) churches. From the Greek word 'charism'—translated usually as 'gift,' persons were challenged as to whether or not they had really received this 'gift' of the Spirit. Those who claimed to have received this special gift of the Spirit became involved with various phenomena associated with the movement, including the 'utterance of tongues,' as both a private and public manifestation of being filled with the Spirit. Churches were torn apart over the issue, and Christians, even within their own family, were pitted against each other in a sort of intramural conflict over who was more spiritual. The older Pentecostal denominations, such as Assembly of God, looked at this phenomenon with some curiosity, as they held from the beginning that a person who did not 'speak in tongues' did not demonstrate the empirical evidence for being filled with the Spirit. This new movement, however, was not about forming a new denomination, or becoming 'Pentecostal.' The impetus was primarily one of spiritual renewal through the charismatic experience.

It was not long before I was confronted by visitors to the church who challenged my own spiritual leadership as deficient because I did not 'have the charismatic gifts.' On one occasion a family entered into our fellowship and appeared to be 'one of us.' It was soon reported however that they were calling teenage children from our members to baby-sit their own children. Instead of leaving the house, they would then remain and attempt to persuade the young person to receive the gift of the Spirit and 'speak in tongues.' When several parents complained about this practice, I called on the family to inquire as to what their purpose was. "Pastor," said the man, "We know that you do not have the Spirit of God so you will not really understand that we have been called here by the Holy Spirit to bring renewal to this congregation." The absolute assurance that he spoke the truth of God was breathtaking, so that instead of it appearing as arrogance it simply was stunning! Without emotion and judgment, he stated what to him was a matter of fact. If there was anything other than conviction on his part it might have been a touch of pity. But even then I could do no more than marvel. I felt somewhat like what Job must have felt when God finally did confront him and say, "Who do you think you are?" I knew that I was defenseless!

I realized that I was not prepared to provide him with the only kind of evidence that he would accept, so agreed that by his definition, I was probably not filled with the Spirit. "I do trust the Spirit however," I replied, "and am very willing for the members of our church to decide for themselves as to whether or not to allow their children to visit your home. I will send a letter to each family of the church informing them that you feel that you were called by the Spirit of God to bring their children into this new experience and that any parent that wishes to participate are free to do so by having their young people go your home to baby-sit." This proposal did not sit well with him as he realized that when his intentions were to be made public the tactic would not work so well! I did send out the letter, but the family left the church immediately and were not heard from again. Apparently the Holy Spirit as he saw it could only work 'under cover,' advancing his own mission under a pretext.

That was my indoctrination into the highly charged atmosphere of the charismatic renewal movement. It should also be said, that there were several members of our congregation who did experience spiritual renewal through receiving of the Holy Spirit as a personal charismatic experience. They were quite satisfied with the spiritual environment of the fellowship and felt no need to force their own experience on others. My teaching and preaching on the Holy Spirit took on a new perspective through this experience and this 'wave' of charismatic renewal passed through and over us, as it did with most churches in the decade of the 1960s and thankfully, with more benefit than bewilderment. My former faculty colleague, Peter Wagner, was to describe this as the 'second wave' of the Holy Spirit, while he himself caught what he called the 'third wave' and rode on ahead of us! The 'third wave,' as Wagner described it, was focused more on the signs of the Kingdom of God expressed in miraculous healing and exorcism of demons. The focus was more on the mission of the church as a beachhead of the Kingdom than with personal and individual competition for the 'higher gifts.'

The third wave is distinguished from the earlier Pentecostal movement, says Wagner, by its emphasis on the filling of the Holy Spirit rather than on a baptism of the Holy Spirit evidenced by the Spirit gift of tongues. The core of the third wave, maintains Wagner, is composed of Christians who are satisfied with their present ecclesiastical affiliation and desire that it remain intact. This leads to a further distinctive of this movement in that it seeks to avoid divisiveness and disunity. By not stressing the Spirit-filled life as against those who do not have the Spirit, this movement seeks to avoid the tendency of the Charismatic movement (second wave) which, in Wagner's judgment, contributed to a 'two-class' Christian experience.

In my judgment, there are some theological inadequacies with the attempt to ground God's power in the Spirit alone. Viewing humanity as only an instrumental vehicle for the Spirit, does not provide for the effect of the Spirit on humanity itself. Humanity is in need of more than its physical or even emotional healing. The power of spiritual renewal is found in the actual humanity of Jesus Christ as the bearer of the very life of the Son as divine logos, not merely as a human instrument through which God displayed his divine power. The emphasis on signs and wonders as a methodology for evangelism and church growth does not grasp the wholistic thrust of the Spirit's life with persons. The miraculous does not violate the natural means by which God's mission finds its way through Christ into the world for the salvation of all. Feeding the hungry, liberating the oppressed, bringing peace and reconciliation to people and between people is never accomplished by the miraculous alone—not in Jesus' ministry, not in Paul's ministry, and not in the church's ministry to the world.

This means that evangelism must not be construed as merely adding members to the church in such a way that the humanity of those evangelized is left unconsecrated. The spiritual renewal of humanity is grounded in the humanity of Christ as a vicarious humanity, by which his priestly ministry includes all who are suffering in their own humanity. Formation of Christ in the world through the Spirit does not take place apart from the world. This can be seen as the thrust of the teaching of Jesus in Matthew 25, where the presence of Christ in the world occurs through ministry to those who are outcasts, through visiting the imprisoned, through ministry to the poor, and clothing the naked.

The authentic *charism* which liberates is not the spirit of power, but the Spirit of Christ. An authentic charismatic theology is one which empowers blacks in South Africa to participate in the franchise of full membership in the human race as defined socially, politically, and spiritually. It is a theology which empowers women to have full parity in every structure of society, especially the church and its ministry. It is a theology which empowers the poor, the marginalized, the weak, and the homeless to live meaningful and comfortable lives as human beings created in God's image. An authentic charismatic theology is one which disarms the church of its pride and privilege, causing it to repent, and to enact repentance toward God through responsible service toward the world which God loves. Thomas Smail has said it well: "[T]he charismatic Christian with his world-affirming approach and his awareness of both the demonic and the prophetic should be among those who can catch the vision. God wants to give in local churches structures of relationship that have their roots in the central relationship to himself, but that express themselves horizontally and practically in such a way as to challenge the oppressive structures of society in which the church lives." Charismatic Christians, Smail continues, should be as much concerned for the socially demonic in the form of oppressive structures as for the personally demonic.

Despite all of the 'craziness' which some profess and act out in the name of the Holy Spirit, it is well to be reminded, as one theologian said, "What is divine is never weird!" The reports that come to me of people possessed by the Spirit making animal noises or bursting out in 'holy laughter' make me hope that God has a sense of humor! When we consider that it was Jesus who was filled with the Holy Spirit 'without measure' we see that this experience did not make him less human but more human. The form of a 'spirit-filled' human being is that of Jesus of Nazareth, and the evidence is not in some form of temporary derangement of mind, emotion, or tongue, but in his inner stability of peace under great stress, and his outer life of compassion and ministry toward the weak and the wounded in the world. When I pray to receive the Holy Spirit it is the Spirit of Jesus that I seek as a counselor and advocate of my own spirit. The evidences, as the Apostle Paul said, are quite clear, to have the same mind that was in Christ Jesus (Phil. 2:5-8).

I suggested earlier that it is highly significant that the ministry of Jesus took place under the power and direction of the Spirit of God. This is important for us to understand as we receive the Holy Spirit in fulfillment of the promise of Jesus: "And I will ask the Father, and he will give you another Advocate [*paraclete*], to be with you forever. This is the Spirit of truth. . . the Advocate, the Holy Spirit, whom the Father will send in my name, will teach you everything and remind you of all that I have said" (John 14:16, 26). We have become accustomed to speak of the Holy Spirit as our advocate or counselor, but it is clear that Jesus is our primary advocate (*paraclete*) for he says that when he leaves he will send 'another Advocate.' The Holy Spirit adds no content to our spiritual life other than that of Jesus Christ. Being filled with the Spirit is being conformed to Christ, and the Spirit is a good mentor and teacher! "When the Spirit of truth comes, he will not speak on his own, but will speak whatever he hears, and he will declare to you the things that are to come. He will glorify me, because he will take what is mine and declare it to you. All that the Father has is mine. For this reason I said that he will take what is mine and declare it to you" (John 16:13-15).

I know that my own spirit is too tame when it should be adventurous. My spirit can be too impulsive and sometimes brash, when it should be measured and modest. My spirit can waver in doubt and uncertainty when I should be brave and bold. This is why I ask for the Holy Spirit to come alongside of my spirit, not to take my place but to make my place more resemble a home where Jesus lives than a college dormitory. I cannot put the image out of my mind created by Irenaeus when he spoke of the Spirit of God becoming "accustomed in fellowship with Him to dwell in the human race, to rest with human beings, and to dwell in the workmanship of God, working the will of the Father in them, and renewing them from their old habits into the newness of Christ." This is the Spirit that I seek when I pray, Spirit of God, Descend Upon my Heart.

I don't want the Spirit of God to wake me up in the middle of the night when I need my rest. I don't want the Spirit of God to make me anxious in order to seek first the Kingdom of God. I don't want the Spirit of God to make me bark like a dog or laugh like a hyena in order to fulfill a craving for 'more of God.' On the other hand, there is something that I desire in being filled with the Spirit. And that is captured in the poignant words of the Psalmist: "I have calmed and quieted my soul, like a weaned child with its mother; my soul is like a weaned child that is within me" (Psalm 131:2-3). I am not sure that I want to go through the weaning process—nor am I sure that God wants to go through it with me! The parent suffers more than the child, I suspect. To be weaned from the kind of relationship with God where my needs for gratification demand his immediate response is to walk alone, it seems. But Jesus went through that process, first in being weaned from the breast of his mother, and then from the power of God as a form of temptation. It was, after all, the Spirit that led Jesus into the wilderness (Matt. 4:1).

The Spirit of Jesus is a 'weaned Spirit' that has returned once more to the Father. My spirit is still too restless. I want every prayer to be answered. I want to keep praying even when there is no answer. In the end, I want to be able to trust God to hold my unanswered prayers like letters from a separated lover, close to his bosom. This is the Spirit of my prayer.

12

Sweet Hour of Prayer

We do not know how to pray as we ought, but that very Spirit intercedes with sighs too deep for words. Romans 8:26

At the midweek Bible study and prayer meeting held in our church for the eleven years that I served as Pastor, we prayed regularly for divine intervention on behalf of those with incurable disease, emotional distress, financial difficulty and other situations for which no ordinary or natural relief seemed available. Most of these prayers were never answered, at least not in accord with the specific nature of our petitions. No records were kept, no accounting was demanded and none given. There seemed to be an implicit conspiracy among us to conceal what was clearly obvious—most such prayers are never answered. For my part, when that thought crossed my mind I immediately brushed it aside. To question the efficacy of prayer seemed as inappropriate as mentioning death in the presence of a dying person.

We often cited the words of Jesus who said that if we had faith as small as a mustard seed we could move mountains (Matt. 17:20). "Ask and it will be given you" (Matt. 7:7). "Whatever you ask for in prayer with faith, you will receive" (Matt. 21:22). To expose the failure of prayer would be to undermine the quality of our faith. God was never on trial in our prayer, it was always our faith. That too is part of the denial process. It is easier to live with unanswered prayer when we are found wanting rather than to believe that God may not be willing.

Surrounding our prayers for divine intervention we packed in plenty of prayers for safe travel, which turned out well for the most part, overcoming the flu, which was virtually a sure thing given enough rest and fluids, and wisdom for our children in making their life choices, which we sort of understood to be as much for the parents as for their offspring. This was all part of how we coped with unanswered prayer, I now believe. The specific prayers for divine intervention could be packaged with prayers of a more general nature when sent off so that no tracking number was required or provided.

"That's unfair," one of my students responded when I raised this discussion in class. "All prayers are answered, we just don't know what kind of an answer God gives, sometimes it's 'no'." Sorry, I responded, 'no' is not an answer. When I pray for a person with an incurable cancer to be healed, I cannot make the funeral service an answer to prayer. When the person dies, that particular prayer was not answered. I move to another level of prayer in which divine intervention is promised on the other side of death, in which our faith is upheld by the Word of God, not demolished by it. Prayer is a sacrament by which we enter the third dimesnion of spiritual reality. That itself is sufficient for the troubled soul.

After leaving this church for two years of study in Scotland for my doctoral degree, I returned to find that my former choir director was stricken with a disease of the liver due to the effects of anesthesia for what was thought to be routine surgery. Several of her friends met to pray for her healing, and even went so far as to take her to a special healing service conducted by a well-known national figure. That failed, and she was brought back in the same condition as before. Her friends rarely visited her, as they did not know how to cope with her failing condition when prayer for her healing seemed itself to fail.

After consulting with her husband, I drove to her home from another city in which we were living. As we talked she expressed frustration and concern over the fact that she did not seem to have enough faith to be healed. After some time, I sensed that underlying her feelings of failure in prayer were more deep-seated feelings concerning the unspoken and seemingly inevitable fact of death. "Has anyone ever talked with you about the fact that you may be dying," I asked her? "No," she replied, "but I think that we need to talk about it."

We did talk about the promises of Scripture which seemed to say that God would answer prayer in the name of Jesus if we had faith. When we talked about the possibility of dying rather than being healed, she herself came up with the insight that it probably required more faith to trust God through the 'valley of the shadow of death' than for a miracle of healing. We agreed that our faith needed to be directed toward God rather than simply on prayer itself. When I left I asked her, "Do you want me to pray for your healing?" "I don't think so," she replied, "I need prayer which connects me with God through this experience, the kind of prayer I have had for healing left me disconnected with God. I have faith enough to leave the matter with God."

Three weeks later I conducted her funeral service. Our prayers were attached to God's promises that the ultimate answer to her prayer was the assurance of resurrection. As I drove home I reflected on what God does with unanswered prayers. I concluded that God holds these close to his heart so that, while the prayer may not be answered, the petition was not ignored.

Even as I write this I am struck by the incredible fact that some prayers for divine intervention are answered! Testimony to answered prayer for healing of an incurable disease or a malignant tumor are often accompanied by confirmation for which no medical reason can be given. Doctors have been known to use the word 'miracle' when they may only mean to say that they have no other explanation for a dramatic turn around in what seemed an inevitable outcome.

How do I explain this? If most such prayers are not answered, how do we account for the fact that some are answered without plunging back again into the downward spiral of weak and ineffective faith? At one of our prayer meetings, a woman gave testimony to a miracle on the part of her daughter who had survived a car accident that totally demolished her car, leaving her without a scratch. "God was in the car with her," the mother said, "We always pray for her when she leaves on a trip and God answered our prayers." I walked over and placed my hand on the shoulder of a man whose son had died in a mountain hiking accident. "We praise and thank God for the power and presence of God who enabled your daughter to survive," I said, "even as we thank God for his presence in the life and family of Joe who lost their son. God was present in their suffering of a loss and we join with you in praise to God who was present with your daughter."

The woman who had the miracle of God's presence did not need my hand on her shoulder. A reported miracle in a prayer meeting sucks all of the oxygen of faith out of the room into that one vortex of divine power. The center of gravity shifts so that all of God's power flows toward the place of answered prayer. My pastoral responsibility was not to be drawn into that vortex and to be caught up in the power flow. Rather, by standing by the person who had no answer to prayer while, at the same time, affirming the answer to prayer on behalf of the mother, I sought to keep God's power more evenly divided between the powerless and those who had been empowered by the miracle. The woman was not in the least put off by my actions, but was affirmed in her own faith in God's power while able to share some of this power with Joe and his family.

Is it possible to keep both answered prayer and unanswered prayer in balance without becoming timid with regard to the 'prayer of faith' that moves God to action?

I use this illustration with my students. God is like a parent, and we have every reason to think in this way. Jesus taught us to pray to "our father in heaven," and the Apostle Paul urged us to think of receiving the Spirit of adoption into God's family whereby we cry, "Abba! Father!" (Rom. 8:15). If God is like a parent, then we must place prayer into that relational context rather than view prayer as 'pulling a lever' and expecting the 'treat to drop.'

When children beg for something from a parent, it is like a petition or prayer for something which they earnestly need or think they need. At least they have their heart set on something which only the parent can provide. Most such begging (praying) goes unanswered if not unheeded. Each time, the answer is 'no' and often the reason given is simply, "Because I said so!" And don't try to tell the child that 'no' is really an answer! Undaunted, the child does not abandon the request but finds ways to persist in the 'prayer' for what is wanted.

Suddenly, the parent will, for no apparent reason, relent and give in to the request. Now the child does not ordinarily say, "I must have asked in just the right way this time, and if I learn how to ask in this way I will always get an answer." No, children simply accept the fact that this is how it is with parents. They just accept the fact that parents sometimes say yes, and sometimes no. Nor do children charge the parents with inconsistency by now saying yes to a request that they have denied many times before. The child does not suffer loss of confidence and trust in the parent through an extended time of unanswered begging (prayer). Nor does the child blame him or herself when the request goes unanswered. Though it must also be said that children can become quite devious with respect to manipulating their parents through insistent begging. Something of the same might be said of how many Christians use prayer in relation to their heavenly father!

In somewhat the same way, our prayers to God seeking divine intervention are offered up most times without an answer. Other prayers we offer to God are in thanksgiving for things we often did not even ask for. "Give us this day our daily bread," is one petition that can pray every day and for the most part, it is answered. The child lives in a virtual cocoon of care, comfort and convenience provided by parents, assuming a healthy and non-abusive family system. Jesus seemed to allude to this when he said, "Therefore do not worry, saying 'What shall we eat?' or 'What shall we drink?'

Or 'What shall we wear?' . . . . indeed your heavenly Father know that you need all these things" (Matt. 31-32). The special kind of prayer by which we seek divine intervention as a miracle of God's power to overcome or overturn a natural course of events, must be kept within the framework of that kind of relationship.

Am I satisfied with this? No, not really.

In no area of the Christian life is there more uncertainty, confusion and even a sense of failure than in our life of prayer. Many of us were taught as children to pray. Later, prayer was urged upon us as a source of spiritual renewal and blessing as well as a way to secure God's answers for our physical as well as spiritual needs. We were reminded of the answers to prayer achieved by many of God's saints as a means of challenging us to a deeper and more sustained prayer life. And yet, we so seldom realize answers for our prayers.

Our children for whom we pray are not always healed of disease and spared the pain of grievous loss. Friends for whom we intercede with fervent prayer still suffer catastrophic illness and lingering, painful deaths. Yes, there are the occasional almost miraculous exceptions to which we cling with nervous faith and of which we speak in a too-shrill voice, as if to fill the void of heaven's silence too long endured. But earnestly inquire of us concerning our confidence in prayer to feed the hungry, heal the sick, salvage broken marriages, produce saving faith in loved ones, and we confess more failure than success.

I remember a woman who came to my office years ago for pastoral counseling. She was distraught and angry. As she talked, I began to feel that she had good reason to be so upset. Her adolescent daughter had a history of drug related problems, had stolen her mother's credit card, had withdrawn a large sum from the bank, and had left home to live with two other teenagers with a man twice their age.

"I am heartsick over this," she told me, "and angry. Angry not only at her for what she has done to me but angry at God for not protecting her." I encouraged her to talk about her feelings toward God. "What has God done or failed to do in protecting your daughter?"

"This is my only child. My husband and I almost gave up trying to have children. I read in the Bible where Hannah, who was without a child, prayed to the Lord and she received a child in answer to her prayer. His name was Samuel. I prayed that God would enable me to conceive, and that if I did I would give this child to God in the same way that Hannah did with her son, Samuel. When my daughter was born I knew that she was an answer to prayer. I named her Samantha."

I waited.

"I kept praying for her, especially when she began to get in trouble. I wonder now if it makes any difference to pray. I wonder if there really is a God, and if there is, why he doesn't put a shield of protection around those who belong to him. I hear stories of other people praying for miracles and they happen! Don't I have a right to expect a miracle too when I pray?" What seemed an answer to prayer turned out to be a disaster, as far as the mother was concerned.

"Should I now pray for a miracle that Samantha be healed of her emotional, moral and spiritual sickness?"

I responded by saying, "yes, but I think that in the meantime we should think about some kind of intervention which may involve placing her under supervised treatment and care."

I told her about the case of a woman, now in her middle 50s who had suffered a paralyzing accident when she was 18, which left her paraplegic and confined to a wheelchair. She went on to earn a Ph. D. in clinical psychology and now works in a rehabilitation center for persons recovering from incapacitating injuries. A young man was admitted who had suffered a spinal cord injury and was in a wheel chair, unable to walk. Being a devout Christian, he insisted that God was going to heal him and that he would get up and walk out of the place as people in his church were praying for him.

Not wishing to destroy his faith which appeared to be the only coping mechanism he had with which to face the devastating loss of bodily function, she asked: "When do you think the miracle will come? Will it probably come tomorrow, or maybe next week?" He responded by saying, "I don't know, but God knows and when he answers our prayers I will be healed."

"That is good," she said. "Now let us see what we can do about learning how to use your fingers to hold a knife and fork so that you can feed yourself, until the miracle comes." With this, he consented to work on his physical therapy routine which he had been resisting based on his expectation of a miracle.

As this woman told the story to my class, sitting in her own wheel chair, she as much as said, "This is what I have accomplished waiting for the miracle to come." She too had been the object of intense prayer for healing at the time of her injury, but had long since given up her faith that God performed miracles. At the same time, as a good therapist, she was wise and supporting in not destroying the faith of the young man while, at the same time, helping him to prepare for a life where there would be no answer to prayer for miracles.

In his high priestly prayer, Jesus not only prays for his disciples, "whom you gave me," but also for all who would come to believe in the Father through Jesus.

"I ask not only on behalf of these, but also on behalf of those who will believe in me through their word, that they may all be one. As you, Father, are in me and I am in you, may they also be in us, so that the world may believe that you have sent me" (John 17:20-21).

The disciples are but the inner core of a circle whose circumference is as extensive as all of humanity.

But we are surprised when we see that the prayer of Jesus when he chose the twelve to follow him resulted in the calling of Judas, his own betrayer (Luke 6). I began musing about Judas years ago. It began with a sermon I preached in the middle 1960s titled "Judas as an Answer to Prayer." After praying all night, Jesus then called all of his disciples and out of them chose the twelve including, as Luke records it, "Judas Iscariot, who became a traitor" (Luke 6:16). I pondered the significance of that choice in light of the night spent in prayer. One could well assume that the purpose of the night spent in prayer was to seek divine guidance in the choosing of the twelve. We would expect Jesus, after a night of prayer, to have discovered what God already knew—Judas would be the betrayer. In the same way, when we pray we often expect to gain an advantage in determining ahead of time the will of God so that we do not fail in some venture, or go in the wrong direction and have to 'backtrack' in order to get back into the will of God. For Jesus, the fact that Judas was an answer to his prayer no doubt enabled him to accept even the betrayal by Judas at the end as bracketed by his prayer which placed all of his life and destiny in the hands of the Father.

This reveals to us how our life of prayer is often based on our misunderstanding of love and grace. When we view God's grace as conditional upon our perfection and success in living by his commandments, we will tend to use prayer as a way of securing God's promises by meeting the right conditions. In this view of God, a failure to produce a result through prayer throws us back upon our own lack of faith or, even worse, some spiritual defect which lies unconfessed and which sabotages God's work. On the other hand, if we view God's providence and foreknowledge as some kind of 'pre-written history,' then we will use prayer to gain access to that secret knowledge of God—to take a peek at the answers in the back of the book, if you please!

What we discover, instead, is that the will of God is grounded in his promise as to the outcome of our lives, not in a detailed plan which remains hidden in the mind of God. Prayer is thus access to the divine promise revealed through the inner relation which the

Son shares with the Father rather than an attempt to avoid the risk of failure. Through his life of prayer with the Father, Jesus could love unconditionally and freely the unknown elements in his disciples as well as the known qualities. In this way, even the actions of Judas as betrayer are included within the divine promise and purpose for Jesus. Prayer, for Jesus, was not for the purpose of excluding the sinful actions of others, but for including all persons, despite their failures, in his own life with the Father as the basis for redemption of sinners.

We are not amazed that the prayers of Jesus were heard and answered by the Father on each occasion when he prayed for others. Yet we have come to expect that our own prayers often seem to go unanswered. We know that we do not pray as we ought, and that our prayers so often are desperate and devoid of the inner certainty which comes from an intimate communion with God, our heavenly Father. How then should we pray for a miracle if most prayers are not answered and miracles are few and far between? Yes, we should pray for divine intervention, but then invest our faith in God rather than in prayer. Do I believe in prayer? No. I believe in God, and pray to God and look to God for the faith to live with unanswered prayer.

This leads me finally to suggest that a miracle of answered prayer, particularly in regard to the healing of the body, be understood as a kind of sacrament. By this I mean that a miracle of healing be viewed as a sign of the ultimate reality of healing in the resurrection of the body, meant to give assurance to the church and to the one who experiences the healing that the resurrection is true. This is not to suggest that we add a third sacrament to the Eucharist and Baptism. These two sacraments are clearly instituted by Christ and are available to all Christians, whereas the miracle of physical healing is apparently not. We can, however, think of a miracle in a sacramental way, without making it into a sacrament. By this is meant that the eschatological reality of the resurrection as the basis for hope is represented in the miracle of healing as a communication of this hope to all Christians, not merely to those who are healed.

Viewing the miracle of physical healing of a person as a kind of sacrament, or sign of the resurrection, delivers the person who is healed from the implied consequence of the healing as some kind of freedom from sickness and disease as a condition of life. The person who is healed may well subsequently die of either a return of the same disease, or another disease, without the effect and meaning of the healing in any way diminished. The effect of the healing is to strengthen faith in the reality of the resurrection and the forgiveness of sins, not to make faith dependent upon the effect of the healing itself.

In the same way, the miracle of physical healing of a person considered as an eschatological sign of the resurrection delivers the church from the temptation to set up physical healing as a special sign of God's grace for those who have sufficient faith. The church is thus delivered from the tendency to make out of physical healing a manipulation of faith and a pragmatic method by which the growth of the church can be assured. That which has the character of a sacrament is an eschatological event and can never be subject to control or manipulation.

Prayer is a way of life 'between the times.' We live by faith and not by sight, said Paul, who knew something about answered prayer and a lot about faith (2 Cor. 5:7). We ought not use faith to turn prayer into magic, nor should we use prayer as a test of faith. In the end, it should be our prayer that we too die in faith "without having received the promises, but from a distance they saw and greeted them" (Hebrew 11:13). Lord, increase our faith! (Luke 17:5)

13

My Faith Looks Up To Thee

Faith can be upset by things to which love pays no attention.
                                        Edward John Carnell

When did I acquire saving faith? The Lutheran pastor who baptized me as an infant would answer, by the same Word of God through which you became a child of God in Baptism. Following a year of catechism study, at the age of 14, I was 'confirmed' in faith by answering correctly the questions directed to me in front of the congregation, and admitted to the Communion Table. It should also be noted that the pastor prepared us for the confirmation by meeting individually with us and having us pray for Jesus to enter our hearts. This was not understood as acquiring 'saving faith' for the first time, but rather confirming personally the 'faith that saves' with which we were endowed at Baptism.

Some years later, as an adult, the connection with that Lutheran congregation lapsed after time spent in the Air Force in the Second World War, and marriage to a Presbyterian! The Presbyterian pastor who admitted me to membership accepted my earlier baptism as authentic, but pressed for a 'confession of faith' as the basis for becoming a member. Thus, 'saving faith' was no longer a supernatural gift but more a matter of personal choice ratified by a community of the faithful.

Still years later, after finishing college and returning to the farm I came into contact with a young farmer who was part of a class I was teaching for the Veterans administration in a program designed to provide continuing 'on-the-farm-education' for veterans. Vic was a Baptist who was never reticent to speak of his own faith in Christ as the opportunity came. In one such discussion, where I was tentatively sharing my own rather ambiguous and unformed convictions of a spiritual nature, he suddenly turned to me and said, "Ray, are you saying that you really do believe in Christ?" My answer, though not as enthusiastic as was his question, gave clear assent, at which he grasped my hand and said, "Now you are really born again!"

This introduced a new vocabulary and a new dimension of faith into my life which began a journey, I am sure, leading to the decision a few years later to leave the farm and enroll at Fuller Seminary and, as they say, the rest is history.

So, when did I acquire saving faith?

The Lutheran pastor who baptized and catechized me, would assure me that I was really born again at my baptism. The Presbyterian pastor would count my adult confession of faith as evidence that I had, through baptism, entered the covenant family of God as a provisional context of faith until I could take upon myself the faith that saves. My Baptist friend, was more pragmatic, You are either saved or you are not—and your personal relation with Christ is the evidence of having saving faith.

In one sense, I felt quite secure, for I seemed to have all the bases covered, even though I could not get all the players on the field at the same time! But I could play well in their own game!

It was during my years spent as a pastor that I began to see how difficult it was for many people to come to grips with the issue of faith. I also found it difficult to preach and teach on the passages of the Bible where faith seemed to be demanded as a condition of answered prayer or, if not a condition, a 'trump card' that could be used to overcome obstacles and clear the landmines from the terrain of everyday life. I never did see a 'mountain cast into the sea' by anyone's faith, not literally nor even figuratively, however one put the spin on it (Mark 11:22-24). At times I wanted to cry out, "Jesus, do you realize what you are doing by telling people that they can do all things through faith? We are all having a crisis of faith down here, and your words are not helping!"

The so-called 'faith' passages in Scripture are especially troublesome as they seem to promise that faith is a key which unlocks in some mysterious way the supernatural power of God (Mark 11:22; Matt. 17:20; Luke 17:6; Mark 9:23; James 1:6). New Testament professor Gordon Fee, an ordained minister in the Pentecostal tradition cautions again using these texts as a means of producing an effect through faith. "The real issue, therefore, when it comes to these texts, is not how 'to get them to work for us,' but how we are to understand them in the light of the full biblical revelation. How do they relate to the reality of God's sovereignty and His overall purposes for mankind?"

I cannot find any reference in scripture where Jesus claimed to produce miracles or answer to prayer based on 'his faith.' Rather, he attributed these miracles to the work of God (John 5:30; 36). Jesus did not say, "my faith I give unto you," but "my peace I give unto you" (John 14:27), and "my joy may be in you" (John 15:11). As Gordon Fee has reminded us, Jesus did not use faith as a device to make God work for him. Rather, his faith was grounded in the inner life of mutual love which he experienced as the Son of the Father. We cannot 'tear these faith texts' out of that context and make out of them a formula for producing supernatural results. I take these texts as a challenge to explore more deeply than we ever have before the depths of divine grace and love available to us through our loving trust and faith in God.

"If you only believe!" I could preach on the text by avoiding drawing out direct implications for people to put into practice. But I could not say the words to a person struggling to accept a doctor's diagnosis that pointed to the inevitability of a long and slow death or, at the minimum, a great deal of suffering and pain. I found myself evasive and noncommittal when challenged by a man who had started a new business venture which was undercapitalized and probably over-visualized to pray with him that he would have the faith necessary to make it work. I instinctively knew that this was a wrong use of faith but he had the text of Scripture on his side. I wanted to tell him that it was not really a matter of faith but of being sure that he had sufficient cash flow and that he was dealing realistically with the profit margin on his product. But I was only his pastor not a financial advisor!

The vision of faith is the open window of new and creative possibility, but when that vision goes out of focus, what was intended to be miraculous becomes monstrous and mean. Fanatical faith is a faith whose vision has gone out of focus, leading to distortion and destruction. Why is it so easy to say that we are justified by faith but so complicated and confusing when we try to live by faith?

Martin Luther triggered the Protestant Reformation with his discovery that we are justified before God by faith alone, apart from enslavement to our works. While that gave him freedom from a guilt-ridden drive to achieve salvation by his own efforts, it also splintered faith into a thousand sectarian versions, not a few of which have even led to bizarre manifestations including snake handling, self mutilation and, in one case, mass ritual suicide.

In 1973, Larry and Lucky Parker, members of a Pentecostal church in Barstow, California, brought forward their eleven-year old son Wesley to be miraculous healed of diabetes at a healing service. Assured that he had been healed by the Pastor and other church members, the Parkers withdrew insulin from Wesley as a sign of their faith in his healing. Three days later, after hours of suffering and agony, Wesley died. As death approached for the tormented boy, the pastor and other church members bailed out, leaving the Parkers to deal with the approaching tragedy alone. They could no longer deny that death might be Wesley's fate, but finding in the raising of Lazarus by Jesus a scripture text to which they could attach their faith, they insisted that even his death would be a test of their faith. When he died, they scheduled a resurrection service to be held three days later, believing that as Lazarus was raised after being in the tomb, their son Wesley would be raised. Arrested, charged and convicted of involuntary manslaughter and child abuse, the Parkers were released on probation.

Seven years later, Larry Parker told their story of misplaced faith in a book, *We Let Our Son Die* (Irvine, CA: Harvest house Publishers, 1980). The book was dedicated "To our beloved son, Wesley, may his death not be in vain." In the book, Parker wrote, "Wesley died needlessly, a victim of our imbalance and misuse of the Bible . . . All healing comes from God—medicine, nature and prayer are methods by which He accomplishes it. . . Ample evidence exists in the Bible for cooperation between medicine and healing by faith."

In 1988, a CBS film for television was produced based on this incident titled, *Promised a Miracle*. In an interview following the release of the film, Larry Parker said, "I knew then that we had allowed what we thought was faith to cause us to forget to love. As we prayed for Wesley and saw him in obvious pain, our love for him wanted to give him the insulin that we knew would stop his suffering. However, we felt that it would be a lack of faith, and could cost him his healing. We learned that our actions were contrary to what the scriptures say. God's word says that love is greater than faith. 1 Cor. 13:13." The story contains a powerful lesson as to the wrong use of faith and the importance of faith being grounded in love. As my former professor, Edward Carnell wisely said, "Faith can be upset by things to which love pays no attention." By that he meant that love is a virtue that can always be practiced, even when faith cannot. The Parkers could not tolerate by faith what love demanded—restore the insulin!

When I show this film to my class, students are unanimous in their horror that parents could so misconstrue faith and allow their son to die. Yet, as the defense attorney at the Parker's trial (in the film), argued, "What they did was clearly a terrible mistake. But it was an honest mistake. They acted in accordance with the teaching of their church and exercised more faith than most of us would attempt. Who of us would have the faith to take the promise of scripture so far?" The attorney was not attempting to justify what they had done, but argued for mercy based on the extraordinary demand placed on faith by a literal reading of scripture.

In the end, the Parker's did receive mercy. The court suspended their sentence and granted them probation allowing them to return home to their other two children. The shattering ordeal of Wesley's death by their own hands brought them close to losing their faith. Instead, as the father has said, we learned that "what we thought was faith" caused us to forget love. They learned what Paul himself taught, "the only thing that counts is faith working through love" (Gal. 5:6).

While the Parker's story is a tragic one and their use of faith not one that any of my students wish to defend, at the same time, they are left uneasy and with more questions than answers. "What are we do with the 'faith promises' in Scripture," they ask? They agree with Larry Parker that love should have prevailed over faith, but is faith then by itself so blind and liable to distortion that we should never trust our faith?

Can faith overcome clinical depression; can it replace a lost love, or repair a broken one? Aside from its religious value as a condition for receiving divine approval, does faith have any practical value for everyday life? Is faith only a psychological crutch meant to give us spiritual consolation when things don't work as we had hoped, or is faith meant to work when nothing else does?

I talk to my students about the difference between folly and faith.

The author of the book of Hebrews defines faith as "the assurance of things hoped for, the conviction of things not seen" (Hebrews 11:1). These two are clearly not visible until they materialize. And 'things not seen' are, by definition, invisible though still 'things.' The evidences on which faith rests are not always visible, though they are real.

Folly is the attempt to 'make visible' what is unreal and so elicit commitment from others and give oneself permission to satisfy greed and grandiosity. Folly manufactures evidence where there is none, while faith sees evidence that is not visible. In retrospect, the difference becomes quite clear. Faith envisions what is real, though not visible, while folly makes visible what is unreal. Folly may be likened to the weeds which grow amidst the wheat, appearing at early stages to be quite similar. It is only at harvest, said Jesus, that the wheat can be separated as it has produced a full head of grain (Matthew 13:24-30).

What are the clues to authentic faith?

Faith, as Edward Carnell, has said, "is the resting of the entire self in the sufficiency of the evidences." In saying this, he stressed the fact that it is not the *kind* of evidences that warrant faith, but the *sufficiency*.

When empirical evidences are sufficient that an airplane can actually lift off the ground, I step aboard. When statistical evidences are sufficient to convince me that a surgeon has been certified and has successfully performed the same kind of operation many times, I submit to his knife. When evidences of another person's moral and spiritual integrity are sufficient I entrust my life to them through vows and promises. The kind of evidences in each of these cases is quite different, but in each case, the evidences must be sufficient for us to release the kind of commitment that faith entails.

There can never be absolute certainty, of course. But 'assurance' and 'conviction' are sufficient for trust and commitment in the everyday course of our lives. The value of this concept of faith is that it relates faith to every aspect of life, not just to a so-called 'spiritual' realm where we abandon rationality and practicality.

I do not fly on airplanes with a bad safety record and whose pilots are known addicts. I do not allow surgeons to operate who have a known history of malpractice suits. I do not trust persons who have proven to be unreliable in the past.

In each of these cases, however, the evidences are more or less visible so that sufficiency can be determined. There are other dimensions of life where the evidences are not so visible. How does one determine sufficiency in these cases?

I have come to believe that the concept of 'saving faith' or 'Christian faith' is a wrong way to think of faith. While there certainly are aspects of faith that are so extraordinary that one can even speak of having the 'gift of faith' (1 Cor. 12:9), there is a generic kind of faith that is characteristic of a person who has learned to trust, to love, and to remain faithful despite adversity and even disaster. 'Becoming a Christian' is not an emotional or spiritual experience that 'fills one with faith' where there was none. 'Saving faith' is not a special kind of faith but a special kind of relationship with a Savior. There are too many 'new believers' who lack the quality and character of faith to make their 'belief' stick. Anxious to try out their new faith, they begin to pray for miraculous solutions to the kind of problems that most people either live with or find other ways of overcoming. They attempt to practice miraculous faith without having learned to live by ordinary faith.

I learned how to have faith long before I developed Christian faith. I was mentored in faith by my parents, not through their own 'confession of faith' articulated in the liturgy of the Lutheran church (though I do not discount the value of that!), but through their 'being faithful' in fulfillment of their task of life. Life itself was the curriculum. The things that inspired hope and sustained their spirits were never really visible. There were crop failures, broken dreams, and even a lot of really bad decisions thrown in amidst sometimes bountiful harvests and successful ventures. Living faithfully meant coping with losses, suffering disappointments, and even personal failures, while finding resources and confidence within to 'stay the course.' The incredible lack of self-doubt on the part of my father could easily be taken as an unrealistic self-concept except for the fact that he also had an unerring instinct for folly. I was mentored in faith by parents who never really questioned the mind of God nor their own sense of devotion to duty. Everything else in between could be questioned and even doubted, for faith, grounded in a healthy love of self and love of God, pays no attention to these things, as Carnell once said.

This is how I learned to be a person of faith. Having assurance of things hoped for, we always had something in which to invest our faith. But, as Paul said, hope that is seen is not hope. "But if we hope for what we do not see, we wait for it with patience" (Rom. 8:25). While hope gives faith endurance, conviction of the reality of things present, but unseen, gives faith nourishment and joy.

What is hoped for is also unseen because it does not exist in the present. This is what gives assurance that one can live a faithful life trusting the promise of God for the future. At the same time, the 'conviction of things not seen' is quite another. 'Things present' but which are invisible but still 'things.' These are the 'things not seen' in a tangible sense, and yet clearly present and real in the one's life.

The spiritual dimension of faith is the capacity of the self to envision evidences which are present but not always visible. This leads to convictions which translate into actions. If I am not convinced that the evidences are sufficient, it would be folly to make the 'leap of faith' The clues which we need to look for in keeping faith in focus are largely within ourselves.

When two people exchange wedding vows, for example, there are 'things hoped for' which are not yet on the horizon of their relationship but which they believe will come to pass. There are also 'things not seen' in a tangible sense, and yet clearly present and real at the occasion.

Part of faith is knowing that it is not our faith but the one in whom we put our trust that turns the key. The test of faith is the capacity to believe when there are no visible evidences on which to rely. It is not the absence of evidences which evokes faith; it is just that some of the evidences on which faith rests are invisible, though real.

When we believe a promise given to us by another person we do so on the basis of evidences which are not always visible. Such qualities as trust, dependability, and even love, are expressions of the spirit of another. It is by actions that we make the invisible intentions of our spirits visible. At the same time, actions alone are insufficient evidences on which to pledge our life to another. A promise is an intention which goes beyond what has already been demonstrated in action, and creates the vision of 'things hoped for' which are still to come. The fact that far too many such unions end up being folly, shows us how difficult it is to really discern the kind of evidences on which a commitment of faith can rest. Those who have not 'learned faith' cannot suddenly 'have faith.'

When Job suffered loss he blessed the name of the Lord and allowed that what had happened was not beyond God's knowledge and ultimate responsibility. Having faith in God allows God to have some responsibility in the matter. We cannot exempt God from the bad things that happen and then trust him for the good things.

When we reserve a separate place in our lives for God, the rest of our lives is devoid of spiritual power. As a result, we suffer a spiritual deficit of faith where we need it the most. Only the Spirit of God can mend a broken spirit and give it new life. What breaks our spirit cannot heal our spirit. Lack of faith is due to a spirit that has been crushed by disappointment, despair and disillusionment experienced in everyday life. What once we named as faith, turns out to be folly.

The human spirit is 'God-breathed' and needs some room to breathe (Genesis 2:7)! Lack of faith may be due to spiritual suffocation—holding our breath in the spiritual vacuum of an anxiety filled chamber of fear. Faith begins with the healing and restoration of our broken and bruised spirit. An anguished spirit is closer to the spiritual core of faith than an anxious spirit. When each day is filled with anxiety over what might happen, we bruise our spirit with bad news that never happens! Faith knows that one moment of pain when something actually does happen is better than a thousand days of anxiety waiting for that which may not happen.

Faith is not the bridge we build to get to God—that is folly!—but it is discovering a path by which God comes to us. When John the Baptist announced the coming of Jesus as the Messiah, he remembered the prophecy of Isaiah and said: "I am the voice of one crying out in the wilderness: Prepare the way of the Lord, make his paths straight" (Matthew 3:3; Isaiah 40:3). The preparing of a pathway for God is the opposite of manufacturing evidence for ourselves.

In the end, faith is not a solitary venture nor a psychological feeling to be generated within ourselves. We are not baptized into faith, but into a community of faith by one Spirit. "There is one body and one Spirit, as you were called to the one hope of your calling, one Lord, one faith, one baptism, one God and Father of all, who is above all and through all and in all" (Eph. 4:4-5). There is one faith upheld in the one body, which is the church, by whatever name and form it appears. I cannot really have this faith without belonging to the one body. Where do I find it?

14

The Church's One Foundation

My companion at our regular Saturday morning breakfast recently said, "I wonder what church Jesus would like to visit if he suddenly returned to earth?" The idea of Jesus having to make such a decision, of course, led to some rather fascinating speculation. I suggested that he might head for the nearest synagogue as that was his custom, according to the gospel writers. Even then, if he scoured the local newspapers for the address of one he would have to make a decision as to whether to attend one that was orthodox, reformed, or liberal! The focus of our discussion was really on the dilemma facing us; we are the ones who have to decide which church among the hundreds of varieties and denominations is the one where Jesus already is present.

In the small village in South Dakota where I grew up, there were three Lutheran churches including the one which my family attended. I remember singing the hymn, The Church's One Foundation, including the verse: "Elect from every nation, Yet one o'er all the earth, Her charter of salvation, One Lord, one faith, one birth." Later I discovered that the same hymn was sung in the other two Lutheran churches as well, though it was always quite clear, each had their own claim to being the true church. The Presbyterians had the same hymn in their book, as well as the local community church. One only crossed over these ecclesial boundaries, however, at the risk of being accused of losing one's faith. Even families were split apart over such transgressions. So much for "One Lord, one faith, one birth!"

It never occurred to us to speculate as to what this sectarian spirit looked like to those who had little interest and no connection to a church. We simply assumed that this was how it was, with only occasional and somewhat humorous comments (always to an insider!) about how Jesus himself probably could not meet the membership requirements of any church!

The Lebanese poet and philosopher, Kahil Gibran, once wrote, "Once every hundred years Jesus of Nazareth meets Jesus of the

Christian in a garden among the hills of Lebanon. And they talk long: and each time Jesus of Nazareth goes away saying to Jesus of the Christian: 'My friend, I fear we shall never, never agree.'" The issue may not be which church is the right one, but which Jesus is the real one!

Jesus never went to church, and he left this earth before having to make that decision! He spoke often of the Kingdom of God but very seldom of the church. He only used the word church (ecclesia) two times, both in the gospel of Matthew (16:18; 18:17). Most scholars think that Matthew introduced the word into the discussion because of his own concern for how the Kingdom of God related to the church. The assumption is that, writing some thirty years after the resurrection and ascension of Jesus and after the Apostle Paul had created local churches throughout the region, Matthew had a bias for the ecclesia as being grounded in Jesus' words to Peter. Even if we assume that Jesus actually said 'church' on those two occasions (remember he spoke in Aramaic not in Greek!), we are left with the virtual absence of any reference on his part to what later became the church in the gospel accounts.

So where did the church come from? From the risen Jesus Christ, of course, as the Apostle Paul assumed and stated so eloquently and convincingly. As the chosen missionary to the Gentiles, by his own account (Gal. 2:8), Paul understood that the Spirit of the risen Christ was calling people into a new community of faith and witness based on the presence of Christ as the head. In writing to the Ephesian church Paul reminded them of this fact. "So then you are no longer strangers and aliens, but you are citizens with the saints and also members of the household of God, built upon the foundation of the apostles and prophets, with Christ Jesus himself as the cornerstone" (2:19-20). What was not revealed through the prophets, Paul said, is now revealed to all, so that "through the church the wisdom of God in its rich variety might now be made known to the rulers and authorities in the heavenly places" (Eph. 3:10). I rather doubt that the 'rich variety' in Paul's mind referred to the variety of churches now presenting their claims to be the one founded by Christ in our day. Rather, the variety included all 'sorts of people,' Jew and Gentile, men and women, slaves and masters (Gal. 3:28).

Long before the gospels were written and the story of Jesus' earthly life and ministry was set forth in the Gospels, the form and content of the church emerged through Paul's ministry in the power of the Spirit of Christ. If the Spirit by which the church emerged through Paul's missionary activity is the Spirit of the Risen Christ, then Christ indeed is the source of the church, and the presence of

Christ in the church constitutes its head and authority. Even when churches disagree sharply over their own origins, polity, and doctrines, most will acknowledge that Christ is the head of the church, regardless of how his authority is mediated. This fact, however, tends to be concealed behind the facade of the church presented to the public through the various forms of worship, criteria for membership, and contemporary marketing methods clamoring for consumer recognition. In driving through a rather blighted urban section of Los Angeles one day I saw the hand painted sign on a storefront church that sought to trump all other pretentious claims to ecclesial authority by calling itself, The Primitive, Apostolic, Holy Spirit Assembly of the Risen Lord Jesus Christ. This has a certain appeal, I suppose, especially when listed alongside the Thirty-Third Presbyterian Church in Philadelphia! I think that even Jesus would be curious about what went on in that fellowship!

But what exactly did Paul have in mind? Would he not also be confused and frustrated at the proliferation of churches in our contemporary society? Paul sometimes refers to 'the churches' when speaking of a larger geographical area (Gal. 1:2), but only to 'the church' when he writes to a large city such as Rome. Even where conflict emerged as to the teaching of the church and its practice, such as in Corinth, Paul assumes that there is "one body and one Spirit. . .one Lord, one faith, one baptism" (Eph. 4:4-5). However many local gatherings of Christians there were on any given week in Rome, as far as Paul was concerned, there was only One Church.

Up until the eleventh century when the Eastern Orthodox churches separated from the Western Church (Rome), and the sixteenth century when the Protestant Reformation resulted in several denominations, the medieval church claimed catholicity (unity) as the one and only church through which salvation could be received. Theologian Emil Brunner, however, cast doubt even upon the claim of the early church to be the true church when he argued that the church which emerged through the Apostle Paul's missionary activity lost is authentic character by the end of the first century. In his book with the provocative title, *The Misunderstanding of the Church,* he asserted that the Pauline concept of the Ecclesia as a community ordered directly by the Holy Spirit had surrendered its distinctive spiritual character to the institutional form of the church as directed by the Bishops (*episcopoi*) and regulated by the sacraments. The true ecclesia argued Brunner, is a primary social unit of believers directed by the Spirit whereas the Church, is an organizational and institutional entity amd only the 'outer shell' within which the ecclesia thrives as the true community of Christ. I tell my students that Brunner's concept is something like a turtle, where the outer shell (the church) is a necessary form of survival, but is really dead tissue, with the living organism, the turtle itself (the ecclesia), the only life form. Brunner did not say that the institutional church was dispensable, but that it was only the 'outer shell' in which the ecclesia lived. In making his case Brunner cited sources from the latter part of the first century and the early second century showing that the ecclesiastical office held authority over the local Spirit-led community, and that the office of the bishop is the central point around which the church is built. Ignatius (Bishop of Antioch who died in A. D. 107) wrote, "where the Bishop shows himself, there let the community also be, just as where Jesus Christ is, there also the universal church is."

Nothing less than returning to the original Pauline concept of the Ecclesia can recover the true nature of the church, argued Brunner. The Ecclesia cannot survive without the 'outer shell' of the institutional church, even as the Holy Spirit can only be present in the Ecclesia, and not in the organizational structure of the church. Karl Barth, who was a contemporary of Emil Brunner, was not convinced and asked, "is not the attempt to discuss the problem of the Church in terms of this criterion a romantic undertaking which makes no serious attempt at theological deliberation? What is the authority for this criterion?"

Though my first response to Brunner's thesis was enthusiastic, I finally had to agree with Barth. The church we see is really the church we get. Whatever the faults and problems with the church as an organization and institution, any attempt to define the ecclesia as an organism apart from the organization is a distinction without a difference. It is really, as Barth said, a romantic undertaking which idealizes the social structure of human relationships as a kind of pure presence of the Spirit. One only has to read Paul's letters to the Corinthian church to realize that the problems besetting that church were not due to its rules and bylaws which defined it as an organized church, but the pervasive and even pernicious spirit of competition over spiritual gifts along with a basic lack of love for each other.

Yet, Brunner's research did reveal a quite radical shift away from what he called the charismatic community led by the Spirit where ministry preceded and created the office and where, as he put it, "The Word surrendered centrality to the sacrament, the fraternity to the hierarchy, the charismatic to the juristic, and the diakoniai to the dogmatic." Citing Ignatius who wrote, "Only the Eucharist may count as the true one which takes place under the bishop's authority,"

Brunner argued that by the end of the first century, personal salvation became a result of the sacrament, and the act of administration of the Lord's Supper became separated from the act of reception, with authority vested in the former.

There was a time in my early ministry as the founding pastor of a church, that I too had a rather ideal vision for what the true church should be. I thought that we could begin with Jesus' words, "where two or three are gathered in my name, I am there among them" (Matt. 18:20). The formal aspects of the church's life, worship and ministry were considered to be dispensable and only viable to the extent that they contributed to the life of the 'fellowship.' We did not call it the ecclesia as Brunner did, we simply called it the church. The theological basis was drawn out of the incarnation where God appeared as an authentic human person, not a religious professional.

In his prayer on behalf of his disciples, Jesus prayed: "As you have sent me into the world, so I have sent them into the world" (John 17:18). I saw the *as* and the *so* as the 'hinge' on which Christians turn toward the world for the sake of manifesting Christ's presence and ministry. I taught that if we explore the content of the *as* we will begin to develop the content of the *so* and the profile of an authentic life of the Christian and the church in the world. I even wrote a short 'manifesto' for an incarnational presence of the church in the world.

As Jesus was: In the midst of a religious culture that prized appearance and cultivated form, Jesus appeared among us clothed simply in grace and truth. He refused to recognize as spiritual that which was artificial and affected. He valued the truth of being and doing over the righteousness of words and prayers. He told it like it was—both in the street and in the temple. He had one language for both the saint and the sinner. He stated divine realities in terms of human experience. His lifestyle was that of a human person living among humans. Because he *was* the truth, he had no fear of exposure, nothing to defend.

So we should be: A real Christian must also be a genuine human being. Spiritual growth is manifested in those who demonstrate the fruit of the Spirit in relationship with others (Gal. 5:22-23). The Christian is to be related to one's own society in the same way that Christ was related to the world (John 17:18). The test for truth in a Christian is what the world sees in us of Jesus Christ, not what other Christians see in us as a Christian.

As Jesus was: In the person of Jesus there was a spiritual integrity that revitalized the spirit of persons amidst the dead weight of tradition and legalism: where Jesus was there was life. In the life of Jesus was a moral integrity that brought an absolute sense of right to specific human situations: where Jesus was there was truth. In the truth of Jesus there was a personal integrity that spoke with authority against the enslaving influences of religious formalism and demonic delusion: where Jesus was there was freedom.

So we should be: Jesus Christ is the truth of God for persons. One whose life is centered on Jesus Christ thereby has spiritual integrity (Col. 2:18-19). There is no Christ other than the Christ of Scripture as present to us in the power of the Holy Spirit. The integrity of Christ exists in the integrity of Scripture as the Word of God written (John 5:39). The integrity of Christian fellowship rests in the person of Jesus Christ as the object of personal faith and the ground of mutual commitment: where Jesus is, there is the church (Matt. 18:20).

As Jesus was: Jesus called men and women out of estrangement and into a redemptive relationship. He came as a Son and introduced God as the Father. Out of this relationship he coined new words to explain human problems and possibilities: prodigal, enemy, reconciliation, friend, brother and sister, flock.

He defined spiritual values in terms of human relationships. God forgives us as we forgive one another; to hate our brother is to hate God; to give of ourselves to another is to love Christ. He gave himself as the new basis for the community of persons. Those who love Christ become his body, with a common life and one heart.

So we should be: There is no such thing as a solitary Christian. One cannot 'come to Christ' apart from coming into the fellowship of his body—the church. This fellowship (koinonia) is not only spiritual, but personal and social. It may not always be structured as an organization, but it will always be an organism. The highest act of the individual is to surrender his or her right to exclusive self-existence in order to create a community of faith and love.

Because each Christian retains individuality, even in community, the community of Christ is a continuing creation—community is broken whenever the individual acts exclusive of others or loses individuality in the group. Personal spiritual growth is measured in terms of the individual's contribution to the common good of the entire body. The fruit of the Spirit are relational realities--love, joy, peace, patience, kindness--and are evidenced in our relationship with others.

We are to give priority to the organism of the church over the organization. Organization is the servant of the organism to carry through the functions that contribute to growth and life: the life of

Chapter Fourteen

one person is of more value than the entire organization. We are committed to maintain the integrity and health of the body of Christ through responsible participation and loving discipline. The life and health of the body of Christ are more vital than the demands of one person. We are committed to set no limits on love that are not intrinsic to the nature of love itself as revealed by Christ. We are committed to go as far as Christ would go, to share as much as Christ would share, to live in fellowship with those in whom Christ lives.

When I look back on these words written more than thirty five years ago, they ring as true now as they did then. The difference is that I no longer see this as a manifesto for creating a more authentic church, but more as a prescription which one would take to any church and have it filled, much as one could take a prescription to a pharmacy to be filled.

I ended the previous chapter by saying, we are not baptized into faith, but into a community of faith by one Spirit. There is one faith upheld in the one body, which is the church, by whatever name and form it appears (Eph. 4:4-5). I cannot really have this faith without belonging to the one body. Where do I find it?

My provisional answer is, Wherever you find it! As I said, we should approach any church with a prescription to be filled. Or, being already in a church by virtue of birth, choice or sheer convenience (it is of some importance to be in easy driving or walking distance!), we still need a prescription with an unlimited number of refills.

It no longer matters to me whether the church robes itself in multicolored vestments and offers a liturgical service with all the 'bells and whistles,' or if the church eschews such trappings and every prayer begins with, "Lord we just want to tell you . . ." One of my favorite authors is Annie Dillard, who wrote, "I know only enough of God to want to worship him, by any means ready to hand. . . . The higher Christian churches—where, if anywhere, I belong—come at God with an unwarranted air of professionalism, with authority and pomp, as though they knew what they were doing, as though people in themselves were an appropriate set of creatures to have dealings with God. I often think of the set pieces of liturgy as certain words which people have successfully addressed to God without getting killed." Perhaps she is right. Whatever the church is, it appears to provide more of insulation than inspiration.

In more than forty five years since taking my first seminary class I have read much of the literature on the origin, nature and form of the church only to come to the conclusion that Jesus probably does not care as much about what the church looks like as much as what we expect from him when we look to the church for the sustenance of the Spirit in our daily life. I am beginning to think that I knew as much about the church before taking my first seminary class than I do now, after more than 40 years of ministry in the church.

In saying that, I am reminded of Dietrich Bonhoeffer who had failed to satisfy the church authorities with what he submitted as sample sermons as part of his ordination process. The examiners report was sent to him by his father while he was in Barcelona (Spain) fulfilling an internship assignment. Along with the report, his father added his own comment quite to the contrary. He cited his own mentor who had supervised him in his clinical work in preparing to be a psychiatrist, who said, "Just don't read any psychiatric literature! It only makes one dumb!" Apparently Bonhoeffer took the advice seriously but still managed to pass his ordination exam. I now realize that the more I read about the church the dumber I got!

As a matter of fact, my reading during the early years of pastoring a church turned more to novels than to theology. I discovered and read all the novels of Thomas Wolfe, among them, *Look Homeward Angel!*, *You Can't Go Home Again*. I read the novels of Dostoyevsky and discovered the agonizing but spiritual core of the human self. I read all of Søren Kierkegaard's works, and pondered the paradox of the existential moment in which the eternal is grasped in time. I read Gibran, the plays of Arthur Miller, Christopher Fry, D. H. Lawrence, the bittersweet and poignant novel, *A Death in the Family*, by James Agee, Nikos Kazantzakis, *Zorba the Greek*, and yes, *The Last Temptation of Christ*! I read the luminous works of Alan Paton, *Cry the Beloved Country*, and *Ah, But your Land is Beautiful*, and discovered the soul of South Africa is close to the soul of God. And through all of this, found the contours of the incarnation of God, a landscape my theology professors never acknowledged if, indeed, they ever saw it.

Even now, I am stunned by the penetrating insights of the contemporary storyteller, Wendell Berry, who lives and farms in Henry County, Kentucky (is that a clue?). In particular, with regard to these musings on the church, I was quite taken by his book, *Jayber Crow*, written in the first person as though by Jayber himself, the local bachelor barber in the southern village of Port William. Early in his life Jayber felt a call to become a preacher, even enrolling as a pre-ministerial student in a Bible college. When confronted by growing doubts as to the theological convictions he was expected to believe and preach, he approached one of professors with his questions, only to discover that if he himself had no answers, he could not preach, and the good professor agreed! So it was, he returned to

Chapter Fourteen

Port William to become the local barber, but also the janitor of the local church. Not being a 'believer' he could not in good conscience become a part of the congregation, but his work as a janitor gave him the opportunity to approach the church on his own terms. Now I must let him tell his own story, so that you can see for yourself what the church could and should be.

> One day when I went up there to work, sleepiness overcame me and I lay down on the floor behind the back pew to take a nap. Waking or sleeping (I couldn't tell which), I saw all the people gathered there who had ever been there. I saw them as I had seen them from the back pew, where I sat with Uncle Orthy (who could not come in any farther) while Aunt Cordie sang in the choir, and I saw them as I had seen them (from the back pew) on the Sunday before. I saw them in all the times past and to come, all somehow there in their own time and in all time and in no time: the cheerfully working and singing women, the men quiet or reluctant or shy, the weary, the troubled in spirit, the sick, the lame, the desperate, the dying, the little children tucked into the pews beside their elders, the young married couples full of visions, the old men with their dreams, the parents proud of their children, the grandparents with tears in their eyes, the pairs of young lovers attentive only to each other on the edge of the world, the grieving widows and widowers, the mothers and fathers of children newly dead, the proud, the humble, the attentive, the distracted—I saw them all. I saw the creases crisscrossed on the backs of the men's necks, their work-thickened hands, the Sunday dresses faded with washing. They were just there. They said nothing, and I said nothing. I seemed to love them all with a love that was mine merely because it included me. When I came to myself again, my face was wet with tears.

Through a lens not quite in focus, we glimpse the continuity of a timeless reality unbroken by the discontinuity of time. Beneath the surface of all that pretends to be the church, there are people whose lives constitute the inner membrane that holds the outer form in place.

Some years ago I knelt at the gravesite of my great grandparents in a mountain village in Norway, behind a church that was more than 800 years old and still in service. Scattered around the church were gravesites, some now invisible, some still to be seen, where eight centuries of people lay bound together by one faith, one baptism, one Lord. The Protestant Reformation came and went; one Sunday a Roman Catholic service, the next Sunday a Protestant Lutheran service. The silent congregation beneath the ground felt nary a ripple as the momentous and sometimes tumultuous changes took place. As I reflect on this, it strikes me that, as with Jayber Crows' mystical congregation, the congregation of God's people are bound to him and thus to one another, despite their contrary convictions and sometimes pointless disputes. The church that Jesus sees may be quite different from the one that we see.

My view of the church changed when I began to look at it from the perspective of the final century rather than the first century. I have come to see that the church can find neither its form nor its purpose by looking back to the first century. The Spirit which comes to the church comes out of the future, not the past. The presence of the Spirit is the anticipation of the return of Christ. Paul makes this clear when he wrote to the church at Ephesus reminding them that in receiving the Holy Spirit they were "marked with the seal of the promised Holy Spirit; this is the pledge of our inheritance toward redemption as God's own people, to the praise of his glory" (Eph. 1:13-14). The "pledge" is literally "the first installment or, the "down payment" (Gr. *arroban*) on the inheritance promised as the future fulfillment of God's promise.

When Christ returns to bring to consummation this pledge made by the gift of the Holy Spirit, it will be the 'final century.' The Spirit is thus preparing the people of God for this final century. The first century of the church is normative for the revelation of Christ as the incarnation of God and the redemption of humans from sin and death. The final return of the same Christ and the resurrection from the dead constitute the reality of the church formed by the Spirit of the risen and returning Christ. The ministry of the Holy Spirit can be understood in light of that which God desires to become a reality at the end, not merely to replicate that form of ministry during the first century.

This is the perspective which Paul had even during the first century. He looked toward the coming of Christ as the final word of approval upon his own teaching and ministry. While the historical Jesus and the cross were central to Paul's theology of redemption and creation, the Spirit of the resurrected and coming Christ was normative for interpreting the past events in light of the coming ones.

This was the argument Paul used in defending his own apostolic authority in the face of those who claimed historical precedence based on their relation to Jesus of Nazareth: "It is the Lord who judges me. Therefore do not pronounce judgment before the time, before the Lord comes, who will bring to light the things now hidden in darkness and will disclose the purposes of the heart. Then each one will receive commendation from God" (1 Cor. 4:4-5).

Theologian Wesley Carr reminds us that, "If the Church is to witness to this constant relevance of the future for its existence and to the breaking in of that future to the present in the act of God in Christ, then that witness must be substantiated in the structures of the Church. These structures need to be charismatic, i.e., they must reflect the Spirit both as formative force in the community and as representing the judgment of the end upon that community." Carr goes on to say, "The dynamic force within this eschatological community is the Spirit, which creates that community and sustains it and at the same time gives to each person within the community his [or her] own individual personhood. . . Christians hope to be one with Christ in the final resurrection and their experience in the Christian community is a partial and anticipatory experience of that end."

What do I look for when I *find* the church that sustains me in the one body, based on the one baptism and the one Lord? I used the metaphor of a prescription earlier in this chapter to suggest that what we seek from the church is what both heals and holds our human existence as bound to the humanity of Christ. Christ is the prescription and the church is to be there for us to fill and renew it. I need healing when my humanity becomes ragged and rough, when I am broken and bitter, when I feel despair and depression. God assumed that humanity in the person of Jesus who, in his own human life healed the wounds and restored humanity to its completeness in the image of God. "We are all born broken," as Eugene O'Neal once wrote, "and the grace of God is the glue." The church which cannot fill this prescription is dispensing a counterfeit product. Or, as Jesus put it, is giving the child a "scorpion when it asks for an egg" (Luke 11:12). Any church that can fill this prescription is one that will lead to your spiritual health, whether it is high or low church, whether blue collar or white collar, whether a cathedral or a chapel.

Let me change the metaphor to make the same point. Nutritionists remind us that there are essential ingredients in our daily diet that are necessary to maintain good health. Consumer protection laws have been enacted which require labels on food products which inform the purchaser in order to make good decisions based on the nutritional value of the product. Here, rather than a prescription which offers a remedy for some distress or dysfunction (though that is still a good idea!), we should each develop our own nutritional guideline which contains the essential ingredients for our spiritual life and growth. It is not the quantity of food intake that is necessary for our health, but the quality. One can suffer serious malnutrition with a full stomach! I have known people who have been so preoccupied with church activities that they are literally 'full' of religion but starving themselves spiritually.

In writing to the Corinthians, Paul warned those who were hyperactive with regard to manifestations of the spiritual gifts, but still infants with regard to their spiritual life and growth. With all of their religious activity they were in effect still living on 'baby food' and this accounted for their lack of spiritual maturity (1 Cor. 3:1-4). In contrasting the works of the flesh with the fruit of the Spirit, Paul points toward a spiritual nutrition guide that should provide criteria in our search for the body of Christ where our spiritual needs are met (Gal. 5:16-26).

I do not expect the church to be my spiritual nutritionist. The Holy Spirit does that quite well! The church can and should provide the kind of 'body life' where the Spirit can reveal to each of us our own particular dietary needs. If I am weak in faith, I need to be in a church where I am not required to profess more faith than I have. Rather, I need the freedom and security to express my faith-deficiency with the expectation that I can draw upon the faith of others as a stimulus for my own growth in faith. If I am starved for love it may indicate that I have a love-deficiency in myself rather than lack of others to love me. The Holy Spirit is a good nutritionist, and will, through the loving care and concern of others, prompt me to growth more in love through a body life where love is offered on the menu (with a variety of flavors!) at every occasion.

The church, however, does not stand alone on a hill nor on the secluded corner of an urban maze. As Jayber Crow discovered, the church is itself cut out of the fabric of the community in which it exists. It was in his barbershop that the crosscurrents of daily life intersected. Without priestly credentials, he touched the head of every person and in doing so, felt with his own hands the membrane that connected one to another and, perhaps, he dared to think, all to God. He looked for divine providence, not in the miracles of the biblical stories, but in the mundane life that holds every person close to the earth. In the storms that threatened to blow apart the fragile bond where each is bond to the other and to God, one could almost see the wings of God, hovering over the children of God.

15

Under His Wings

It was Saturday evening, and harvest time. I was but a young boy, and had to stretch my legs to match my father's stride as we walked out into the barley field. The ripening grain flowed almost to my father's waist, and to my shoulders, as we waded into this river of gold.

"It's about ready," my father said, as much to himself as to me. "Come Monday we will begin cutting."

I don't know what his dreams were that night, but mine were of the excitement of following the horse-drawn harvester around the field, watching the bundles spew out, each tied with rough twine by the clicking fingers of the mechanical apparatus. My job was to stack them into shocks with the grain ends on top, forming a bearded bouquet of sunlit straw.

But it was not to be. On Sunday afternoon, a thunderstorm marched across the prairie stabbing the ground with lightening strokes and pelting all that lay within its glowering stride with the mercilessly pounding hail stones. The frozen pellets of ice drove animals under cover, tore shingles off the roof, and cut the standing grain to a mangled mass of broken straw.

When the storm had passed, we walked once more out into the field. He surveyed the sodden field with eyes as practiced in measuring chaos as they were in envisioning a harvest. When he spoke, it was directly to me, as though he were depositing the words, like seeds, into a freshly plowed field.

"Son," he said, "when this field dries out we will begin to work it to keep the weeds down. A fall rain is good for the subsoil. We still have seed for planting in the spring, and it will grow a better crop next year for all of this."

This was surely not his first crop loss, nor would it be his last. I have often wondered about his feelings at the time which, if they were expressed, were beyond my capacity to perceive. This I remember. There was no cursing of the earth and no angry gestures toward heaven. There was no apparent self-recrimination for failing to have begun the harvest earlier.

I first learned to sing the Hymn, Under His Wings, in the Lutheran church my family attended every Sunday. I suspect that it may have been one of the hymns we sang the Sunday following the hailstorm. If so, there appeared to be no contradiction or question in my father's mind.

> Under his wings I am safely abiding,
> Tho the night deepens and tempests are wild;
> Still I can trust Him, I know He will keep me,
> He has redeemed me and I am His child.

As I reflect back upon that incident as well as many others where storms, drought, and the unpredictable weather cycle were the constant and inevitable factors against which the community in which I lived sowed their dreams and reaped their harvest, I remember no charge raised against the Deity when misfortune struck. Nor was I aware of any suggestion from the church that God's providence could be invoked to deflect the hazard's of nature or guarantee a bountiful harvest. We prayed for rain during the drought but then bought hail insurance for the wheat when the weather turned stormy.

In the third stanza of the hymn we sang were the words, "Sheltered, protected, no evil can harm me." We did not count a hailstorm as evil, nor did we attribute an untimely death in the family as an attack of the evil one. In the baptismal ritual we did promise to "renounce the devil and all his ways," but that seemed to take care of it. Later I discovered that Luther had a running battle with the Devil and even threw his inkwell at him, but we heard little about the Devil in our church and no one gave him credit for causing misfortune in our daily lives. We gave thanks to God for the good things, and took the bad things in stride as part of life. Were we naive and theologically illiterate? Probably. But we lived close to the soul of God.

I think it was in High School that I first learned that Providence was a city in the state of Rhode Island. Some years ago I was there, in Providence, so that I know that it is a real place. If the word 'providence' slipped into our vocabulary from time to time, it was more of an adjective than a noun. "The rain last night was providential, the crops were about finished for this year." Or, "That was a providential gift, the check arrived the day before the final payment was due on the mortgage." Actually, it was mostly the school teachers or those in our community who had a bit more education than their local schooling who knew when and how to use the word. I suppose that I had some thought of divine providence lurking in my mind from catechism instruction and an occasional sermon on the topic but, unlike Providence, Rhode Island, I have never been there and would find it hard to explain to someone else where and what it is.

It was only years later, during my first classes in theology at seminary that I learned about God's providence and entered into debates as to why God, who is altogether good, should permit evil to strike those who trust in him. The traditional concept of God's sovereignty viewed God as controlling (causing) every detail and event in human history. The alternative to this, it was felt, was to be subject to chaos and confusion, leaving humans subject to the capricious winds of fate and fortune. Even the ancients looked to the stars, if not the entrails of animals, for an explanation and cause of what appeared to be random events. To live in a world without a supervening order and cause was more than the human spirit could bear. Where religion took away freedom, it gave back certainty, which, in the end, made fatalism more comforting than faith.

In reading the theological books on divine providence I was stunned to discover that many theologians attributed every event that occurs, both good and bad, to the providence and will of God. While most theologians subscribed to the view of God's general providence—he sustains and orders the universe—some went so far as to argue for God's specific providence—he orders (or permits) every event which occurs in the universe, including the actions of human beings. Martin Luther, for example, argued that God's will is "measure of all things," so what takes place "must take place because He so wills it." John Calvin was even more specific when he wrote: "there is no erratic power, or action, or motion in creatures, but that they are governed by God's secret plan in such a way that nothing happens except what is knowingly and willingly decreed by him." He went on to say that, "in times of adversity believers [may] comfort themselves with the solace that they suffer nothing except by God's ordinance and command, for they are under his hand."

It sounded plausible at the time; I was looking for good grades, not comfort.

The argument that God's providence lies behind every event, good or evil, implies the doctrine of God's foreknowledge—he knows in advance every event that occurs. Those who hold this view base their argument on the concept that if God is omniscient—knows all—then that knowledge must include future events as well as past events. William Craig, for instance, says that, "this aspect of divine omniscience underlies the biblical concept of history, which is not that of an unpredictable unfolding sequence of events, rather, God knows the future and directs the course of world history toward his foreseen ends."

If this is true, then it also follows, as Douglas Grivett says, "It is logically possible that God has a morally sufficient reason for permitting every evil there is, including heinous inscrutable evils. This we may know even if we do not know that there actually are morally justifying reasons for God's permission of the evils that exist. Still less are we required to know what reasons actually do justify God's permission of each instance of evil, if indeed they are justified." In other words, even if we do not know the specific reason that God has for allowing the sexual abuse of a child or the senseless slaughter of innocent men and women by a terrorist bomber, this theologian asks us to think that there may be a perfectly logical reason that God has for allowing this when he has the power to prevent it, even though we may never know in this lifetime what that reason may be.

As I say, I was stunned to discover that theologians actually could argue these concepts of God with impeccable logic and with little, if any, emotional affect in their writing. I suppose that I began my pastoral ministry with this view of divine providence safely tucked away in some corner of the cortex of my brain where passion goes to die. But I was soon to undergo brain surgery!

During the early part of my pastoral ministry, a woman came to me with a tragic and disturbing story. Six months earlier her seven-year old daughter had died of a brain aneurysm on a Sunday evening while she and her husband were attending a service in their church. The child had been left home with a babysitter and they were summoned out of the service by paramedics who responded to the call for help.

Tragic as this sudden death was and her grief over the loss of their only child, what happened next was more deeply disturbing and the cause of her outrage directed against God. The funeral service for the girl was held in the church with the pastor officiating. During the service, in an attempt to bring some meaning and comfort to the parents, he suggested that God wanted to bring spiritual renewal to the members of the church and had selected one of their most prominent families and had taken their daughter home to be with the Lord, where she was far better off than to live in this world. God's purpose in doing this, the Pastor went on to say, was to cause the members of the church to reflect upon the brevity of life and to call them to repentance and renewed commitment to the Lord. He then gave an invitation for those who wished to acknowledge their new commitment to Christ to come forward for a prayer of dedication. Following the service she never again went back to the church.

As the woman told me this story, her face flushed with anger and she said, "I could never worship a God who would do that!" She went on to express her anger at God for killing her child, even expressing feelings of unbelief in God's existence. I remained silent, except to agree with her that a God who would do such a thing in order to coerce others into a response of deeper commitment was not the God that I could worship. I moved my chair alongside hers and took her side against God. After many minutes during which she poured out her anger at God, she paused and, taking a deep breath, said, "I really don't believe that God killed my child. But what other reason could there be for her death? Isn't God in control of everything that happens? If he loved her in the way that we do, why could he not have intervened and saved her?"

At the time, I was only a year or two out of seminary, and no discussion in my theology classes had ever dealt with this question, other than to affirm the importance of upholding the attributes of both God's sovereignty and goodness. Now, faced with this question, in the face of this woman's grief and suffering, I found the traditional arguments for God's goodness and sovereignty quite inadequate.

To my surprise, she did not really demand an answer to her question. She only wanted the permission to ask it. As I directed her to consider the tears of Jesus at the tomb of his friend Lazarus as the very tears and grief of God, she left feeling closer to God than when she came. But it was a different God than the one she carried into the room on the crest of her anguish and anger.

Years later, I discovered the book by Rabbi Harold Kushner, *When Bad Things Happen to Good People*. His son died at the age of fourteen, following extended illness due to progeria, the rapid aging disease. Failing to reconcile this tragedy with the theological concepts of God's power and love with which he had been trained, he wrote the book in which he raised the question as to whether God could be both all powerful and good. "I believe in God," he wrote, "But I do not believe the same things about Him that I did years ago, when I was growing up or when I was a theological student. I recognize His limitations. He is limited in what He can do by laws of nature and by the evolution of human nature and moral freedom. I no longer hold God responsible for illnesses, accidents, and natural disasters, because I realize that I gain little and I lose so much when I blame God for those things. I can worship a God who hates suffering but cannot eliminate it, more easily than I can worship a God who chooses to make children suffer and die, for whatever exalted reason."

To tell a woman that the death of her young child was God's plan to develop in her a deeper spiritual life and a stronger character will likely provoke the response, "I would rather have my child and remain weaker in character, given the choice." Some who have gone through the cycle of self-development, experiencing grief and loss and who finally survive, may well testify to a faith and hope that is stronger by virtue of having stood the test. But only those who have suffered such grief have the right to make such a statement.

Can we believe in a God who permits evil that good may come?

Ivan Karamozov, a character in one of Dostoyevsky's novels, does not think so. Ivan challenges the theology of his brother Alyosha, a novice in residence to become a monk. Ivan recounts incidents of the torture of children, and one case of a general who set his dogs on a boy chewing the child to bits before the eyes of his mother. When Aloysha protests and suggests that this horrible crime can only be explained by submitting to the inscrutable will and purpose of God, Ivan responds with outrage bordering on blasphemy in his brother's eyes. "Listen! If all must suffer to pay for the eternal harmony, what have children to do with it, tell me, please? It's beyond all comprehension why they should suffer, and why they should pay for the harmony. Why should they, too, furnish material to enrich the soil for the harmony of the future? I understand solidarity in sin among men. I understand solidarity in retribution, too; but there can be no such solidarity with children."

Sensing the protest mounting in Aloysha, Ivan continues: " Oh, Aloysha, I am not blaspheming! I understand, of course, what an upheaval of the universe it will be, when everything in heaven and earth blends in one hymn of praise and everything that lives and has lived cries aloud: 'Thou art just, O Lord, for Thy ways are revealed.' When the mother embraces the fiend who threw her child to the dogs, and all three cry aloud with tears, 'Thou art just, O Lord!' then, of course, the crown of knowledge will be reached and all will be made clear. But what pulls me up here is that I can't accept that harmony."

What Ivan cannot accept is the theological answer to the problem of evil that God will finally reconcile all things to himself and reveal a pattern of perfect justice that will vindicate him and produce a final harmony. Not even retribution against the offender will satisfy the injustice that this horrible evil was permitted. No forgiveness and no atonement can wipe away the *fact* that a grievous wrong was done. "I don't want harmony," Ivan cries out, "From love for humanity I don't want it. I would rather be left with the unavenged suffering. I would rather remain with my unavenged suffering and unsatisfied indignation, *even if I were wrong*. Besides, too high a price is asked for harmony; it's beyond our means to pay so much to enter on it. And so I hasten to give back my entrance ticket, and if I am an honest man I am bound to give it back as soon as possible. And that I am doing. It's not God that I don't accept, Alyosha, only I must respectfully return Him the ticket."

With less eloquence, but with equal passion, the woman who had lost her child was close to "giving back her ticket," if it meant being asked to believe that God had a reason and the power to weave the death of her child into some eternal harmony of peace and joy. While I had not found in my earlier theological training a response to her question, I had read Dostoyevsky and understood well the complaint of Ivan against a too simplistic explanation for the evil which afflicts the human condition.

In the face of the grief and outrage against God I experienced from the woman who had been told that God had actually caused the death of her child in order achieve his own good purpose, I could no longer defend this doctrine. She was pressing toward the soul of God and I followed her. I told her that the death of her child was not predetermined by God, was not known by God in advance, and was not caused by God.

But then what are we to make of the biblical promises that seem to assure us of nothing less than permanent well-being and blessed prosperity for those who belong to God? It must have been a warm day, with the gentle breeze blowing, after a good meal, when the Psalmist wrote: "I have been young, and now am old, yet I have not seen the righteous forsaken or their children begging bread" (Psalm 37:25). Really? What planet has he been living on! Job probably found comfort in such platitudes, but when the storm struck leaving him bankrupt, childless and in utter misery, he sang a different tune. "I cry to you and you do not answer me; I stand, and you merely look at me. You have turned cruel to me; with the might of your hand you persecute me" (Job 20-21). The three so-called comforters of Job brought to bear with a vengeance the traditional theology of direct cause and effect with regard to righteousness and reward. They insisted that if Job would only confess that he deserved all of the misfortune for the evil things he had done then the Lord would heal and restore him. Though Job had been comfortable with that theology during the days of his prosperity, he refused to acknowledge it when catastrophe struck. For to acknowledge that he deserved such terrible misfortune was to commit a falsehood against his own spirit and sacrilege against the soul of God. In the end, he pushed through the rhetoric and ridicule and demanded a response from God. He got it, but it was a mixed blessing. He was affirmed for his own integrity but rebuked for the lengths he went to maintain it in the face of his friend's attack.

Habakkuk also found the gospel of prosperity lacking. He has seen quite enough suffering of the righteous and prosperity abounding for the unrighteous. And he is not afraid to question God's own sense of justice. "Your eyes are too pure to behold evil, and you cannot look at wrongdoing; why do you look on the treacherous, and are silent when the wicked swallow those more righteous than they" (Habakkuk 1:13)? The answer that Habakkuk received offered no explanation; God simply reminded him that "the righteous live by their faith" (2:4). Faith in God, it seems, has little to do with providing a cushion against the sharp edges of injustice, but a great deal to do with living with grace. "My grace is sufficient for you," was the Lord's reply to the Apostle Paul's earnest plea for healing from his affliction (2 Cor. 12:9). Living by faith in God enables one to endure what must be endured by the grace of God. God is neither a distant bystander nor a personal security service. But what is he then?

Jeremiah likewise was not afraid to challenge God in the face of the reality of human suffering, daring to attribute to God the calamities which struck him. "He has made my teeth grind on gravel, and made me cower in ashes; my soul is bereft of peace; I have forgotten what happiness is; so I say, 'Gone is my glory, and all that I had hoped for from the Lord'" (Lamentations 3:16-18). But when he had finished his tirade and drew near to the soul of God, he was given a new song, "The steadfast love of he Lord never ceases, his mercies never come to an end; they are new every morning; great is your faithfulness" (3:32-33). I suspect that most people who now sing the familiar hymn, Great is Thy Faithfulness, have forgotten, if they ever knew, that these words of assurance are to be sung most vigorously when misfortune seems our only fortune.

Job asks of God, "Don't you hear me when I cry out to you?" Habakkuk demands of God, "It's not fair, don't you see what is happening to us?" Jeremiah complains, "God, what you are doing hurts me, can't you make it stop?" I have heard these questions in my rounds of pastoral care. Sometimes I myself have asked them. They are ancient questions and they are contemporary questions. All of them have to do with the soul of God more than the doctrine of God.

Does God permit suffering and allow evil to impact our lives in order to produce some good? The answer is no. The fact that "all things work together for good for those who love God" (Romans 8:28), cannot mean that God uses evil things to bring about good. Rather, in spite of evil, God works through all things to bring about good as the outcome of his faithfulness so that we may trust in him.

I now believe that there is a theology of God's providence that balances in a more realistic way the openness of God to the actual events with which we struggle in our lives with the assurance that God is in control and in the end, will achieve his redemptive purpose in spite of evil.

For the Hebrew people, it was sufficient to know that God was not only one who could enter into the story at will, but who also had their story under his control. Ultimately, their trust in God was grounded in his love and his covenant promise. They understood God's providence to be aligned with his covenant promise, not with nature. Attempts to read God's purpose out of the events which occur in the natural world always leads to futility or fatalism. They knew that the source of salvation is not in a perfect world, but in God who keeps us under his wings and who can be trusted to preserve our lives in the end.

The Hebrew concept of providence is not concerned with divine power, but with covenant promise. Providence is a confession of God's faithfulness and power to accomplish his promise and will. God accomplishes his gracious will in spite of human sin and failure. For the Israelite, as well as for the Christian, God's providence is attached first of all to promise, with promise embodied in God's participation in our struggles and in our ambiguous existence for the sake of the ultimate realization of his purpose. "God's plans are not cast-iron molds to which the course of history passively and perfectly conforms," writes theologian Richard Rice. "They are goals that God pursues over time and in different ways. At times, God acts to bring things about unilaterally, as it were. Some things God wants done, so he does them... At other times, however, God interacts with creaturely agents in pursuing his goals. He works in and through situations where people are variously receptive and resistant to his influence." The will of God in this view is not an irresistible, all-determining force. Rather, God works with and through human agents and he interacts and reacts with the random events of nature. The fact that most of the events which occur within the natural world are random rather than predetermined, does not mean that we are confronted with chaos and disorder.

The fact is, many things that occur in life are often nothing more than coincidences. Though I have long held this view, I was encouraged by John Boykin to think that this is precisely how God arranged for the world to be. "The ways God operates in our lives mesh perfectly with the ways He designed us to operate. He does not normally determine, cause, and control our circumstances, because He could do so only by controlling *us* to the *n*th degree. He does not, for instance, give us jobs or customers, rig elections, or cause certain people to be in certain places at certain times. Circumstances are people's doing, not God's. He *can* intervene in them, He *has*, and on occasion He may choose to—but He normally does not. His kingdom is not of this world."

To live in the shadow of God's wings means being able to hold fast to God's providence as his sovereign control over events in order to insure that his ultimate redemptive purpose is accomplished. This frees us from the fatalism and determinism of an abstract and alien sovereignty and opens us to the freedom and purpose of God. Through God's grace we can endure events for which there is no interpretation or explanation.

Within the providence of God there is room for a tragic dimension as well as a triumphant vision. Theologian Wendy Farley reminds us of this when she writes, "Created perfection is fragile, tragically structured. The tragic structure of finitude and the human capacity for deception and cruelty together account for the possibility and actuality of suffering and evil. Because of its independence, history constitutes a 'surprise center' even for God." She goes on to say, "The potential for suffering and evil lie in the tragic structure of finitude and cannot be overcome without destroying creation. The power to create must therefore include the power to redeem. The fragility of creation of creation requires the continual presence of divine power to resist the evils resident in history."

David Basinger suggests that when a tragic event occurs, such as a death, we can assume that "God is often as disappointed as are we that someone's earthly existence has ended at an early age or that someone is experiencing severe depression or that someone is being tortured... We remain free to assume that such evil was an undesired by-product of misguided human freedom and/or the normal outworking of the natural order."

God's providence is expressed through his partnership with human persons in suffering, which is the divine power to be present as our advocate in the context of suffering and for the purpose of redeeming those who suffer. The providence of God is bound to his promise. This promise is a miracle and mystery of divine love.

Suffering and injustice can produce a crisis of faith, leading us directly to God as the one who must ultimately take responsibility. In his taking responsibility through participation in the dilemma of evil, God provides redemption from evil, not simply treating it as a problem to be solved.

When we undertake to love so as to bring forth life, such as the birth of a child, we participate in creating some of the very pain and sorrow which is inevitable for love to exist in this world. For example, in bringing our three daughters into the world through our love, my wife and I ensured that there would someday be three graves at the end, many tears along the way, and even some inexplicable sufferings for them and for us. To embrace possibility with love is to embrace the tragic as well as the triumphant. Love does not dwell on this, but in the end, love knows how to accept it.

"This movement of God's holy love into the heart of the world's evil and agony is not to be understood as a direct act of sheer almighty power," says Thomas Torrance, "for it is not God's purpose to shatter and annihilate the agents and embodiments of evil in the world, but rather to pierce into the innermost centre of evil power where it is entrenched in the piled-up and self-compounding guilt of humanity in order to vanquish it from within and below."

That God is in control, is certain, at least as one reads the Scriptures. But being 'in control' does not mean 'controlling every event,' I tell my students. The root metaphor of God's relation to the world is not power, as in being Creator, but love, as in being parent. When God's power is grounded in God as Creator, it becomes mechanical and merciless.

If we conceive of God's control more like that of a parent who loves rather than a creator who coerces, we can find a helpful analogy in the way that parents often relate to their children. For example, parents may take their children in a car with the purpose of an outing at a recreation park. As they depart everything is going on schedule until some unforeseen events begin to transpire, such as a highway construction project which forces a detour or a flat tire on the car which requires the assistance of a tow truck. These events are unpredicted and purely random, out of control of the parents in the sense that they could have neither predicted or prevented them. The children do not blame the parents for these happenings, but are only concerned that they really do arrive at their destination. The parents assure the children that they are 'in control' of the situation even though changes will occur which will affect their arrival time, etc.

The point of this analogy is that in somewhat the same way we can say that God is in control of the world and of our lives, but does not control, or cause, every event to take place. This allows for both the freedom to initiate and complete actions within the limitations of our finite and temporal existence, but also ensures that in God's providence, his purpose for our lives will be completed.

If my father were alive he would not need to read this, for he lived it. This is why he could sing, "Under His Wings," without a murmur of complaint, for the loss of a barley crop was part of a bargain between him and the soil, not between him and the soul of God.

16

All the Way My Savior Leads Me

On a hot July day in 1955, I stopped my tractor in the middle of a cornfield in South Dakota and pondered the question that had preoccupied me for the past several weeks. A month earlier on a Sunday afternoon broadcast of the Old Fashioned Revival Hour, Charles E. Fuller mentioned that he had founded a new theological seminary in Pasadena, California only a few years earlier. This came at a time when I had been growing increasingly aware of a rather strong feeling that my life destiny was somehow being altered from ending as a retired farmer to something more related to full-time Christian ministry. With a degree in Agriculture, a wife and two daughters, and solidly entrenched in developing my own farming career, it seemed rather preposterous to think that such a mid-career move was possible, or even desirable. What possibly could I do with such a background—perhaps become an agricultural missionary in some foreign country? That seemed logical but not very attractive. I was also involved in teaching on Sundays in a local church and had even given a few sermons when asked at other churches. I felt deeply involved in both my farming career and in ministry. But there was still something lacking. Hearing Charles Fuller expand on the newly formed seminary with the purpose of training 'young men' for ministry (yes, that was in 1955!), I wondered what would happen if I should apply with my B. S. Degree in Agricultural science on my transcript.

As I sat there on the tractor, I suddenly found myself saying out loud, "I'm going to do it. I'm going to apply."

While I remember the occasion and my exact words with precision, I have no recall as to what transpired when I communicated the decision to my wife! I expect that she had grown accustomed to the manner in which I made decisions and, besides, she was not unaware of my growing interest in some form of full-time ministry. She was probably more prepared than I was for the move. In any event, the application was submitted to Fuller seminary for admission to the fall class of 1956 and to my surprise, was accepted.

Now the questions came from friends and extended family. "Are you sure that this is the will of God for your life?" Even more difficult was the question, "How did you determine that you were actually called of God to do this?" In my own thinking, I had not really thought about my decision being the result of a specific calling of God. Nor did I claim to have discerned the will of God for my life as a solution to my own inner searching. All of this, of course, made it even more difficult to provide the expected evidence that it really was God calling me and not some wild idea that Ray Anderson had concocted for himself!

I had been thinking about the will of God, but the more I thought about it the less sure I was that I could find it, and if I did, that it would fit in with my own will. At the time, in my daily Bible reading I came to Paul's admonition in Philippians 2:12-13. "Therefore, my beloved, just as you have always obeyed me, not only in my presence, but much more now in my absence, work out your own salvation with fear and trembling; for it is God who is at work in you, enabling you both to will and to work for his good pleasure." I was reading from a modern translation of the New Testament which paraphrased the text as: "Work out your own salvation with awe and reverence, for God is at work in you both to help you desire as well as do it." If this was true, that God was already at work in my life, and that my desire was also how he was working in my life, I decided that I would trust my desire to be his will. I believe that it was the next day that I sat on the tractor and said, "I'm going to do it."

The sermons that I heard in those days on the will of God were strong on exhortation but weak on practicality. One preacher asked us to envision God as having created a perfect plan for our life with every detail drawn in. When we die and go to heaven, this preacher said, God is going to take the actual form that my life took and lay it over the top of his perfect will to see where I followed it and where I missed it. My reaction was that this is grotesque and even absurd! To think that God would have such a plan scripted in advance, first of all, eliminated the freedom that I would have in working out my own life. Secondly, for God to conceal such a plan until he could spring it on me at the end when it was too late was not only unfair but cruel. I thought of how I as a parent would want my own children to 'do my will.' I concluded that they would know that my love for them desired a good outcome in all their decisions along with the freedom to discover and find this for themselves. The Psalmist wrote that God is like a parent who has compassion for his children (Psalm 103:13), and such a device as the preacher described did

Chapter Sixteen

not originate in the soul of God but in the mind of man.

Other sermons urged us to think of God's will as an arrangement of certain external things in our life, along with biblical principles, and finally our own desires. Only when our desires lined up with the biblical principles and the so-called 'open doors' could we conclude that we were in God's will. I had as much trouble finding biblical principles as in finding which open door was the right one! Then I found that even the Apostle Paul did not go through a door "opened for me in the Lord." He did not go through it but instead, followed his own pastoral instincts and went in a different direction (2 Cor. 2:12). So much for the theory of open doors!

During my time in seminary I become friends with two other students who confided to me their dilemma. They had come to love each other and believed that it would be God's will for them to marry. However, Bob said that he had answered a call in his church at the age of 16 to surrender his life to the Lord as a missionary to a foreign land. Susan, on the other hand, said that she gone forward in a meeting in her church at the age of 13 surrendering her life to the Lord as a missionary to the native American Indians in Arizona. They were now conflicted. If they were to follow the will of God for their lives as determined in their calling it would make their marriage impossible. On the other hand, if they really believed that it was the will of God for them now to marry, then they risked being disobedient to the will of God expressed in their calling. As I shared with them my own story, I suggested that their understanding of the will of God as teenagers was sufficient to get them to the same seminary and to discover each other in order that they could now join their lives in fulfilling the will of God together. Whether or not my advice was the determining factor, they did marry and went off to another land as missionaries. When I saw them again years later, they were satisfied that the will of God was indeed being worked out in their lives as God enabled them to desire as well as do it. If, however, they arrive in heaven and God lays out the blueprint for their life and marriage is not on it, I will be in deep trouble!

I have found that the concept of the will of God is confusing and ambiguous for many Christians. We can sing the hymn, All The Way My Savior Leads Me, but if we understand this to mean that we are led to do God's perfect will in every decision, we will as often feel misled as led. I interpret this to mean that Christ leads us toward God's will as the outcome of our life, not from the standpoint of knowing God's will in advance..

For several years, as a faculty member, I team-taught a class on Strategic Planning for upper level leaders and managers of

Christian organizations. What these leaders were most concerned about when it came to applying biblical principles to the running of their organizations was how to determine the will of God. Their assumption was that if the strategic plan they developed was based on God's will, it could not fail. When so many plans did fail, they either had to conclude that God's will was the cause (and how could they trust such a God?) or that they had attached the wrong plan to God's will.

God's will is not the plan, I told them, but the outcome of the plan. In other words, you should not attach God's will to the plan but to the goal which the plan is designed to reach. God's will is what we discover at the end, not at the beginning. This was viewed as quite radical and contrary to what they were hearing in their churches. They asked for biblical support.

The strategic plan of the Apostle Paul is laid out in the fifteenth chapter of his letter to the Roman church. Writing from Ephesus he told them that he planned to visit them for the sake of seeking their support for his mission to Spain (15:24-25). First, he said, he must go to Jerusalem to fulfill his promise to gather funds from the churches in Macedonia and Achaia and take them to Jerusalem for aid to the poor. When he has completed this, he told them that he will then come to Rome and then, with their assistance go on to Spain (15:25-29). This is Paul's mission plan, laid out clearly. When we turn to the book of Acts, we can trace the development of this plan step by step. First, Luke writes that "Paul resolved in the Spirit" to go through Macedonia and Achaia, and then to go on to Jerusalem. After that, he said, "I must also see Rome" (Acts 19:21). Luke then provided an account of Paul's travels through the area finally arriving on the east coast of Palestine at the port city of Tyre. The Christian believers there confronted Paul directly with an admonishment from the Spirit—"Through the Spirit they told Paul not to go on to Jerusalem" (21:4). Paul apparently did not heed this direct word from the Spirit and proceeded down the coast toward Jerusalem. Coming to Caesarea, Paul again sought out the local assembly of believers.

During this time at Caesarea, Agabus arrived from Jerusalem with an even stronger message from the Spirit. He took Paul's belt, bound his own hands and feet with it, and said, "Thus says the Holy Spirit, 'This is the way the Jews in Jerusalem will bind the man who owns his belt and will hand him over to the Gentiles.'" Luke then wrote, "When we heard this, we and the people there urged him not to go up to Jerusalem." Paul's response was, "What are you doing, weeping and breaking my heart? For I am ready not only to be bound but even to die in Jerusalem for the name of the Lord Jesus." Luke then adds, "Since he would not be persuaded, we remained silent except to say, 'The Lord's will be done'" (Acts 21:10-14).

What is important to note is that up to this point no one, not even Paul, claimed to know the will of God. Paul never claimed that he was doing this as the will of God, but only as he was 'constrained in the Spirit' (19:21). Even those who sought to dissuade him did not claim that they knew better than he what the will of God was. They only spoke out of their own sense of the Spirit. It was only at the end, that Luke and the other believers said, "The Lord's will be done." The will of God is the outcome of the plan, not the basis on which the plan is developed. The will of God is not something that we can use to make our plans 'fail-safe.' Nor is the will of God something that we can use to overcome our own inner sense of being led by the Spirit. In their attempts to dissuade Paul by their own sense of the Spirit, they came up against Paul's own deep resolve in the Spirit.

And so what was the outcome? As it turned out, Agabus was right. Within a few days after arriving in Jerusalem Paul was arrested, almost lost his life, and then spent the next two years in a Roman prison in Caesarea (23:23-24). After two years Paul appealed to the Emperor Caesar in Rome and was then led in chains as a prisoner to the boat which set sail for Rome, spending the better part of the next year getting there, with a shipwreck along the way. When he did finally arrive at Rome after three years, it was as a prisoner (28:16). An epilogue to this story can be found in the letter Paul wrote from the prison in Rome to the church at Philippi which had sent him money to ease his situation while in custody. Rather than expressing a sense of failure or even regret at not listening to his friends who had attempted to keep him from going to Jerusalem, he wrote: "What has happened to me has actually helped to spread the gospel, so that it has become known throughout the whole imperial guard and to everyone else that my imprisonment is for Christ" (Philippians 1:12-13). In other words, it has all turned out in such a way that the Lord's will was done, even though Paul apparently never did get to Spain.

We should not conclude from this that one should not think about the will of God. On the contrary, because the will of God will be the final verdict on one's life it should be part of our planning and decision making as something toward which we are moving.

In my teaching to the leaders of Christian organizations I suggested the proper sequence of the biblical paradigm that I drew out of Paul's life is that we must seek first of all the wisdom of God by claiming his promise to lead us through the indwelling presence and power of the Holy Spirit. The wisdom of God then informs our common sense so that we do not attempt what is fantastic or unrealistic in order to test whether or not we are in the will of God. There is an interesting footnote to the story of Paul's voyage to Rome as a prisoner. When the ship docked at the port of Fair Havens, Paul advised against setting sail due to unpredictable winter storms. He advised the officials, "sirs, I can see that the voyage will be with danger and much heavy loss, not only of the cargo and ship, but also of our lives" (Acts 27:10). The captain of the ship went ahead anyway with what turned out to be a foolhardy decision. Paul did not claim to have a direct word from the Lord, but knew well the weather patterns in that part of the sea and acted out of common sense, which in many cases, may be one of the best ways of determining the wisdom of God! Informed by the wisdom of God, we then formulate a plan by which the work of God can be done in and through our lives. A vision and a promise is not enough. We need plans inspired by spiritual wisdom and carried out through practical steps of action. All of this has the intention of bringing us to the point where we can look back and say, "The will of God was done"—despite some shipwrecks and change of plans along the way!

While this model was developed as a way of helping Christian leaders discern and carry out the will of God in their organizations, I have found it helpful in my own life and as a guide to others in being led by Christ. I have found the book, *Decision Making and the Will of God* by Gary Friesen to be very helpful. He suggests that all decision making takes place within the circle of God's moral will; where there is specifically revealed moral direction, obedience is demanded; where no specific moral direction is revealed, there is freedom to make decision within God's overall moral will. Friesen says that we should not try to 'read providence' or look for an 'open door' as a command for what God wants us to do. "In short," he writes, " for all practical purposes, *sovereign guidance has no direct bearing on the conscious considerations* of the decision maker." In other words, the principle of God's sovereign will does not relate to decision making directly, but only indirectly. God does not 'overpower' our own moral will and free choice, though he 'leads' us toward the ultimate goal and good for each of us, and through his sovereign grace and power, upholds that as his will.

When we sing the hymn, All the Way my Savior Leads Me, we are not expecting the Savior always to show us the way but to lead us in the way. The *way* is something for us to choose, or to accept as circumstances dictate for us. Through the Spirit Christ leads us 'in the way.' For example, when we took a trip to Norway some years ago to teach and travel, I looked to my former student and friend who lived there to guide us in the way. He did not dictate where we should go, but along the way, opened up possibilities at every turn for us to explore, leaving it to us to decide. In somewhat the same way, the Spirit of Christ leads us in the way by revealing possibilities which we would not discover on our own, and by warning us of consequences which might turn out contrary to the will of God in other directions.

In teaching and mentoring students in a theological seminary for more than 27 years, I have discovered that the concept of God's will is one of their most common concerns and often the source of their greatest anxiety. Some arrive with absolute certainty that they are in seminary because it is God's will. Underneath such certainty, however, lurks a hidden and persistent anxiety; What if I am wrong? Have I misunderstood God's will? These questions often arise during the time when they find the work most difficult, or when they are approaching graduation and discover that they must then choose a vocation and find a job! Others come with no real certainty about God's will but faced with the choices that they must make concerning their degree program and curriculum, suddenly become concerned because they don't know how to determine God's will.

When I share with them my own experience, I make clear the difference between a 'call of God' to a particular vocation or task, and the calling that we have in Christ which is the basis for our very salvation. Our calling is to serve Christ and to live our lives in conformity to him. Paul exhorts us to "live a life worthy of the calling to which you have been called." He goes on to say, "There is one body and one Spirit, just as you were called to the one hope of your calling, one Lord, one faith, one baptism, one God and Father of all, who is above all and through all and in all" (Eph. 4:1, 4-6).

Bob and Susan, of whom I wrote above, each identified the will of God with what they felt was a call to a specific mission place in the world. They came to understand that there is basically one calling which every Christian has by virtue of baptism into Jesus Christ by the one Spirit. We are *called* to serve God in Christ and *sent* into the world to fulfill that calling. Could I have fulfilled my calling in Christ by staying on the farm with the understanding that this was the place to which I was 'sent' to work out the will of God for my life? Absolutely. My decision to pursue another direction was not based on a 'call' to ministry, but the choice of another *way* to fulfill that calling. After eleven years of pastoral ministry, I chose another *way* and am now closer to the will of God than at the beginning! But only because I am closer to the final destination of my life-journey. The Spirit of Christ has led me in each of the ways that I have chosen.

As a practical device to help my students reframe the concept of the will of God I often ask them to consider what they will be doing five or ten years later if they were to pursue the direction they are now taking. I tell them, "Each of us has a destiny here on earth that will be defined by where we are and what we are doing when our own death suddenly comes upon us." I ask them to visualize and experience in the depths of their feelings what that will be like. Will they have regrets, and cry out for more time and more opportunity to do what they deeply desire to do but have for some reason, delayed hoping for more time? Or, will the feeling be one of satisfaction, as with the Apostle Paul, no regrets, my life is fulfilled even though I could long for it to go on.

I explain to them that thinking of their destiny rather than their calling arouses in them their deepest desires and moves them out of the ambiguity and anxiety of trying to discern the will of God for their lives in the present moment.

Dietrich Bonhoeffer, the Lutheran pastor and theologian who was killed by Hitler in April of 1945 just weeks before the end of the war, had chosen to return from the United States in September of 1939 to enter the conspiracy against Hitler. Within two weeks after escaping from Germany to avoid being put to death for resisting being drafted into the army, Bonhoeffer said, "I have made a mistake in coming to America." If he had stayed, he could have avoided the very circumstances that took his life in the end, when he was only 39 years of age. During the two years that he spent in prison prior to his execution, he never expressed any regrets about his return. Eberhard Bethge, his former student and friend wrote his biography after the war. In that book, Bethge commented on this critical point in his life. "In 1932 he found his calling, in 1939 his destiny." It was in 1932 that Bonhoeffer first 'became a Christian,' by his own admission. Prior to that he had undertaken his theological work without any personal relationship to Christ. It was that transforming experience that became his calling to live as a disciple of Christ. The route of discipleship took many different *ways* for him, but each was grounded in his one calling to serve Christ.

Several years ago one of my students who made a mid-life career decision to come to seminary to be trained for pastoral ministry, was stricken with cancer during his first year. He was told that he had only a few weeks to live. I called on him in the hospital. "I don't understand what God is doing to me," he said. "I left my business because I felt called to enter full-time Christian ministry. I was obedient to his will and left everything to come here." As we talked about this, he suddenly said, "You know, I would have had cancer if I had stayed in Idaho. Just think if this had happened to me there when I was just doing my own thing. Thank God that I am here, in just the right place for my life to end. I have no regrets about my decision." He did not speak of having found his destiny, but what he said expressed it more profoundly than I ever could. At his memorial service, a few weeks later, I pondered what he said and asked of myself, "Am I in the place that might well become my destiny?" If so, then I will know the will of God.

My students complain, "This is getting pretty morbid!"

"Only if you think of death rather than destiny," I respond. I elaborated further. When you view life from the present, you spend more time looking back than ahead. And if you do look ahead you see only uncertainty and dread. When you view life from the final destination, you can really live in the present with freedom from anxiety about finding your calling. The Latin word for anxiety is *angustia*, a word which means narrowness. Anxiety is the result of our life being narrowed to the present moment. Anxiety about finding the will of God in the present moment restricts us from viewing our life as moving toward the will of God as a destination. Kierkegaard, who argued that the self exists always in the present moment, also said that, "life must be understood backwards but lived forwards." I take this to mean that if we attempt to understand life by projecting the will of God forward, we will end in despair. But if we place ourselves by faith at our destination, then we can 'look backwards' to the present moment and move forward with faith in our choices.

Living toward the will of God as our destiny is something like booking a trip with a travel agent who agrees also to go along as a tour guide. The agent assumes that you will begin the trip from your present situation and then assists you in choosing the *way* you will take to reach your destination. Where will you be when you arrive? What will you do when you get there? Is this where you really want to go if you reach it?

The Holy Spirit is our travel agent and guide. All the Way My Savior Leads Me. The excitement builds, the possibilities are endless (it is an open fare ticket!), and there will be no regrets.

17

Abide With Me

> I am deeply grieved, even to death; remain here, and stay awake with me. Matt. 26:38

The tears of God flowed down the cheeks of Jesus at the tomb of Lazarus (John 11:35). When the Son grieves the Father groans. What touches the soul of Jesus touches the soul of God. This is the inner meaning of the theological assertion that the eternal Son (Logos) of God became flesh and dwelt among us (John 1:1; 14). The Son and the Father are two dimensions of one soul, and the Spirit is the soul of the Father and the Son. Theologians who torture the language in order to speak of the triune God as one substance comprised in three persons, are as far removed from the divine reality when they finish as when they began. We are here dealing with soul, not substance.

"Believe me that I am in the Father and the Father is in me," Jesus told his disciples (John 14:11). "When the Spirit comes," Jesus assured his disciples, "we will come to them and make our home with them" (14:23). The soul of God is the "we of God." The tears of Jesus at the tomb of Lazarus are the tears of the Father as much as of the Son. The compassion of Jesus expressed in audible groans when confronted with human deformity and distress is as much the compassion of the Father as of the Son. The suffering (passion) of the Christ is not encapsulated in the final hours of physical and mental pain leading to the crucifixion of Jesus as a victim of human sin and divine judgment. It is the very soul of God, Father and Son, that is rent from within, of which the tearing of the curtain in the temple was but a sign and symbol (Matt. 27:51). What rends the soul of Jesus rends the soul of God.

The Apostle Paul has a clear vision of this truth when he writes, "When we cry, 'Abba! Father!' it is that very Spirit bearing witness with our spirit that we are children of God . . . that very Spirit intercedes with sighs too deep for words" (Rom. 8:15-16; 26). In this way, Paul reminds us that the language of the Spirit is the language of Jesus—it is the 'wordless' language of the soul of God. The soul can bear things which seem unbearable to the mind. The soul can speak of things for which there are no words. But the soul cannot abide alone.

What the soul dreads goes deeper than what the soul fears. Fear can be cast out with love (1 John 4:18). Dread arises in the soul when love appears to withdraw. Dying is a dreadful thing for the soul to face. What Jesus faced at the end was not merely a painful death on the cross but the dread of the darkness which creeps into the soul when the light of life is extinguished. He knew well the words of despair and the language of dread. As a boy he 'learned by heart' the first lines of Psalm 22, "My God, My God, why have you forsaken me?" Now, with death and darkness looming before him, he feels in the soul what he once learned in the heart. "Now my soul is troubled," he cried out in Gethsemane (John 12:27).

Abide with me, he begs of his disciples, "I am deeply grieved, even to death; remain here, and stay awake with me" (Matt. 26:38). "Abide in me," Jesus had once urged his disciples, in order that they might be connected to the vine and bear fruit (John 15:1-5). He was their paraclete (advocate) when they suffered rejection and abuse. Now that dread is penetrating the soul of God, with darkness beginning to eclipse the face of the Father, Jesus reaches out to those with whom he felt the closest intimacy, seeking to make them his paraclete in a time of need. It was not lack of courage that caused him to seek companionship as he faced his mortal hour—courage can itself be an individual virtue. Difficult as it is to dare the thought, it is the very soul of God that reaches out to human souls for sustenance in grieving his own death. Dietrich Bonhoeffer, who experienced his own Gethsemane while in prison awaiting execution, understood very well Who it was that sought the solace of human help when he wrote:

Men go to God when he is sore bestead,
Find him poor and scorned, without shelter or bread,
Whelmed under weight of the wicked, the weak, the dead;
Christians stand by God in his hour of grieving.

We are each one a mortal being, created from the dust of the ground and destined by nature to return to the dust. "By the sweat of your face you shall eat bread until you return to the ground, for out of it you were taken; you are dust, and to dust you shall return" (Genesis 3:19). Lest one think that our mortality is only the consequence of human disobedience, the story of creation reminds us that humans were originally taken from the dust. "The Lord God formed man from the dust of the ground, and breathed into his nostrils the breath of life; and the man became a living being" (Genesis 2:7).

Is death then part of our human nature, or is it God's punishment for the sin of the first humans? I have found this analogy helpful in discussion with my students.

Imagine that an astronaut on a space ship orbiting the earth has been assigned the duty of taking a 'space walk' in order to repair some exterior part of the shuttle in which they are riding. A pressurized space suit is donned and the astronaut leaves the craft through a hatch, but is attached to the shuttle with a long cord so as to prevent him or her from drifting off into space and certain death. The astronaut is warned by the commander, "Do not damage or cut this cord because you will then be separated from us and you will certainly die." The astronaut agrees, but during the space walk becomes overly enthused about the experience and, wanting freedom to explore beyond the length of the tether cord, cuts the cord. Alas, the consequence becomes immediately clear as the astronaut drifts helplessly out into space, still alive, but with the limited resources provided by the space suit, doomed to death.

Now, I ask my students, "is the inevitable death for the astronaut a punishment for disobedience or a consequence of the disobedient act?" The answer is quite obvious, the astronaut was always under threat of death if disconnected from the shuttle, but this only became a reality as a consequence of the act, and not as punishment.

I then take the analogy one step further. Imagine that the commander of the shuttle contacts the astronaut by radio who is now drifting helplessly out into space and makes clear what the consequence of the willful act of disobedience is. The astronaut is contrite, remorseful, and confesses the 'sin' of disobedience. The commander offers forgiveness and assures the astronaut of complete absolution and forgiveness. While this relieves the guilt of the astronaut, the situation remains unchanged—death is still an inevitable outcome, forgiveness has not changed that, for the consequence of the act of disobedience was not merely guilt, but death.

This is exactly the situation that Adam and Eve found themselves in when their act of disobedience severed, as it were, their 'lifeline' connection to their Creator. The consequence of their act was death. Death was not imposed as a punishment, but death was a consequence of the nature of their mortal bodies, taken from the dust of the ground. The consequence of sin is death, not merely guilt (Rom. 6:23). As long as Adam and Even remained 'tethered' to their

Creator by the spiritual lifeline with which they were created, they had a certain degree of freedom to explore the created world without fear of death. However, they were told, "In the day that you eat of it you will die" (Gen. 17). Don't cut the lifeline!

When Adam and Eve did cut their 'lifeline,' God did not have to impose death as a punishment. Rather, death became a consequence of the fact that they were created with mortal bodies—out of the dust of the ground. As long as they remained connected to God, their mortality could not have a fatal effect on them. Without disobedience, we can assume that their mortal bodies would be somehow transformed into immortal ones, as Paul affirmed would take place in resurrection (1 Cor. 15:43).

We can also now see why forgiveness of sin is necessary but not sufficient to overcome the consequence of sin. As in the scenario I created with regard to the disobedient astronaut, confession of sin and absolution from sin did not itself overcome the consequence of now being under 'sentence of death' due to natural mortality. In some way that is difficult for us to understand, the consequence of the sin of Adam and Eve not only plunged them into death as a consequence, it had an effect upon all humanity that issued from them. Paul makes this clear in his own analogy of the 'first Adam' and the 'second Adam' (Romans 5). "Therefore, just as one man's trespass [Adam] led to condemnation for all, so one man's act of righteousness [Christ] leads to justification and life for all" (5:18). It was not just that guilt was passed on through Adam and Eve to all humanity, death was passed on as a consequence of their disobedience. This is why death has become 'unnatural' for all humans, for God did not intend that our mortal bodies should determine our destiny. When death became destiny through the disobedience of Adam and Eve, God intervened and recreated the lifeline through the promise that he himself would undergo that human death in order to destroy its power over humans. The sacrificial system installed immediately after their sin pointed forward to the death and resurrection of Christ. God summoned Adam and Eve out of their 'flight into death' and clothed them with the skin of animals as a sacrament of grace and promise that life could now come through death—not merely the death of animals, but the death which God assumed in becoming human.

This is why, while the Bible takes death seriously, it does not develop a theology of death. The theme of death is expressed descriptively (as history), poetically (as lamentation and complaint), theologically (as the outcome of sin) and eschatologically (as overcome through the resurrection of Jesus Christ). Yet there is no single theology of death to be found as a thematic development in Scripture. There is no view of death in the Bible as inherently evil. Death *can* be a peaceful end to life, and thus part of the good of human life. Death is not intrinsically a curse and an arbitrary power that stands over and against human life. Yet, it is also a threat to the very humanity of life because it separates the individual in three ways: from oneself in the dissolution of the body and soul and loss of vital power; from the community of God through which the individual gains personal identity; and from God, who is the very source of life itself. Death can never be a consolation in and of itself. God desires life, not death, and therefore death is never considered as having meaning or significance in itself.

Apart from relation to God, says Helmut Thielicke, our death could not be a personal death and it could not be a human death. Physical death is the 'biological mask' which, for all of its literalness, does not 'literally' destroy my life in partnership with God. I sink into death, but not in such a way that I will stay in it, "For God has called me by name and will call me again on his day. . . I am not immortal, but I am one who awaits the resurrection."

While we live in this mortal body, we should not reject our mortal existence in this body as having no meaning or value. Dying is woven into the fabric of living but we should not live as though we are dying every day, but receive every day as a gift and live it with gratitude. Dietrich Bonhoeffer, in his reflections on Psalm 119:19 wrote:

> I am a stranger on earth. Therefore, I confess that I cannot remain here, that my given time is brief. Nor do I have any claim here to houses and possessions. The good things which I enjoy I must thankfully receive, but I must also endure injustice and violence with no one to interceded for me. I have no firm hold on either persons or things. As a stranger, I am subject to the laws of the place where I sojourn. The earth, which nourishes me, has a right to my work and my strength. I have no right to despise the earth on which I live. I owe it loyalty and gratitude. It is my lot to be a stranger and a sojourner, but this cannot become a reason for evading God's call so that I dream away my earthly life with thoughts of heaven. There is a very godless homesickness for the other world which is not consistent with really finding one's home there. I ought to behave myself like a guest here, with all that entails. I should not stay aloof and refuse to participate in the tasks, joys and sorrows of earth, while I am waiting patiently for the redemption of the divine promise. I am really to wait for the promise and not try to steal it in advance in wishes and dreams.

Alan Lewis, a former colleague in graduate studies at the University of Edinburgh in Scotland, and later professor of theology at Austin Presbyterian Theological Seminary until his untimely death in 1994 due to cancer, echoed the theme of Bonhoeffer when he wrote, "The eschatological vision of the human body, redeemed and resurrected, healed of its diseases, freed from tears and pain, raised in glory though sown in weakness, is the gospel's ultimate demand that, while rejoicing in God's victory over death, we accept and not reject, enjoy as blessing and not disdain as curse, our mortality itself."

We are not first of all mortal beings who happen also to be human, we are human beings who happen also to be mortal. It is our humanity that bears the divine image, not our mortality.

For all creatures but the human, their earthly nature determines their destiny. For humans, their destiny is determined by their Creator God. After the fall, while human mortality became a condition of life, the promise of God is that the seed of the woman (Genesis 3:15), Jesus born of Mary, will triumph over death and through his resurrection "this mortal body must put on immortality" (1 Cor. 15:54). From the very beginning of the creation story the theme of redemption from death and reconciliation to God as the source of life was introduced. The sacrifice of animals was instituted as a provisional sign pointing to the sacrifice of Christ which put an end to all sacrifice and instituted life instead of death (Hebrews 9:23-28).

Once death has entered the soul of God, it is "swallowed up" as Paul said, not through an act of dying, but by immersion in life (1 Cor. 15:54). The life of God assumed death in order to extinguish it as light 'swallows up' darkness. The redemption of humans from the fate of death has its origin in the soul of God and its completion in the resurrection of God. God, who cannot die, assumed human death in order to die that death and be raised from the dead.

The reconciliation of humanity to God began with the assumption of mortal humanity in the womb of Mary. In becoming human, the divine Son of God brought human mortality into the very soul of God. I have often told my students, Jesus of Nazareth came under sentence of death in assuming mortal human nature. Jesus did not have a sin nature, but he had a death nature. Jesus will inevitably die, because he assumed death in becoming human. The common assumption that Jesus could not die because he is without sin, except by voluntarily giving himself over to death, is simply not true. The author of the book of Hebrews puts it plainly: "Since, therefore, the children share flesh and blood, he himself likewise shared the same things, so that through death he might destroy the one who has the power of death, that is, the devil, and free those who all their lives were held in slavery by the fear of death" (Hebrews 2:14-15).

The moment that Jesus is born he will die of something, sooner or later, because his human nature is mortal and subject to death as a consequence of the sin of the first humans. God warned Adam and Eve, concerning the forbidden fruit, "in the day you eat of it you will die" (Genesis 2:17). The consequence of sin is not merely that humans became guilty of sin for which divine forgiveness was the remedy. The consequence of sin was death, for which resurrection into new life was the gift of God. "The wages of sin is death, but the free gift of God is eternal life in Christ Jesus our Lord" (Romans 6:23).

We are those of whom the author of Hebrews wrote, "those who all their lives were held in slavery by the fear of death." We too are 'under sentence of death,' though this is an unbearable thought. In his Pulitzer Prize winning Book, *The Denial of Death*, Ernest Becker, uses a surgeon's scalpel to cut away the defenses we create against this truth in order to push back the reality of our own mortality. Becker argues that a good deal of the anxiety that causes what he calls neurotic behavior is due to an underlying sense of our own mortality. That is, it is not so much a fear of the experience of dying, but the knowledge that we are mortal beings and that despite all of our efforts to avoid or to conceal that fact, death will inevitably overtake us. While death was at one time a visible and recognized part of normal life, our contemporary culture has repressed death and made it virtually invisible. Our older societies and culture, he maintains, had rituals built into life so that every individual growing up and living in that society had ready-made rituals which served to lead the self through the entire life-cycle, from birth to death. Modern persons, he writes, "no longer know what were the proper doses of experience. This safe dosage is exactly what is prescribed by traditional customs, wherein all the important decisions of life and even its daily events are ritually marked out." In our modern urban society, individuals are cut off from these built-in rituals and customs which once served to mediate anxiety and provide objective and communal patterns in which each person could find a refuge from the 'terror of being alive,' as he put it.

As a result, individuals need to create their own rituals which tend to be addictive, repetitive and restricting. "Neurosis," says Becker, "is the contriving of private obsessional ritual to replace the socially-agreed one now lost by the demise of traditional society."

The need to 'immortalize' the self in the face of one's own mortality, he argues, leads us to develop coping mechanisms which deny most threats to our lives—it will never happen to me—or to project our own identity upon our cultural heroes—those who appear to us to be 'larger than life' or represent the 'ideal human figure.' We can even use religion, he suggests, to clothe ourselves with a kind of 'character armor' which enables us to achieve a form of piety or spirituality which is, at its base, a denial of the reality of our mortality. No person, he warns can look fully into the face of our mortality without being paralyzed by dread. Consequently we need some form of illusion in order to push back the knowledge that we are mortal in order to function somewhat normally in every day life.

I know something of what Becker speaks when he describes the rituals of traditional communities by which reality and illusion were fused together in such a way that the boundary between life and death became transparent and even friendly.

On a lazy summer Sunday afternoon, without apparent premeditation, my parents would suddenly announce a visit to the local rural cemetery for the purpose of tending some family gravesites. Of course we children were included. It was not a long trip, for the cemetery adjoined the farm on which we lived on the flat prairie-land of middle America. The simple rituals of pulling some weeds, clipping some grass and digging up the soil around a straggling, flowering plant were quickly accomplished, and served only as a pretext for the visit, as it usually turned out.

Trailing behind, as my parents wandered from gravesite to gravesite, I heard the litany of their commentary on the dead. "Here's where the Torstensons are buried. Wasn't she a Carlson girl who came over with her parents from the old country, and didn't they homestead the quarter section next to the old Anderson farm where I was born?" my father would ask. Of course he already knew the answer, but it was as if he were tracing out once more the landscape of his soul in order to find himself in a familiar place.

And so it went. These were not questions, but statements. Statements about a community in which the boundary between the living and the dead lost its sharp edge of terror. This was a mystery which was part of the fabric of life. What this small boy experienced was the easy familiarity with which this uncanny boundary was traversed. But even more, what was experienced was the wordless testimony that this excursion was an event in which their faith was enacted. Implicit in this patriarchal pageantry was a statement about what they believed; and death was not alien to this belief system.

What did my father think about when he tended the gravesites, and contemplated the plot where he himself would one day be buried? Did he have anxiety? Did he fear that death would annihilate all of the meaning of his life to that point? Did he have the feeling that he was sinking into an oblivion which would be a place of peace and rest from the self-conscious worry and fretful toil of every day life? Or did he have in his mind a hope for continuing self-consciousness life beyond the grave, and if so, how did he envision this life?

What went though his mind when he passed the small grave marker and commented, "Yes, and here is the two year-old Peterson boy; he was kicked in the head by a cow and died that very night." Had he ever questioned the fairness of that? Had he ever questioned God about that?

I don't know. He never said. Death and God were the two subjects that were never openly discussed, even though both were woven into the fabric of their lives. Perhaps the question and the answer had become so fused that faith was as simple as a Sunday afternoon walk in the cemetery and planting a straight row of corn.

The final stop, before getting into the car, was always a quiet moment spent tidying a green plot of sod with no graves yet dug, marked only with the single headstone—ANDERSON. This space has now been filled, of course. And not too far away there is another plot which has been purchased, not only as a sign of my own anticipation of joining this 'processional,' but which is also a statement about what I believe, about life and about death. I am not, because of distance, granted the privilege of being the 'caretaker' of my own place of burial, nor can I take my own children on Sunday afternoon walks to this place.

I sense a disconnect in our culture and even in our own lives that would not be so serious if it were recognized. I scanned the titles of the hymns in several hymn books looking for the songs that would connect us with our mortality in a meaningful and healthy way. There were songs in every category of this life and the next, but scarcely one that allows us to embrace our mortality with spiritual maturity. Perhaps it is easier to sing of Amazing Grace and the Love of God than to express in song our common mortality.

Wendell Berry, in his book, *Jayber Crow*, allows Jayber, the bachelor barber in the southern village of Williams Port to tell his own story. Jayber is an observer but not a participant in the local church where he serves as janitor. He cannot with integrity confess his faith in the traditional language of the church, but he draws spiritual nourishment from the services indirectly. He does not like the sermons, but relishes the occasional moments of silence. "What I liked least about the service itself," he commented, "was the prayers; what I liked far better was the singing. . . I liked the sound of the people singing together, whatever they sang, but some of the hymns reached into me all the way to the bone: 'Come, Thou Fount of Every Blessing,' 'Rock of Ages,' 'Amazing Grace,' 'O God our Help in Ages Past.' . . . I thought that some of the hymns bespoke the true religion of the place. . . And in times of sorrow when they sang, 'Abide with Me,' I could not raise my head."

> Abide with me! Fast falls the even-tide.
> The darkness deepens; Lord with me abide!
> When other helpers fail and comforts flee,
> Help of the helpless, oh, abide with me!

There are many kinds of death, each different in their own way, yet all profoundly human in the same way. Whether death comes quietly with old age, (he died of natural causes), as a result of a lingering and devastating disease (it was a blessing), in a tragic accident (we still cannot believe it), to a young person (she had so much to live for), or by one's own hand (we never realized), death is one thing, not many. Each tears at our own humanity and makes visible for a time at least, our own mortality. The English poet John Donne, put it as well as it can be said: "No man is an island, entire of itself; . . any man's death diminishes me, because I am involved in mankind, and therefore never send to know for whom the bell tolls; it tolls for thee."

The soul cannot abide alone, not ours, nor God's. We repress the knowledge of our mortality because we sense that death is something that isolate us; others can surround us, but not enter into it with us. Abide With Me, is a scarcely disguised lament as much as it is a prayer. Like Jayber, when we sing it, we can hardly raise our head.

A few years ago a member of our congregation suffered a stroke which left him unable to walk or speak. For more than a year he lay, helpless and barely responsive to words and touch of love. When he died, at the funeral service his adult son spoke and told of being with him during those last days. Not being able to communicate with his father, he said that he got into the bed alongside him and held him in his arms for a time. He sensed that his father was saying without speaking it, abide with me.

In his telling of this, I thought how difficult it is for us to break through the almost impenetrable barrier of even the most profound intimacy, and hold each other in an 'abiding way.' My own father died at home, in his own bed. The cancer which relentlessly destroyed body tissue finally caused him to slip in and out of a coma. The physician made an occasional visit to the house, but his dying, like his birth, was a domestic and familial affair. While he was unable to speak, he gave indication that he could hear and understand what we were saying by the movement of his eyes and small gestures with his hands, as if to punctuate sentences which were in his mind but impossible to express with the tongue. Within a few hours, even those responses ceased and he lay motionless, except for an occasional raising of his hand to rub his lower lip, a ritual familiar to us and so common to him that it required no conscious thought. At the end of 36 hours or so, there was no response and the doctor who made a brief visit said that the end was not far away.

At the time I felt a compelling need to be there with him, holding his hand, listening to his faltering heartbeat. In all the years that I knew him since being a child, there was never a moment that I felt free to hold or even touch him. The intimacy was too powerful to risk a gesture that would break the code of silence that kept each of us from even a gesture that would unleash a torrent of unspoken love. Even the day when I left for the service when I turned 18, when we arrived at the train station, he could not reach out to me, not even a handshake, but could only say, "Son take care of yourself." And then I saw it, a single tear moving down his cheek. The only time I ever saw him weep. And I did not see it—that is, in such a way that he knew that I saw it.

Even as I write this it seems so unnatural and likely to be misunderstood that I hesitate to leave it stand. Most people that I know express their feelings for family members through touch and embrace without awkwardness or uncertainty. But this is what I wanted to say. At the moment when my father was dying, this barrier seemed to be removed. It was as though the words of the hymn, which he had sung so many times in the security of the sanctuary, now became liberated by the reality of our common mortality. His hands, which at one time could hold my infant life, were now the hands that I could hold. If he had felt my heartbeat as a child held closely to his breast, I could now feel his heartbeat with my own hands. There is a time when hearts begin to beat and there is a time when they stop. So begins and ends our allotted time on earth. We are joined to each other by a heartbeat, in birth as well as in death. Father and son, a heartbeat away from each other, closes the distance between heaven and earth. Now I wonder if the door behind which we keep our mortality hidden even from ourselves is the same door which keeps us from true intimacy in the summertime of life?

Can we find a way to keep the mystery of death connected to the miracle of birth? If it is my death that I will eventually die, it should not come as a stranger in the night to steal my heart and destroy my life. My death belongs to me. It was given to me in birth and will take place within my lifetime. It requires faith to live as well as to die. Living by faith, God's hand joins our first heartbeat to our last to encompass our life as the gift of his faithfulness.

In the soul of God there is a place where we can abide, yes. But there is also in our souls a place where God can abide. We need to sing Abide with Me with uplifted head and, like Jesus, with tears that come from our living spiritual soul not merely from repressed emotion. "If mortals die will they live again" (Job 14:14)?

"See, the home of God is among mortals. He will dwell with them; they will be his peoples, and God himself will be with them; he will wipe every tear from their eyes. Death will be no more" (Rev. 21:3-4).

18

Jesus Lives, and So Shall I

> I go to prepare a place for you . . . Because I live, you also will live. John 14:2;19

Some years ago I talked with a young man who was dying with AIDS and who had only a few more weeks to live. As we talked he wondered what would happen when he died and if there was life after death, what it would be like. I shared with him the words of Jesus, "I go to prepare a place for you. . . I will come again and take you to myself, so that where I am, there you may be also" (John 14:3). "I want to believe that," he said, "but what really will it be like?" In his mind he was attempting to picture a continuation of his present self-identity but in a strange environment.

I asked him to visualize with me the time when he was in his mother's womb. A place where he was secure, nourished and attached to a place that was his very own. Then I asked him to visualize having a moment of self-awareness in that state, fully aware of where he was and what it felt like. Then a voice came to him saying that it was time to leave this place and to be drawn out into another life which would enable him to move freely on his own, to breathe, walk and embrace with love other people just like himself. "It will be necessary for you to leave this place where you are firmly attached," the voice said, "and that part of you through which you now receive nourishment will be cut off. Yet, in this new place, there will be experiences that you have never dreamed of and could never imagine, but it is a good place, and you will be happy and fulfilled in it."

As he pondered this, I went on to say, if you were to hear this and understand it while still in the womb of your mother, your first thoughts would be of uncertainty and apprehension, and you would feel some anxiety. The voice will tell you, "The womb cannot be taken with you, but you will be the person that you are now and will live forever." The voice you hear will be a familiar voice, one that you can trust, and you will know the way to go (John 14:6; 10:14).

Dying is somewhat like being born. We are drawn out of the world where we live with the body given us by our Creator into a new place, where we are given a new body which we will experience as our very own. And we will live forever.

There was a long silence. Then a beautiful smile came across his face and he said, "I want to believe this and I can believe this. It makes perfect sense to me!" A few weeks later as he lay dying, attended by his sister and mother, he lay quietly as though in a deep sleep, but with a smile on his face. "Look how beautiful he is," his sister exclaimed, just like Jesus." Then he spoke, "Yes, Jesus," and he was gone. I wrote a poem in order to capture the moment:

Oh Todd, you are beautiful! My child, my joy.

Perfect was your birth; unblemished,
every finger and toe alive with eager longing.
You arrived wearing your very own face,
a mirror reflecting human love,
and a window into the face of God.
You outgrew boyhood boundaries;
searching the silence of mountains' majesty
and the wordless love of common humanity
for an echo of your own voice. At last,
you heard it through the pain
 and found it where it had ever lain,
at home.

Oh Todd, you are beautiful! My son, my teacher.

Perfect was your entrance into life eternal
wearing your very own face, so loved on earth,
so dear in heaven that Angels wept with joy
at your arrival.
"Come!" Said your new-found friend. "Come with me
to the place I have prepared."
"Yes Jesus," you replied.
Your final words of love, a benediction,
 released to live again with our permission,
at home with God.

At the memorial service held for him in the garden of his mother's home, I told his story, shared the poem and read the words of Jesus—"I go to prepare a place for you . . . Because I live, you also will live" (John 14:21;19). If we *want* to believe this, we *can* believe. Not because we can make it true by wishing it to be so, but there is an uncommon sense that reaches through what is visible to touch what is invisible. How else would we reach the core of love and trust our souls to the keeping of another?

In reciting the Nicene Creed, composed by the early church (4th century), we confess our belief in God, "Maker of heaven and earth, and of all things visible and invisible." Common sense tells us that if something is invisible it must not be real, for what cannot be experienced through our senses lacks substance and may only be a delusion and fantasy of the mind. The soul, however, has an uncommon sense which goes beyond comprehension to contemplation, and even communion. The English poet, Francis Thompson, who himself heard the footsteps of Jesus in the dark night of his own soul, reminds us that what seems incomprehensible might, after all, be very real.

O world invisible, we view thee,
O world intangible, we touch thee,
O world unknowable, we know thee,
Inapprehensible, we clutch thee!

Not where the wheeling systems darken,
And our benumbed conceiving sours!—
The drift of pinions, would we hearken,
Beats at our own clay-shuttered doors.

The Angels keep their ancient places;—
Turn but a stone and start a wing!
'Tis ye, 'tis your estranged faces,
That miss the many-splendoured thing.

The resurrection of the body and life after death, however, are not merely invisible dimensions of the created world, but are an entirely new and different order. For this reason, resurrection is more than a 'light at the end of a tunnel,' which some have claimed to see in a 'near death experience.' It is resurrection of *the body* which the Bible tells us was fashioned out of the dust of the ground and will return to dust (Genesis 3:19). The ancient Greeks, who held to the immortality of the soul, viewed the human body as merely a temporal container which imprisoned the soul. Therefore, death was viewed as a liberation of the soul to return to its eternal existence, allowing the mortal body to fall back into the dust. The Hebrews, however, viewed the body and soul as bound together in such a way that the death of the body was virtually the death of the soul. They had no concept of a disembodied soul continuing to exist after death.

Those who claimed to have encountered Jesus alive after his death were convinced of the reality of the resurrection by touching as well as seeing his body. Even Thomas, who doubted at first, was finally convinced when he himself could touch with his fingers the hands and side of Jesus (John 20:26-29). "It makes perfect sense to me," he might have said!

But it does not make sense to many people who only have the words of Scripture and the creeds of the church as a testimony to the fact that, even though our bodies fall back into the dust of the ground, there will be a resurrection *of the body!* It takes more than common sense to make this leap of faith. For this reason, while some may be able to envision some sort of continuation of life after death, the resurrection of the body is truly inconceivable from a human point of view. Let me suggest why this might be so.

We all live in the age of reason. After the so-called Enlightenment which occurred in Europe during the eighteenth century, human reason became the criterion for what is objectively true with faith viewed as mere subjective feelings. The biblical version of Jesus as the very incarnation of God and his resurrection from the dead were held to be logically impossible and therefore unbelievable. For the rational mind, the resurrection of the body and life after death, even if one might wish it to be true, makes no sense. I understand this. Fear of being irrational is what keeps reason within bounds. The 'light of reason' from within does not fear the darkness without, that is its virtue. But what it cannot abide is a light source other than its own. Rationalism is itself a kind of secular faith based on fear. Our faith in reason is what keeps even the most profound minds from falling into the abyss of irrational and delusional thinking. But this is to live behind 'clay-shuttered doors' where the spirits are never permitted to speak in 'unknown tongues.'

We all live in the age of science. While few of us are trained to be scientists, we are all influenced by scientific thinking. We expect the medication we take to be tested and approved after strict scientific research and study. We have a bias toward products which offer a scientific basis for their claims. We know that the human brain controls our emotions as well as our thoughts because we can literally 'see' the brain cells light up on the computer screen when aroused by what we once thought were only feelings aroused by external stimuli. In the same way, we 'know' that human cell tissue is broken down to its rudimentary elements when subject to death and decay.

And as for resurrection from the dead, where are the evidences that would compel, must less permit, such a belief?

There is no logical progression from death to life, that is the truth of reason. And there is no biological evolution from mortality to immortality, that is the truth of science. At the same time, we must acknowledge that unbelief in God as Creator does not cause the natural world to crumble into chaos. It appears to run very well on its own without God, where even the occasional catastrophes that ravage human life are accounted for as 'part of nature.'

In the same way, unbelief in God as the power of resurrection from the dead does not in and of itself shorten the human life-span. Humans can live an apparently healthy and normal life without belief in life after death. The universality of death appears to make it normal, even though it often comes as a tragic end. There are many causes of death, but in the end, all humans are mortal and each die the same death. Those who die in unbelief appear to die in quite the same way as those who believe in God. Though we are often shocked by death, we are not surprised that death occurs, we are but mortal beings.

I said that the resurrection of the dead is the most difficult thing to believe, in fact, it is not merely difficult, it is impossible. It defies human logic and is a scandal to the scientific mind. I understand why those who view religion as one of the greatest threats to the so-called freedom of the human spirit have an almost irrational fear of holding as real that which cannot be resolved in a rational way. I completely understand why even those who claim to be adherents to the Christian faith can recite as a creed in church what they cannot respect as a conviction of the mind when faced with the relentless reality and apparent finality of death. I too live in the culture and context of a world-view which has harnessed my spirit to technology (we have walked on the moon), but at the same time, surrendered my soul to secularism (we are no longer a nation 'under God'). But this kind of thinking makes no sense to me.

In the face of this, how then can one continue to believe in God and in life after death without appearing to surrender reason to emotion? Are the normal people really the secular minded folk where atheism is a sign of maturity and unbelief a mark of sanity? What if the reverse were true? Suppose that ultimate meaning and hope based on a Creator God were considered to be normal constituents of the human spirit, then unbelief might be considered as a form of insanity. Theologian Emil Brunner thinks so:

> It is the *heart* which feels the disharmony of existence in its 'sorrow-of-heart.'... [The] inward unity which still exists we call spiritual or psychological 'health' or 'normality,' to distinguish it from madness, or insanity. Yet all this health is in itself mad and insane. To place the central point of existence outside God, who is the true Centre, in the 'I' and the world, is madness; for it cannot be a real centre; the world cannot provide any resting-place for the Self; it only makes it oscillate hither and thither.

What Brunner wants us to consider is that what we consider to be mental and emotional health may be an illusion if it lacks the essential spiritual component which relates us to God. In the previous chapter I used the analogy of a spacewalker who cuts the cord that serves as a lifeline to the space ship. While there is sufficient oxygen and pressure to maintain life for a while, eventually the condition will lead to certain death. The person in the space suit may be enthusiastic about the experience of being free to the point of exuberance, even in denial (unbelief) that he or she is doomed. Those in the space ship, however, will not interpret this sense of well being as healthy or normal. Unbelief can be fatal, if we are spiritual beings.

In the end, we must see that the barrier to belief in the resurrection and life after death is neither human reason nor science, but unbelief. This is as true today as it was in the first century. Though Jesus performed many miracles and revealed God's power over disease, demons, and death, it was unbelief that blinded many to the reality of God in their midst. Mark tells us that even in his hometown, he could do no great works. "And he was amazed at their unbelief" (Mark 6:6).

Unbelief is not a modern phenomenon though atheism is. Following the age of reason, as noted above, it became possible to conceive of a world without a God to uphold its laws and influence the events of history. Atheism made unbelief a viable secular lifestyle. Unbelief in the reality and power of God counts reason and science as allies in holding to a purely materialistic and naturalistic view of reality. Actually, unbelief is not a necessary consequence of either reason or science; there are many who believe in God who also hold reason in high esteem and view science as a tool for exploration of God's created world. However, many modern persons use reason and science to support their unbelief in somewhat the same way as the contemporaries of Jesus used religion and even the law of Moses to justify their unbelief.

The difficulty of believing in the resurrection and life after death is not because we have outgrown the 'adolescence' of a medieval world-view where the supernatural and natural appeared to share the same space. It is not as though the concept of resurrection and life after death were at one time readily believed by a pre-scientific human culture where, like children, magic is as real as mystery. It was never so. In the ancient world, Job protested against the rampant rationalism of his day. Though it was cloaked with the pretension of religious certainty, the message was the same—don't expect to escape your own mortality. Humans are mortal beings, Job was warned. "Even though they mount up high as the heavens, and their head reaches to the clouds, they will perish forever like their own dung. . . Their bodies, once full of youth, will lie down in the dust with them" (Job 20:6-7; 11).

Job well knew the truth of that, but asked the question anyway, "If mortals die, will they live again?" (14:14). He pushed logic to the point of despair, and yet did not end with despair. He argued with logic as far as logic could go: "For there is hope for a tree, if it is cut down, that it will sprout again, and that its shoots will not cease. . . You would call, and I would answer you; you would long for the work of your hands" (14:7; 15). If he could not find a place in his own mind to answer the question, he could find it in the mind of God. If God thinks of him with longing, then logically (it makes sense!) that there is within God a reason for hope.

Here is our clue. It is not in our own souls that we find the truth of resurrection but in the soul of God. Because Job believed that he was valuable to the soul of God, it made perfect sense that God would "long for the work of his own hands." What is inconceivable to the human mind, is conceivable for God. David the Psalmist had the same conviction in his own soul when he wrote, "Therefore my heart is glad, and my soul rejoices, and my body also rests secure. For you do not give me up to Sheol, or let your faithful one see the Pit" (16:9-10). After the resurrection of Jesus, Peter cites this passage in his sermon on the day of Pentecost in support of the fact that David, inspired by the Spirit, "spoke of the resurrection of the Messiah, saying, 'He was not abandoned to Hades, nor did his flesh experience corruption'" (Acts 2:25-31).

But in order for this to 'make sense' to us, we must allow for the Spirit of God to reveal to us the innermost depths of God's own soul. No one comprehends what is truly of God, wrote the Apostle Paul, "except the Spirit of God. Now we have received not the spirit of the world, but the Spirit that is from God, so that we may understand the gifts bestowed on us by God" (1 Cor. 2:11-12).

My point is this: because resurrection of the body and life after death are only possible as a creative act of God, those who reject the possibility of resurrection are not merely skeptics, but unbelievers. Unbelief is more a matter of the will than of logic. Jesus did not face skeptics who lacked sufficient evidence to believe, but *willful* unbelievers. "Anyone who resolves to do the will of God will know whether the teaching is from God or whether I am speaking on my own" (John 7:17). The lack of willingness to believe in God is not because such belief is an offense to reason, but it is a challenge to the self-sufficiency of the human ego. Belief in God involves the willing surrender of the self as being sufficient unto itself. The lifeline to God connects our soul to God and needs to be maintained from our end as well. This is why one cannot believe in the resurrection without believing in God.

But what is it that we believe when we believe 'in the resurrection of the body?' My young friend, Todd, said that it made 'perfect sense,' but did not live long enough to press me further on just what a resurrected body might be like. As I have said, the Hebrew people in biblical times thought of the soul and the body as an interactive whole. The idea of the resurrection of the soul without a body was unthinkable. The contemporary theologian, Thomas Grentz, is consistent with this view when he says, "The resurrected reality is not that of a disembodied immaterial substance, but an embodied psychosomatic human person. Consequently, our essential nature is wholistic. The human person is by divine design one indivisible reality."

But what does this mean? Are we to believe that in the resurrection the very elements of our physical body, no matter how widely dispersed back into the earth, are somehow gathered together in order to be reassembled as a resurrection body? Will we literally 'come out of the grave' in the resurrection? Is there some kind of 'spiritual DNA' which was embedded in humanity as the image of God which God can use to 'clone' our resurrection body? I do not think so. "Flesh and blood cannot inherit the Kingdom of God," wrote Paul, "nor does the perishable inherit the imperishable" (1 Cor. 15:50).

Perhaps it is even misleading to think of the resurrection of the body. It would be more consistent with Paul's teaching to speak of being given a 'resurrection body' rather than the resurrection of this physical body. Paul uses the metaphor of sowing a seed in the ground which emerges in an entirely different form above the ground, as a way of explaining how the physical body which dies remains in the soil, while the resurrection body has is own spiritual form. "What you sow does not come to life unless it dies. And as for what you sow, you do not sow the body that is to be, but a bare seed, perhaps of wheat or some other grain. But God gives it a body as he has chosen, and to each kind of seed its own body . . . It is sown a physical body, it is raised a spiritual body" (1 Cor. 15:36-39; 44).

The resurrection body is 'given' by God, says Paul. This suggests that it is created rather than cloned. The fact that "each kind of seed has its own body" implies that the resurrection body 'given' to us will be just as much 'our body' as is our present physical body. Thus, despite the fact that the concept of resurrection seems to imply the raising of the physical body itself, Paul points in a different direction. The physical body returns to the earth—it dies. It is not dug out of the earth again, for what is perishable cannot become imperishable. What is mortal cannot become immortal. What is a physical body cannot become a spiritual body. Paul is quite clear about this. Any attempt to suggest that the present physical body reappears in a different form is foolish, says Paul (15:36). When he says that this perishable body must 'put on' imperishability, he is careful not to say that the perishable can in some way 'become' imperishable. What is 'put on' as a resurrection body is a new creation—but it will have our label on it!

This makes perfect sense to me!

Furthermore, we have present assurance of this through the Spirit of the resurrected Christ given to us as a pledge or a 'down payment' on our own resurrection (Eph. 1:14). We are given not only the Spirit of Christ in becoming children of God, we have the Spirit of the resurrected Christ as the inward witness of our own resurrection. What Job hoped for and what Jesus promised, the Apostle Paul claimed with a conviction bordering on certainty. "For if we have been united with him in a death like his, we will certainly be united with him in a resurrection like his" (Rom. 6:5). The hope of resurrection was so deeply grounded in Paul's own life that he could say, "If for this life only we have hoped in Christ, we are of all people most to be pitied" (1 Cor. 15:19). Belief in our own resurrection as a gift of the Spirit has such present value and gives us such hope that if it were not true (God forbid!), we would be viewed by others as having lost what is of the greatest value. Paul wants us to dare to live in the power and Spirit of the resurrection as the defining content of a life of faith.

One question Paul did not answer was, When will this resurrection body be given to us, immediately after we die or only at the end of the age, and the "resurrection of the dead" (Phil. 3:11)? Perhaps he would also call this question foolish! What prompts the question is the apparent interval between death and resurrection from the perspective of our existence in time. I can count the years since my parents have died, but this does not reckon with the relation of time and eternity. Eternal life is not simply the extension of temporal life without end, though we might have no other way to picture it. The idea that my parents exist as disembodied souls waiting (passing the hours!?) until they are given their resurrection bodies borders on absurdity. There will be no earthly hours in eternity. Consequently, my parents and I will receive our resurrection body immediately after death and at the same time! My former professor, Thomas Torrance, reminds us that, "Looked at from the perspective of the new creation there is no gap between the death of the believer and the *parousia* of Christ, but looked at from the perspective of time that decays and crumbles away, there is a lapse of time between them."

But this is how theologians talk! We have our own language of faith which allows for our loved ones who die to be held secure in God's time. On the marker of my grandparents who came to this country from Norway, I found this inscription, engraved in the Norwegian language:

SOV SØDT OG HVIL HOS GUD DIG UD
NAAR HAN TROR BEDST, HAN
SENDER BUD

Freely translated, it reads: Sleep well, and rest with God. In his best time he will send for you.

I find it easy to believe in the resurrection of Jesus. It is a belief that has been passed from generation to generation for almost two thousand years. I am part of those people who lived and died confessing that truth as the power of the gospel of Christ. I find it easy to make the resurrection of Jesus the center point of my theology, believing along with the Apostle Paul that if he did not rise from the dead our faith is futile and the cross is meaningless (1 Cor. 15:17). I find it easy to sing, Jesus Lives and So Shall I. His Spirit sings along with my spirit, and we are in perfect harmony (Rom. 8:16).

Maranatha!

References

The Quotation from Dag Hammarskjold is from *Markings*, New York: Knopf, 1966 p. 110.

Preface

The reference to Thomas Moore is from, *Care of the Soul: A Guide for Cultivating Depth and Sacredness in Everyday Life,* New York: Harper Collins, 1992, p. xi.

The reference to Karl Barth is from, *Evangelical Theology: An Introduction*, London: Weidenfeld and Nicholson, 1968, p. 64.

The reference to Emily Dickinson is from, *The Complete Poetry of Emily Dickinson*, Boston: Little Brown and Company, 1989

The reference to David Hubbard is from *Incarnational Ministry: The Presence of Christ in Church, Society and Family,* Essays in Honor of Ray S. Anderson, Christian D. Kettler, Todd H. Speidell, editors. Colorado Springs: Helmers and Howard Publishers, 1990. p. xi.

The term 'maverick' originated on the cattle range in Texas. Samuel Augustus Maverick (1803-1870) was a prominent Texas pioneer, rancher and statesman, who helped establish the republic of Texas. In 1845 he took a herd of 400 cattle in payment of a debt. He did not brand the cattle. They strayed, and neighboring ranchers called them mavericks. While the name was first given to all unbranded range cattle, it became a term used to describe calves who had lost their mothers. Those calves, in order to survive, had to go from one cow to another in order to steal some milk. As a result, these maverick calves were usually more vigorous than others but were also inherently promiscuous!

Chapter One: *I Have Decided to Follow Jesus--No Turning Back!*

The quotation from Søren Kierkegaard is from *The Journals of Kierkegaard*, New York: Harper Torchbook, 1958, p. 89

Chapter Two: *From the Prairie to the Pulpit*

The reference to Karl Barth is from, *Church Dogmatics*, I/1, Edinburgh: T & T Clark, 1975, p. 79.

The reference to Helmut Thielicke is from, *A Little Exercise for Young Theologians*, Grand Rapids: Eerdmans, 1962, pp. 8, 36.

The reference to Dietrich Bonhoeffer is from, *Spiritual Care*. Philadelphia: Fortress Press, 1985. pp. 67-8.

The reference to Karl Barth is from, Eberhard Busch, *Karl Barth—His Life from Letters and Autobiographical Texts*, Grand Rapids: Eerdmans, 1993, p. 97.

The reference to C. S. Lewis is from, *Letters to Malcolm: Chiefly on Prayer*, New York: Harcourt, Brace, & World, p. 187

The quotation from Christopher Fry is taken from, *Three Plays*, "A Sleep of Prisoners," New York: Oxford University Press, 1961, p. 209.

The reference to my book on the soul of ministry is, *The Soul of Ministry: Forming Leaders for God's People*, Louisville: Westminster Press, 1997.

Chapter Three: *The Soul of a Preacher*

The quotation from G. J. Hamann is from: "J. G. Hamann and the Princess Gallitrzi," *Philomathes*, Robert Palmer and Robert Hamerton-Kelley (eds). The Hague: Martinus Nijhoff, p. 339.

The reference to Edward John Carnell is from, *The Burden of Søren Kierkegaard*, Grand Rapids: Eerdmans, 1965.

The reference to the book by Dag Hammarskjold is *Markings*, New York: Knopf, 1966.

The reference to Søren Kierkegaard is from: *The Journals of Kierkegaard*. New York: Harper Torchbook, 1958, p. 56

The quote from Kierkegaard on the poet is from: *Either/Or*. New York: Anchor Books, 1959, Frontispiece.

The quotation from Bonhoeffer is from a letter to E. Bethge, dated June 25th, 1942. Cited by Andre Dumas in "Religion and Reality in the Work of Bonhoeffer," in *A Bonhoeffer Legacy: Essays in Understanding*, A. J. Klassen, editor. Grand Rapids: Eerdmans, 1981, p. 258.

The quotation from K. Gibran is from, *The Prophet*, New York: Alfred Knopf, 1962.

The quotation from Kierkegaard on desire is from: *Journals*. New York: Harper Torchbook, 1959.

The quotation from Edward John Carnell is from, *Christian Commitment: An Apologetic*, New York: The Macmillan Company, 1957, p. 79.

Part Two

The quotation from Christopher Fry is taken from *Three Plays*, "A Sleep of Prisoners." New York: Oxford University Press, 1961, p. 209.

Introduction

The quotation from Karl Barth concerning Kierkegaard is from, *Evangelical Theology: An Introduction*, Karl Barth, Grand Rapids: Eerdmans, 1963, p. 154.

The reference to Geoffrey Wainrwright is, *Doxology—A Systematic Theology*, New York: Oxford. 1980.

The reference to James McClendon is, *Systematic Theology—Ethics*, Nashville: Abingdon Press, 1986.

Chapter Four: *Guide Me, O Thou Great Jehovah*

The reference to Abraham Heschel is from, *The Prophets*, Vol. II. New York: Harper and Row, 1962. Heschel writes:

"The anger of God must not be treated in isolation, but as an aspect of the divine pathos, as one of the modes of God's responsiveness to man. It shares the features that are characteristic of the pathos as a whole: it is conditioned by God's will; it is aroused by man's sins. It is an instrument rather than a force, transitive rather than spontaneous. It is a secondary emotion, never the ruling passion, disclosing only a part of God's way with man... For all the terror that the wrath of God may bring upon man, the prophet is not crushed or shaken in his understanding and trust. What is divine is never weird. This is the greatness of the prophet: he is able to convert terror into a song. For when the Lord smites the Egyptians, he is both 'smiting and healing' (Isa. 19:22)." (p. 63)

"The divine pathos, whether mercy or anger, was never thought of as an impulsive act, arising automatically within the divine Being as the reaction to man's behavior and as something due to peculiarity of temperament or propensity. It is neither irrational nor irresistible. Pathos results from a decision, from an act of will. It comes about in the light of moral judgment rather than in the darkness of passion." (p. 78)

The reference to Karl Barth is from, *Church Dogmatics*, II/1, Edinburgh: T & T Clark, 1957, pp. 257ff.

The citation from Kornelis Miskotte is from, *When the Gods are Silent*, London: Collins, 1967, p. 218.

The reference to C. S. Lewis is from: *Letters to Malcolm: Chiefly on Prayer*, New York: Harcourt, Brace, & World, p. 187

The reference to my former theology professor is from Carl F. H. Henry who held that human reason is univocal (identical) with divine reason: "Does the truth of God, which meets us through the Logos this side of man's conjectural speculations about invisible reality, mesh us in an activity of rationality that comprehends the Infinite and the finite in one and the same logicality?. . . Only univocal knowledge is, therefore, genuine and authentic knowledge. . . Only a univocal element in analogical affirmation can save it from equivocation. Unless we have some literal truth about God, no similarity between man and God can in fact be predicated; . . . The alternative to univocal knowledge of God is equivocation and skepticism." *God, Revelation and Authority*, Vol. III, Waco, TX: Word Books, 1976-1983, pp. 221-222, 364.

The quotations from Thomas F. Torrance are from; *God and Rationality,* Oxford: Oxford University Press, 1971, pp. 188, 189.

The citation from Kornilis Miskotte is from, *When the Gods are Silent*, London: Collins, 1967, p. 194.

The citation from John Pedersen, is from: *Israel: Its Life and Culture*, Vol. I, London: Oxford University Press, 1973. The full text for the quotation is as follows:

"For the Israelite *thinking* was not the solving of abstract problems. He does not add link to link, nor does he set up major and minor premises from which conclusions are drawn. To him thinking is to grasp a totality. He directs his soul towards the principal matter, that which determines the totality, and receives it into his soul, the soul thus being immediately stirred and led in a certain direction. In the Hebrew dictionary we look in vain for a word which quite corresponds to our 'to think.' There are words which mean 'to remember,' 'make present,' and thus to act upon the soul. There are words expressing that the soul seeks and investigates;

but by that is not meant an investigation which analyses and arranges according to abstract views. To investigate is a practical activity; it consists in directing the soul towards something which it can receive into itself, and by which it can be determined. One investigates wisdom, i.e. makes it one's own." (pp. 108-109)

"When modern logicians have characterized the correct manner of thinking as an interplay of simple, i.e. essentially empty but sharply defined space images, then we see at once the contrast between this and the Israelite way of thinking. The Israelite does not occupy himself with empty nor with sharply defined space images. His logic is not the logic of abstraction, but of immediate perception... The most important word for thinking contains the plan, the direction of the mind towards action." (pp. 124-125)

The reference to Karl Barth is from, *Church Dogmatics*, II/1. Edinburgh: T & T Clark, 1964, p. 353.

Chapter Five: *Thou Didst Leave thy Throne*

The reference to Barth is from: *Karl Barth: His Life from Letters and Tests*, by Eberhard Busch, London: SCM Press, 1976, p. 44

The reference to Dorothy is from *The Wizard of Oz* (film, 1939). Attribution: Noel Langley (1898-1981), U. S. author, Florence Ryerson, and Edgar Allen Wolfe.

The reference to Thomas Torrance and the inner relation of Son and Father is expressed more fully in this quotation:

"Our knowledge of the Father and the Son, of the Father in the Son and of the Son in the Father, is mediated to us in and through Jesus Christ in such a way that in a profound sense we are given to share in the knowledge which God has of himself within himself as Father and Son or Son and Father, which is part of what is meant by our knowing God through the Spirit of God who is in him and whom he sends to us through the Son. Now it is because we do not know the Father or the Son except through the revealing and reconciling work of Jesus Christ, that our knowledge of the Father and of the Son and of the Holy Spirit is, as it were, a function of our knowledge of Jesus Christ. Because God has revealed himself to us and given himself to us in him, Jesus Christ constitutes in his own incarnate Person the mediating centre of that revelation whereby all our knowledge of God is controlled." T. F. Torrance, *The Mediation of Christ*. Colorado Springs: Helmers and Howard, 1992, p. 55

The reference to my doctoral dissertation is found in, *Historical Transcendence and the Reality of God: A Christological Critique*. Grand Rapids: Eerdmans, 1975, p. 252.

The reference to James Torrance is from, "The Vicarious Humanity of Christ," in *The Incarnation--Ecumenical Studies in the Nicene-Constantinopolitan Creed A. D. 381,* Thomas F. Torrance, Editor. Edinburgh: Handsel Press Ltd., 1981, p. 141. Todd Speidell reinforces this when he adds: "Christ presents himself in the depths of human need—the hungry, the thirsty, the naked, the sick, the imprisoned (Mt. 25:31ff). The stranger among us, the homeless and psychologically debilitated, may be the place of Christ's presence among us. The Gospel of Matthew does not exhort us simply to be like Christ—ministering to the needy 'as Jesus would' (which implies that he is not actively present but merely serves as a model for our social action)—but attests that Christ discloses himself through the stranger. We must be where Christ is, and act where he acts." "Incarnational Social Ethics," in *Incarnational Ministry—The Presence of Christ in Church, Society, and Family*, Colorado Springs: Helmers and Howard, publishers, 1990, p. 146.

The reference to Karl Barth on Jesus as the primary sacrament is from, *Church Dogmatics* II/1, p. 54. Barth goes on to say that there is a primary objectivity connected with the sacramental attestation of Jesus' life and death which can only be represented in a secondary way. There is a concealment as well as a revelation of this sacramental reality, "even as the man Jesus as such is always enigma as well." Ibid, p. 56. C. Norman Kraus expresses much the same when he writes: "We need to know that this one who mediates God's presence is one with him. It is not enough to think of shared spiritual or rational divine substance. His unity with the Father must be such that we can be confident that he represents God's inner character and attitude toward us. This, of course, was the essence of apostolic faith in Christ, and our theological language struggles to express adequately the content of this faith." *Jesus Christ Our Lord: Christology from a Disciple's Perspective.* Scottdale, PA: Herald Press, 1987, p. 117.

Chapter Six: *The Love of God*

The quotation from Edward John Carnell is from, *The Kingdom of Love and the Pride of Life.* Grand Rapids: Eerdmans, 1960, p. 18.

The quotation from Thomas Wolfe is from, *Look Homeward Angel!* New York: Charles Scribner's Sons, 1930, from the Frontispiece.

The quotation from John Macmurray is from, *Reason and Emotion.* London: Faber and Faber, 1935, p. 32.

The source for the hymn, *The Love of God*, is: Text and Music by Frederick M. Lehman. Copyright 1917, Renewed 1945 by Nazarene Publishing House, *The Hymnal for Worship & Celebration*, Waco, TX: Word Music,

1966, p. 67.

The reference to Barth's views on *agape* and *eros* are from, *Church Dogmatics*, IV/2. Edinburgh: T & T Clark, 1958, pp. 736-37.

The reference to the book by Anders Nygren, *Eros and Agape* is London: S.P.C.K., 1953.

The reference to the book by C. S. Lewis is, *The Four Loves*, New York: Harcourt, Brace, 1960

The citation by Thomas Torrance is from, *A Passion for Christ: The Vision that Ignites Ministry*, Gerrit Dawson and Jock Stein, eds. Edinburgh: The Handsel Press, 1999, pp. 13, 14.

The quotation from Catherine Mowry LaCugna is from, *God For Us: The Trinity and Christian Life*, San Francisco: HarperCollins, 1991, pp. 352, 354. In this connection, Paul Fiddes suggests that there might be a sense in which God has freely decided to be God *with us*, implying that he has *chosen* to need us, thus preserving his own freedom. *Participating in God: A Pastoral Doctrine of the Trinity*, London: Darton, Longman & Todd, 2000, pp. 210-215.

The citation from Francis Thompson is from: *The Hound of Heaven*, New York: Peter Pauper Press, nd, p. 26.

The citation from Arthur Miller is from, "Death of a Salesman," *Arthur Miller's Collected Plays*, Volume I. New York: The Viking Press, 1957, 1987, pp. 221-222. Miller traces the desperate unraveling of the dream for Willy Loman with unerring insight. The quiet desperation of Willy to succeed is projected upon his two sons, Biff and Happy who, at first, are captivated by the dream and then are forced to become accomplices in the charade. At the end, unable to maintain the pretense, Willy precipitates an accident in which he is killed in the midst of a delusion that he will be viewed as a hero when the $20,000 insurance check arrives for his family. Following the funeral service, a postmortem on his life is conducted by Biff, one of his sons who could no longer sustain the pretense, while his brother, Happy, and Willy's friend, Charley, continue to defend Willy's self image.

BIFF: He had the wrong dreams, All, all, wrong.
HAPPY: Don't say that!
BIFF: He never knew who he was.
CHARLEY: Nobody dast blame this man. You don't understand; Willy was a salesman. And for a salesman, there is no rock bottom to the life. He don't put a bolt to a nut, he don't tell you the law or give you medicine. He's a man way out there in the blue, riding on a smile and a shoeshine.

And when they start not smiling back—that's an earthquake. And then you get yourself a couple of spots on your hat, and you're finished. Nobody dast blame this man. A salesman is got to dream, boy. It comes with the territory.

The citation from Wendy Farley, is from *Tragic Vision and Divine Compassion*. Louisville: Westminster John Knox Press, 1990, pp. 125-127. Divine power is conditioned by divine love which operates within the tragic structures of the created world. "Omnipotence is the power to do whatever can be done absolutely, that is, whatever is logically possible. But to overcome the tragic structure of finitude, to be free animate beings from all suffering, to determine finite freedom so that it will always love the good and have the courage to pursue it—these things are not possible. The potential for suffering and evil lie in the tragic structure of finitude and cannot be overcome without destroying creation. The power to create must therefore include the power to redeem. The fragility of creation requires the continual presence of divine power to resist the evils resident in history. But it is the virtue of this power that it is not absolute, it is interactive. If this mutuality is construed as a limitation upon divine power, it is the limitation that is entailed by the alterity of finite existence and by the nature of love. It is the nature of love to desire the freedom and well-being of the beloved rather than domination. Omnipotence is not *limited* at all, but its power is to shape life and mediate love. Yet because of the inexorable fragility of creation and the potential for sin, the infinite abyss of divine power and love is destined to disappointment."

The reference to Lewis Smedes is to his book, *Love within Limits: A Realists View of 1 Corinthians 13*. Grand Rapids: Eerdmans, 1978, p. 1.

The reference to Karl Barth is from, *Church Dogmatics*, III/1, p. 312.

The quotation from Christopher Fry is from, *The Boy With a Cart*. New York: Oxford University Press, 1959, pp, 4-5, 8.

Chapter Seven: *There's a Wideness in God's Mercy*

The source for the hymn, "There's a Wideness in God's Mercy" is: *The Hymnal for Worship & Celebration*, Waco, TX: Word Music, 1966, p. 68.

The reference to William Shakespeare is from *The Merchant of Venice*. IV i.

The quality of mercy is not strain'd,
It droppeth as the gentle rain from heaven
Upon the place beneath. It is twice blest:
It blesseth him that gives and him that takes.

'T is mightiest in the mightiest: it becomes
The throned monarch better than his crown;
His sceptre shows the force of temporal power,
The attribute to awe and majesty,
Wherein doth sit the dread and fear of kings;
But mercy is above this sceptred sway,
It is enthroned in the hearts of kings,
It is an attribute to God himself;
And earthly power doth then show likest God's,
When mercy seasons justice. Therefore, Jew,
Though justice be thy plea, consider this,
That in the course of justice none of us
Should see salvation: we do pray for mercy;
And that same prayer doth teach us all to render,
The deeds of mercy.

The reference to costly grace in Dietrich Bonhoeffer is from: *Discipleship*. Minneapolis: Fortress Press, 2001 edition, Chapter One. "Cheap grace was very unmerciful to our Protestant Church. Cheap grace surely has also been unmerciful with most of us personally. . . . .Blessed are they who in this sense have become Christians, for whom the word of grace has been merciful." Pp. 53, 56.

The source for the story of Amy Biehl is, *The Orange County Register*, Orange County California, July 29, 1998, pp, 1, 16.

Chapter Eight: *Amazing Grace*

The quotation from Eugene O'Neill is from, "The Great God Brown," in *The Plays of Eugene O'Neill*, Vol. 1. New York: Modern Library, 1982, p. 318

The quotation from Karl Barth is found in *Church Dogmatics* IV/2, p. 579. Barth also said of God's work of grace through Christ, "He kills the old man by introducing the new, and not conversely." P. 577.

The source for the hymn, *Amazing Grace* is: text by John Newton. *The Hymnal for Worship & Celebration*, Waco, TX: Word Music, 1966, p. 202.

The reference to Karl Barth is from, *Church Dogmatics*, II/1. Edinburgh: T & T Clark, 1964, p. 353.

The quotation from Thomas Torrance, is from: *God and Rationality*. New York: Oxford, 1971, p. 72

The source for the quotation on love is: Hans Urs von Balthasar. *A Theo-*

logical Anthropology. New York: Sheed and Ward, p. 87.

The source for the paraphrase of grace 'dying the death of a thousand qualifications,' is A. Flew and A. MacIntyre, *New Essays in Philosophical Theology*. London: SCM Press, 1955. "A fine brash hypothesis may thus be killed by inches, the death of a thousand qualifications." P. 96.

Chapter Nine: *When I Survey the Wondrous Cross*

The source for the hymn, "When I Survey the Wondrous Cross" is: *The Hymnal for Worship & Celebration*, Waco, TX: Word Music, 1966, p. 185.

The reference to Wolfhart Pannenberg, is from, *Christian Spirituality and Sacramental Community*. London: Dartman, Longman and Todd, 1983, pp. 20, 25. Pannenberg goes on to say: "The good Protestant knows that the only chance for righteousness is to put oneself in the place of the sinner, of the tax collector, rather than that of the Pharisee. The consciousness of sin must be kept at a boil. It usually goes unnoticed that these very efforts put the good Protestant in the place of the Pharisee."

"At the Cross," copyright, 1916, by R. E. Hudson. *Church Service Hymnal*. Winona Lake, IN: The Rodeheaver Hall-Mack Co., 1948.

The quotation from Thomas Wolfe is from, *Look Homeward, Angel!*, New York Charles Scribner's Sons, 1930.

Chapter Ten: *I Serve a Risen Savior*

The source for the references to Lessing is from, *Historical Theology: An Introduction*, by Geoffrey Bromiley. Grand Rapids: Eerdmans Publishing Company, 1978, pp. 344-45.

The reference to Bultmann is from, *Jesus Christ and Mythology*. London: SCM Press, 1966.

The quotation from Thomas Torrance is from his book, *Space, Time and Resurrection*, Grand Rapids: Eerdmans, 1976, p. xi.

The second quotation from Thomas Torrance is from *Space, Time and Resurrection*. Grand Rapids: Eerdmans, 1976, p. 60

The source for the quotation from Maria von Wedemeyer is from: *Love Letters from Cell 92: The Correspondence Between Dietrich Bonhoeffer and Maria von Wedemeyer 1943-1945*. Edited by Ruth-Alice von Bismarck and Ulrich Kabitz. Nashville: Abingdon Press, 1992, p. 198.

Chapter Eleven: *Spirit of God, Descend Upon My Heart*

The citation from Irenaeus is from: *Irenaeus Against Heresies*, Volume 1, p. 334 (III/17/1)

The citation from Thomas Torrance is from, *Theology in Reconstruction*. Grand Rapids: Eerdmans, 1965, p. 247; see also, Michael Green, *I Believe in the Holy Spirit*. Grand Rapids: Eerdmans, 1975, pp. 47; 105-6;

The references to Karl Barth are from, *Church Dogmatics*, IV/2, pp. 320-21; 325-26.

The source for Karl Barth's discussion of the filioque clause can be found in *Church Dogmatics*, I/1, pp. 473ff. For other sources regarding this discussion see: Alisdair Heron, *The Holy Spirit*, Philadelphia: Westminster Press, 1983, pp. 90-99; 176-178; Lukas Vischer, editor, *Spirit of God, Spirit of Christ—Ecumenical Reflections on the Filioque Controversy,* WCC. Faith and Order # 103, 1981.

The source for reference to C. Peter Wagner, is from: *How to Have a Healing Ministry Without Making Your Church Sick*, Ventura, CA: Regal Books, 1988, pp. 23ff.

The quotation from Thomas Smail is from, *The Forgotten Father*. Grand Rapids: Eerdmans Publishing Company, 1980, p. 179.

It was the Old Testament theologian, Abraham Heschel who said, "What is divine is never weird. This is the greatness of the prophet: he is able to convert terror into a song. For when the Lord smites the Egyptians, he is both 'smiting and healing' (Isa. 19:22)." *The Prophets*, Vol. II, New York: Harper and Row, 1962, p. 63.

Chapter Twelve: *Sweet Hour of Prayer*

My reference to "Judas as an answer to prayer," became the chapter in a book on Judas which I wrote titled: *The Gospel According to Judas: Is There a Limit to God's Forgiveness*. Colorado Springs: NavPress, 1994, pp. 43-56.

Portions of this chapter on prayer were drawn from my book, *Dancing with Wolves: The Musings of a Maverick Theologian*. Eugene, OR: Wipf and Stock Publishers, 2001, pp. 90-100.

The two lines at the end of the chapter are from the hymn, "Sweet Hour of Prayer," *The Hymnal for Worship & Celebration*, Waco, TX: Word Music, 1966, p. 433.

Chapter Thirteen: *My Faith Looks Up to Thee*

The quotation from the hymn, "My Faith Looks Up to Three, is from *The Hymnal for Worship & Celebration*, Waco, TX: Word Music, 1966, p. 410.

The quotation from Edward John Carnell is from his book, *The Kingdom of Love and the Pride of Life*. Grand Rapids: Eerdmans, 1960, p. 125.

The quotation from Gordon D. Fee, is from his book, *The Disease of the Health and Wealth Gospels*. Costa Mesa, CA: The Word for Today, P.O. Box 800, 1979, p. 17.

Sources for the story of Larry and Lucky Parker are from, *ACTS*, Burbank, CA 5 (May-June 1977) 3 18-20; *The Los Angeles Times*, May 17, 1988.

The reference to Edward John Carnell is from his book, *Christian Commitment: An Apologetic*. New York: Macmillan Company, 1957, p. 76.

Chapter Fourteen: *The Church's One Foundation*

The quotation from the hymn, "The Church's One Foundation," is from *The Hymnal for Worship & Celebration*, Waco, TX: Word Music, 1966, p. 97.

The reference to Emil Brunner's book is, *The Misunderstanding of the Church*, London: Lutterworth Press, 1952.

The quotation from Brunner regarding Ignatius is from, *Dogmatics*, III, *The Christian Doctrine of the Church, Faith and Consummation*, London: Lutterworth 1963, p. 67.

The quotation from Annie Dillard is from, *Holy the Firm*, New York: Harper and Row, 1977, pp. 55, 59.

The reference to Kahil Gibran is from his book, *Sand and Foam*. New York, Alfred Knopf, 1954, p. 77.

The quotation from Karl Barth is from *Church Dogmatics* IV/2, pp. 686-7.

The citation about Bonhoeffer is from, Thomas Day, *Dietrich Bonhoeffer on Christian Community and Common Sense*. New York: The Edwin Mellen Press, p. 183.

References 225

The quotation from Wendell Berry is from his book, *Jayber Crow*, Washington, D.C.: Counter Point, 2002, pp. 164-65.

The quotation from Wesley Carr, is from, "Towards a Contemporary Theology of the Holy Spirit," in *Scottish Journal of Theology,* Vol. 28, No. 7, 1975, pp. 506, 507-8. W. Pannenberg stresses the eschatological nature of the apostolic character of the church based on the fact that the Holy Spirit is the presence of the Christ who is coming as well as of the historical Christ. "In this age of historical consciousness, therefore, the church needs a new concept of apostolicity that will allow it to recognize without reservation the difference between the age of the apostles and its own day, without thereby losing its connection with the mission of the apostles. Attention to the eschatological motif in the early Christian apostolate can help us do this. The only criterion of apostolic teaching in this sense is whether and to what degree it is able to set forth the final truth and comprehensive universality of the person and work of Christ in the transforming and saving significance of his resurrection and its power that gives light to the world. To demand that the teaching of the church be apostolic cannot mean that everything that is known from the age of the apostles should be normative for the present day, nor can it mean that only that which is derived from the age of the apostles can be regarded as valid today. It follows that the true *vita apostolica* is to be sought in the life of the church's leaders and in the life of individual Christians who let themselves be permeated by the final all-encompassing, liberating, and transforming truth of Jesus. The *vita apostolica* does not mean copying the way of life of the apostolic age or what we think that way of life was, and it certainly cannot be lived by borrowing this or that form of life from the regulations of the apostles. That which was apostolic then may be irrelevant today or may even be a hindrance to our apostolic tasks. This insight enables the church to be free to live in its own historicity as opposed to that of the apostolic age and still remain in continuity with the mission of the apostles." W. Pannenberg, *The Church*, Philadelphia: Westminster Press, 1983, pp. 56-57.

The quotation from Eugene O'Neill, is from, "The Great God Brown.' *The Plays of Eugene O'Neill*, Vol 1. New York: Modern Library, 1982, p. 318.

Chapter Fifteen: *Under His Wings*

The quotation from the hymn, "Under His Wings," is from *The Hymnal for Worship & Celebration*, Waco, TX: Word Music, 1966, p. 356.

The quotation from Martin Luther is from, *The Bondage of the Will in Erasmus-Luther: Discourse on Free Will*, New York: Frederick Ungar, 1961, p. 106.

The reference to Calvin is from, *Institutes of the Christian Religion*, 1.16.3, Philadelphia: Westminster, 1960, 2 volumes, 1.200-201. Cited in *God Under Fire: Modern Scholarship Reinvents God*, Douglas S. Huffman and Eric L. Johnson, editors. Grand Rapids: Zondervan, 2002, p. 190.

The quotation from William Craig is from, "What Does God Know?" in *God Under Fire: Modern Scholarship Reinvents God*, Douglas S. Huffman and Eric L. Johnson, editors. Grand Rapids: Zondervan, 2002, p. 138

The quotation from Douglas Geivett, is from "How Do We Reconcile the Existence of God and Suffering," in *God Under Fire: Modern Scholarship Reinvents God*, Douglas S. Huffman and Eric L. Johnson, editors. Grand Rapids: Zondervan, 2002, p. 186.

The reference from Harold Kushner can be found in his book, *When Bad Things Happen to Good People*. New York: Avon Books, 1981, p. 134.

The citation from Fyodor Dostoyevsky can be found in *The Brothers Karamazov*. New York: Random House, 1950, pp. 290-291.

The quotation from Richard Rice is from, *The Openness of God*, Clark Pinnock *et al*, editors, InterVarsity Press, 1994, pp. 38-39.

The quotation from John Boykin is from, *The Gospel of Coincidence—is God in Control?* Grand Rapids: Zondervan, 1996, p. 201

The quotation from Wendy Farley is from, *Tragic Vision and Divine Compassion*. Louisville: Westminster JohnKnox Press, 1990, p. 127

The quotation from Thomas Torrance is from, *Divine and Contingent Order*. Oxford, New York: Oxford University Press, 1981, p. 136.

Chapter Sixteen: *All the Way My Savior Leads Me*

The source for the quotation from Gary Friesen is, *Decision Making and the Will of God*, by Gary Friesen, with J. Robin Maxson. Portland, Or.: Multnomah Press, 1980, p. 233.

The reference to Dietrich Bonhoeffer is from, *Dietrich Bonhoeffer: A Biography*, by Eberhard Bethge. Minneapolis: Fortress Press, revised edition, 2002, p. 677.

The reference to Søren Kierkegaard is from, *The Journals of Kierkegaard*, New York: Harper Torchbook, 1958, p. 89

Chapter Seventeen: *Abide With Me*

The quote from Dietrich Bonhoeffer is from, *Letters and Papers From Prison*. New Greatly Enlarged Edition. New York: Macmillan, 19721, p. 349.

The quotation from Helmut Thielicke is from, *Living With Death*. Grand Rapids: Eerdmans, 1983, pp. 138; 163

The quotation from Dietrich Bonhoeffer is from, *Dietrich Bonhoeffer: Meditating on the Word*. Cambridge, MA: Cowley Publications, 1986, p. 139.

The quotation from Alan E. Lewis is from, *Between Cross & Resurrection: A Theology of Holy Saturday*. Grand Rapids: Eerdmans, 2001, pp. 434-5.

The references to Ernest Becker are from, *The Denial of Death*. New York: Simon and Schuster. Free Press Paperbacks, 1997, pp. 199, 202.

The quotation from Wendell Berry, is from, *Jayber Crow*. Washington, D. D.: Counterpoint, 2002, pp. 162-3.

The source for the hymn, *Abide with Me*, is: *The Hymnal for Worship & Celebration*, Waco, TX: Word Music, 1966, p. 419.

The quotation from John Donne is from, *The Poems of John Donne*, edited by H. J. C. Grierson. London: Oxford University Press, 1964, 1933.

Chapter Eighteen: *Jesus Lives, and So Shall I*

The quotation from Francis Thompson is from: 'The Kingdom of Heaven,' *Selected Poems of Francis Thompson*. London: Burns and Oates, 1907, pp. 132-133.

The source of the quotation from Emil Brunner is, *Man in Revolt,* London: Lutterworth Press, 1939, reprint, Philadelphia: Westminster Press, 1979, p. 235.

The source for the quote from Stanley Grenz is from, *Theology for the Community of God*. Grand Rapids: Eerdmans 1994, p. 163.

The citation from Thomas Torrance is from: *Space, Time and Resurrection*. Grand Rapids: Eerdmans Publishing Company, 1976, p. 102. See also, Helmut Thielicke, *Being Human. . . Becoming Human*. Garden City, NY: Doubleday, 1984, pp. 116ff.

Bibliography

Anderson, Ray S. *Dancing with Wolves: The Musings of a Maverick Theologian*. Eugene, OR: Wipf and Stock Publishers, 2001

Anderson, Ray S. *The Soul of Ministry: Forming Leaders for God's People*, Louisville: Westminster Press, 1997

Anderson, Ray S. *The Gospel According to Judas: Is There a Limit to God's Forgiveness*. Colorado Springs: NavPress, 1994

Barth, Karl. *Evangelical Theology: An Introduction*. London: Weidenfeld and Nicholson, 1968

Barth, Karl. *Church Dogmatics*, II/1, Edinburgh: T & T Clark, 1957, 1964

Barth, Karl. *Church Dogmatics*, IV/2. Edinburgh: T & T Clark, 1958

Becker, Ernest, *The Denial of Death*. New York: Simon and Schuster. Free Press Paperbacks, (1973) 1997

Berry, Wendell. *Jayber Crow*. Washington, D.C.: Counter Point, 2002

Bethge, Eberhard. *Dietrich Bonhoeffer: A Biography*, Minneapolis: Fortress Press, revised edition, 2002

Bonhoeffer, Dietrich. *Discipleship*. Minneapolis: Fortress Press, 2001

Bonhoeffer, Dietrich. *Spiritual Care*. Philadelphia: Fortress Press, 1985

Bonhoeffer, Dietrich. *Letters and Papers From Prison*. New Greatly Enlarged Edition. New York: Macmillan, 1972

Bonhoeffer, Dietrich. *Meditating on the Word*. Cambridge, MA: Cowley Publications, 1986

Boykin, John. *The Gospel of Coincidence—is God in Control?* Grand Rapids: Zondervan, 1996

Bromiley, Geoffrey. *Historical Theology: An Introduction*, Grand Rapids: Eerdmans Publishing Company, 1978

Brunner, Emil. *The Misunderstanding of the Church*. London: Lutterworth Press, 1952.

Brunner, Emil. *Man in Revolt,* London: Lutterworth Press, 1939, reprint, Philadelphia: Westminster Press, 1979

Brunner, Emil. *Dogmatics*, III, *The Christian Doctrine of the Church, Faith and Consummation*. London: Lutterworth 1963

Bultmann, R. *Jesus Christ and Mythology*. London: SCM Press, 1966

Busch, Eberhard. *Karl Barth—His Life from Letters and Autobiographical Texts*, Grand Rapids: Eerdmans, 1993

Calvin, John. *Institutes of the Christian Religion*, Philadelphia: Westminster, 1960

Carnell, Edward John. *The Burden of Søren Kierkegaard*, Grand Rapids: Eerdmans, 1965

Carnell, Edward John. *Christian Commitment: An Apologetic*, New York: The Macmillan Company, 1957

Carnell, Edward John. *The Kingdom of Love and the Pride of Life*. Grand Rapids: Eerdmans, 1960

Carr, Wesley. "Towards a Contemporary Theology of the Holy Spirit," in *Scottish Journal of Theology*, Vol. 28, No. 7, 1975

Craig, William. "What Does God Know?" in *God Under Fire: Modern Scholarship Reinvents God*, Douglas S. Huffman and Eric L. Johnson, editors. Grand Rapids: Zondervan, 2002

Day, Thomas. *Dietrich Bonhoeffer on Christian Community and Common Sense*. New York: The Edwin Mellen Press, 1982

Dickinson, Emily. *The Complete Poetry of Emily Dickinson*, Boston: Little Brown and Company, 1989

Dillard, Annie. *Holy the Firm*, New York: Harper and Row, 1977

Donne, John. *The Poems of John Donne*, edited by H. J. C. Grierson. London: Oxford University Press, 1964

Dostoyevsky, Fyodor. *The Brothers Karamazov*. New York: Random House, 1950

Dumas, Andre. "Religion and Reality in the Work of Bonhoeffer" in *A Bonhoeffer Legacy: Essays in Understanding,* A. J. Klassen, editor. Eerdmans, 1981

Farley, Wendy. *Tragic Vision and Divine Compassion.* Louisville: Westminster John Knox Press, 1990,

Fee, Gordon D. *The Disease of the Health and Wealth Gospels.* Costa Mesa, CA: The Word for Today, P.O. Box 800, 1979

Fiddes, Paul. *Participating in God: A Pastoral Doctrine of the Trinity.* London: Darton, Longman & Todd, 2000

Flew, Anthony and A. MacIntyre, *New Essays in Philosophical Theology.* London: SCM Press, 1955

Friesen, Gary. *Decision Making and the Will of God*, with J. Robin Maxson. Portland, Or: Multnomah Press, 1980

Fry, Christopher. *Three Plays*, "A Sleep of Prisoners." New York, Oxford University Press, 1961

Fry, Christopher. *The Boy With a Cart.* New York: Oxford University Press, 1959

Geivett, Douglas. "How Do We Reconcile the Existence of God and Suffering," in *God Under Fire: Modern Scholarship Reinvents God*, Douglas S. Huffman and Eric L. Johnson, editors. Grand Rapids: Zondervan, 2002

Gibran, Kahil. *The Prophet*, New York: Alfred Knopf, 1962

Gibran, Kahil. *Sand and Foam.* New York, Alfred Knopf, 1954

Green, Michael. *I Believe in the Holy Spirit.* Grand Rapids: Eerdmans, 1975

Grenz, Stanley. *Theology for the Community of God.* Grand Rapids: Eerdmans 1994

Hammarskjold, Dag. *Markings*, New York: Knopf, 1966

Henry, Carl. *God, Revelation and Authority*, Vol. III, Waco, TX: Word Books, 1976-1983

Heron, Alisdair. *The Holy Spirit*, Philadelphia: Westminster Press,

1983

Heschel, Abraham. *The Prophets*, Vol. II. New York: Harper and Row, 1962

Huffman, Douglas S. and Eric L. Johnson, editors. *God Under Fire: Modern Scholarship Reinvents God.* Grand Rapids: Zondervan, 2002

Kettler, Christian D. and Todd H. Speidell, editors. *Incarnational Ministry: The Presence of Christ in Church, Society and Family,* Essays in Honor of Ray S. Anderson. Colorado Springs: Helmers and Howard Publishers, 1990

Kierkegaard, Søren. *The Journals of Kierkegaard,* Harper Torchbook, 1958

Kraus, C. Norman, *Jesus Christ Our Lord: Christology from a Disciple's Perspective.* Scottdale, PA: Herald Press, 1987

Kushner, Harold. *When Bad Things Happen to Good People.* New York: Avon Books, 1981

LaCugna, Catherine Mowry. *God For Us: The Trinity and Christian Life*, San Francisco: HarperCollins, 1991

Lewis, Alan E. *Between Cross & Resurrection: A Theology of Holy Saturday.* Grand Rapids: Eerdmans, 2001

Lewis, C. S. *Letters to Malcolm: Chiefly on Prayer*, New York: Harcourt, Brace, & World, 1964

Lewis, C. S. *The Four Loves*, New York: Harcourt, Brace, 1960

Luther, Martin. *The Bondage of the Will in Erasmus-Luther: Discourse on Free Will*, New York: Frederick Ungar, 1961

McClendon, James. *Systematic Theology—Ethics.* Nashville: Abingdon Press, 1986.

Miller, Arthur. "Death of a Salesman," *Arthur Miller's Collected Plays*, Volume I. New York: The Viking Press, 1957, 1987

Miskotte, Kornelis. *When the Gods are Silent*, London: Collins, 1967

Moore, Thomas. *Care of the Soul: A Guide for Cultivating Depth and Sacredness in Everyday Life.* New York: Harper Collins, 1992

Nygren, Anders. *Eros and Agape.* London: S.P.C.K., 1953

O'Neill, Eugene. "The Great God Brown," in *The Plays of Eugene O'Neill*, Vol. 1. New York: Modern Library, 1982

Palmer, Robert and Robert Hamerton-Kelley (eds). "J. G. Hamann and the Princess Gallitrzi," *Philomathes*, The Hague: Martinus Nijhoff, 1971

Pannenberg, Wolfhart. *Christian Spirituality and Sacramental Community*. London: Dartman, Longman and Todd, 1983

Pedersen, John. *Israel: Its Life and Culture*, Vol. I, London: Oxford University Press, 1973

Rice, Richard. "Biblical Support for a New Perspective," *The Openness of God*, Clark Pinnock *et al*, editors, InterVarsity Press, 1994, pp. 11-58

Smail, Thomas. *The Forgotten Father*. Grand Rapids: Eerdmans Publishing Company, 1980

Smedes, Lewis. *Love within Limits: A Realists View of 1 Corinthians 13*. Grand Rapids: Eerdmans, 1978

Speidell, Todd. "Incarnational Social Ethics," in *Incarnational Ministry—The Presence of Christ in Church, Society, and Family*. Colorado Springs: Helmers and Howard, publishers, 1990

Thielicke, Helmut. *A Little Exercise for Young Theologians*, Grand Rapids: Eerdmans, 1962

Thielicke, Helmut. *Living With Death*. Grand Rapids: Eerdmans, 1983

Thielicke, Helmut, *Being Human... Becoming Human*. Garden City, NY: Doubleday, 1984

Thompson, Francis, *The Hound of Heaven*, New York: Peter Pauper Press, nd,

Thompson, Francis. "The Kingdom of Heaven," *Selected Poems of Francis Thompson*. London: Burns and Oates, 1907

Torrance, James. "The Vicarious Humanity of Christ," in *The Incarnation—Ecumenical Studies in the Nicene-Constantinopolitan Creed A. D. 381,* Thomas F. Torrance, Editor, Edinburgh: Handsel Press Ltd., 1981

Torrance, Thomas F. *God and Rationality,* Oxford: Oxford University Press, 1971

Torrance, Thomas F. *The Mediation of Christ*. Colorado Springs: Helmers and Howard, 1992

Torrance, Thomas F. *A Passion for Christ: The Vision that Ignites Ministry*, Gerrit Dawson and Jock Stein, eds. Edinburgh: The Handsel Press, 1999

Torrance, Thomas F. *God and Rationality*. New York: Oxford, 1971

Torrance, Thomas F. *Space, Time and Resurrection*, Grand Rapids: Eerdmans, 1976,

Torrance, Thomas F. *Theology in Reconstruction*. Grand Rapids: Eerdmans, 1965

Torrance, Thomas F. *Divine and Contingent Order*. Oxford, New York: Oxford University Press, 1981

Vischer, Lukas, editor, *Spirit of God, Spirit of Christ—Ecumenical Reflections on the Filioque Controversy*. WCC. Faith and Order # 103, 1981

von Balthasar, Hans Urs. *A Theological Anthropology*. New York: Sheed and Ward, 1967

von Wedemeyer, Maria. *Love Letters from Cell 92: The Correspondence Between Dietrich Bonhoeffer and Maria von Wedemeyer 1943-1945*. Edited by Ruth-Alice von Bismarck and Ulrich Kabitz. Nashville: Abingdon Press, 1992

Wainwright, Geoffrey. *Doxology—A Systematic Theology*, New York: Oxford. 1980

Wagner, C. Peter. *How to Have a Healing Ministry Without Making Your Church Sick*. Ventura, CA: Regal Books, 1988

Wolfe, Thomas. *Look Homeward Angel!* New York: Charles Scribner's Sons, 1930

Index of Names

Anderson, Ray S. 8, 182
Barth, Karl 7, 19, 21, 51, 59, 62, 70, 73, 79, 83, 97, 99, 121-3, 129-30, 160
Basinger, David 178
Becker, Ernest 196, 198
Berry, Wendell 198
Bethge, Eberhard 188
Bonhoeffer, Dietrich 188, 192, 195-6
Boykin, John 178
Bultmann, R. 120, 122
Brunner, Emil 158, 160-1, 207-8
Busch, Eberhard 217
Calvin, John 58, 92, 170
Carnell, Edward John 31, 55, 75-77, 147, 150, 152-3
Carr, Wesley 167
Dickinson, Emily 58, 213
Dillard, Annie 163
Dostoyevski, Fyodor 174
Farley, Wendy 82, 178, 220
Fee, Gordon D. 148-9
Fiddes, Paul 218
Flew, Anthony 102
Friesen, Gary 186
Fry, Christopher 22, 30, 55, 57, 84, 164
Gibran, Kahil 48, 157, 164
Hammarskjold, Dag 6
Henry, Carl 216
Heschel, Abraham 59, 215

Hubbard, David 8
Ignatius 160-61
Irenaeus 129, 135
Kierkegaard, Søren 9, 11, 30, 31, 33-36, 39-40, 44, 46, 53-5, 57, 76, 82-3, 164, 189
Kraus. C. Norman 218
Kushner, Harold 173
LaCugna, Catherine Mowr 81, 219
Lessing, Gotthold 120, 133
Lewis, Alan E. 196
Lewis, C. S. 23, 61, 79
Luther, Martin 59, 149, 171
MacArthur, Douglas 8
McClendon, James 59
Miller, Arthur 82, 164, 219
Miskotte, Kornelis 61, 62
Moore, Thomas 7
Nygren, Anders 79
O'Neill, Eugene 77, 167
Pannenberg, Wolfhart 114, 115, 225
Parker, Larry 149-50
Pedersen, John 62, 216
Rice, Richard 177
Roddy, Clarence 87, 89, 90
Smail, Thomas 133
Smedes, Lewis 84
Speidell, Todd 218
Thielicke, Helmut 21, 195
Thompson, Francis 80, 205

Torrance, James 73, 218
Torrance, Thomas F. 80-1, 94, 97, 99, 108, 113, 117, 121, 129, 179, 212, 217
von Balthasar, Hans Urs 102
von Wedemeyer, Maria 123
Wagner, Peter 132-134
Wainwright, Geoffrey 58
Wolfe, Thomas 75, 116, 164

www.ingramcontent.com/pod-product-compliance
Lightning Source LLC
Chambersburg PA
CBHW070313230426
43663CB00011B/2107